QUICKSANDS OF PTSD

Stories
by veterans and
their partners, healing through
post-traumatic stress disorder

First published by Busybird Publishing 2020
Republished 2024

Copyright © 2020 Remain with the individual authors

ISBN: 978-1-922954-93-0

This work is copyright. Apart from any use permitted under the *Copyright Act 1968*, no part of this publication may be reproduced, stored in a retrieval system or transmitted in any form or by any means, electronic, mechanical, photocopying, recording or otherwise, without the prior written permission of individual authors.

Cover design: Busybird Publishing

Layout and typesetting: Busybird Publishing

Busybird Publishing
2/118 Para Road
Montmorency, Victoria
Australia 3094
www.busybird.com.au

CONTENTS

Introduction	1
I'm the Guy Who Buries His Head in the Sand *Chris Hodder*	5
Beyond the Brokenness *Susannah Newman*	17
Candle in the Window – The Stokerman's Journey *Garry Daly*	35
The Enemy Within *John Marks*	74
There's Nothing Wrong With Me … Or Is There? *Marty Miles*	124
Love you! Love you more! *Laurel Miles*	128
My Challenge with the Abyss *Nikko Nicholas*	136
Riding the Rollercoaster *Marney Nicholas*	176
A Journey of Hope *Pekka Hirvonen*	184
Our Journey On My Own *Robyn Hirvonen*	220
For What It's Worth *Terry Wolff*	227
Glenda's Story – Sadly Interrupted *Glenda Wolff*	237
The Boy at the Gate *Trevor McLean*	245
Just a Few More Words	269
Acknowledgments	273
Footnotes	275
Glossary	277

INTRODUCTION

Participants in the PTSD Group Treatment Program at the Heidelberg Repatriation Hospital, Melbourne, 2005.
Left to right Back row: Laurel Miles, Marty Miles, Terry Wolff, Trevor McLean, Chris Hodder, Pekka Hirvonen, Garry Daly.
Front Row: John Marks, Christine Marks (vale), Glenda Wolff (vale), Robyn Hirvonen, Marney Nicholas, Mike 'Nikko' Nicholas.

The past is never dead. It's not even past.
William Faulkner

William Faulkner's words are most true for those who have lived through trauma. Memories of horrors past continue to intrude: the sights, sounds, smells and emotions of the trauma are relived, nightmares disrupt sleep and the body stays in a state of heightened alert, anticipating the return of danger and need for protective action at any moment. Enormous energy goes into appearing normal in the face of internal turmoil. One's life becomes restricted by attempts to avoid the thoughts, feelings and situations that act as reminders of the past and cause memories, emotions and thoughts associated with the trauma to come flooding back. Despite the enormous energy expended to keep the past locked away, these strategies rarely succeed in the long term and often make things worse. Unfortunately, our past cannot be denied, and our efforts to deny its truth, suppress its memory, and avoid its consequences only increase its stranglehold on the present. Perhaps unjustly, the only way to heal trauma is to find a way to face its reality and integrate its occurrence into the narrative of one's life. That is, we must find a way to live with it; it can't be erased. Having traumatic memories take their rightful place in the past, thereby allowing people the freedom to live their lives in the present, and to pave a path of hope for their futures, is the key endeavour of trauma treatment.

People who have endured trauma suffer predictable psychological harm. There is a spectrum of traumatic symptoms, ranging from the effects of a single overwhelming event to the more complex effects of prolonged and repeated traumatic experiences.

While we can say much about what the impact of trauma has in common amongst its victims, we also need to honour the complexities of how these impacts manifest in varied ways for each individual. In the personal stories related herein, you will recognise the commonality and the incredible variety in how people come to experience the trauma of military experiences and how this variation is inexorably linked to the personal histories each person brings with them. One sad commonality reflected herein is the instance of childhood adversity compounding the traumatic experiences endured during military service.

In 2005, eight veterans of war confronted their emotional demons by embarking on a Post Traumatic Stress Disorder (PTSD) Group Treatment Program. This program was run at the Heidelberg Repatriation Hospital in Melbourne. The program began in 1995 and similar programs are still running today. It's staffed by a multidisciplinary team, including psychiatry, psychology, social work, occupational therapy and psychiatric nursing. In 2005, it was delivered over twelve weeks, with an initial four-week intensive phase. During this intensive phase, the veterans attended Monday to Friday for a full day of group treatment and twice weekly individual therapy. During this month they lived in accommodation close to the hospital. After this intensive phase the program ran weekly for a further eight weeks. The group treatment involved a combination of psycho-educational and skills-based groups (e.g., anxiety management, anger management, communication skills), as well as a more unstructured group therapy for discussion of topics of most concern to the group.

When this group of eight embarked on the program, I was an eager student of psychology in my last year of training. Not as nervous as the men courageously coming together to get treatment, I was still anxious about whether I would have anything useful to offer these men who'd seen and experienced so much. I was individual therapist to John Marks during the program and afterwards. I was honoured when he asked me to write an introduction for this collection of stories.

The key question I reflected upon in writing this introduction was: how did this group of veterans create such strong bonds, lasting years post-treatment and culminating in this book? How did they develop the courage to write their personal stories for the benefit of others?

This is an important question for all trauma survivors because ongoing social support and a sense of connection and belonging are amongst the most powerful predictors of recovery. Rarely do individuals with PTSD walk out of a twelve-week program stating they are healed. The journey towards a happy and meaningful life requires ongoing work and support. If we, as professionals, can do anything to increase the chances of a group making lifelong connections and providing years of support to each other, this is among the most important benefits any treatment program could offer.

I asked the men and their partners to reflect on this question themselves. In their responses, two themes were dominant. First, having the opportunity to stay together during the intensive month of treatment allowed personal connections to develop and intensify. The men were able to socialise outside of the treatment context, and got to know each other more fully. Being together over this time also allowed them to provide support to each other as they each went through difficult phases during the treatment. Second, the inclusion of their partners in the program was key to allowing ongoing catch-ups to occur, with the women often the driving force and organisational masterminds behind the regular meetings. This is unsurprising. PTSD is characterised by avoidance, shame and social isolation. So much of trauma occurs in the context of interpersonal relationships and can severely undermine the ability to trust and feel safe with others, and makes participating in the ordinary give-and-take of relationships fraught with difficulty. Difficulties with memory and concentration also make it hard to plan and organise. It is incredibly difficult for someone with PTSD to take on the challenge of organising ongoing catch-ups, no matter how dearly they want the support. The partners, however, are a group not afflicted by such difficulties but also in need of the kind of social support you can only get from those who are in the same position as you.

From my perspective, this group also utilised the treatment program to its full potential. It's possible to complete a treatment program without fully facing your demons; but this group, from the beginning, made a commitment to each other to be honest and to fully participate in the activities the group program was asking of them. This takes incredible courage. Group treatment asks veterans to do exactly what they've been avoiding since encountering trauma: remember and talk about what happened, allow yourself to feel emotions, trust others with your vulnerabilities, face the situations you've been avoiding. This goes against what their survival brain was telling them was necessary: be strong, don't fall apart, keep it in, don't let others see you falter, and so forth. But by making this commitment, this group of eight spent twelve weeks sharing their darkest thoughts, deepest feelings, greatest fears and their greatest hopes. Slowly but surely, this group attempted to make some sense and meaning from what they had experienced and, in finding each other, this search for meaning and healing continued well beyond the twelve weeks and continues today. The writing of their stories is yet another way of trying to integrate and makes sense of one's life. I hope, as they do, that it will inspire others to seek support and treatment.

Dr Tarni Jennings
Clinical Psychologist

I'M THE GUY WHO BURIES HIS HEAD IN THE SAND

Chris Hodder

Explosive Ordnance Disposal operations in Northern Ireland during the conflict known locally as 'the Troubles' 1

I grew up in Matabeleland in Rhodesia. My parents had a very comfortable home in the suburbs of Bulawayo and in hindsight my two older brothers and I had a remarkably privileged upbringing. Both of my parents were professionals: my father was company secretary of an asbestos mining company and my mother was a physiotherapist with her own practice. Our home was on a one and a half-acre block and we had a swimming pool, an orchard and what seemed like an enormous garden in which to play. I guess the most remarkable thing, particularly for people from parts of the world other than Southern Africa, was that we had domestic servants in the house. We had a cook (Echeke), a housemaid (Lucia) and a gardener (Ronnie), all of whom lived on the property. This has, over the years, generated considerable comment from people who believed that the white population in Africa was wholeheartedly exploiting the locals. With the benefit of thirty years living away from Africa, I can see their point. At the time, it was merely the norm and I had neither the maturity nor insight to question the status quo.

Our childhood was idyllic. We had endless freedom to roam the surrounding bush land and as long as we were home by the time the streetlights came on, all was well. This in itself was slightly surreal as the country had been fighting a counter-insurgency war against black Nationalist factions since 1965, and by today's standards it seems strange that our parents were so relaxed about our being out of sight for the majority of our free time. The schooling in Bulawayo was based on the English model, with prefects, frequent beatings and a somewhat nonsensical curriculum that included English and European history, Latin and geography, with topics such as a detailed study of the Steppes of Russia. Our education of our own land was woefully lacking. It did, however, include a generous helping of sport!

In short, my childhood was a wonderfully carefree and happy time. Sadly, this came to an abrupt end when I left school and was faced, as was every other male of school-leaving age, with conscription into military service. Again, this was the norm, and despite the slight trepidation of being thrust into the unknown, it was a source of some excitement and anticipation. Following basic training, I was posted to the Rhodesia Regiment and served in a number of the tactical areas around the country as an infantryman. The action I saw in my two years of National Service never really troubled me as I was well schooled in the notion that the army was merely assisting the government in maintaining law and order by preventing terrorist cells from inflicting civilian casualties. There was something meaningful about the role, something that I don't think my Vietnam veteran friends enjoyed. I reacted quite well to the structure of the army, probably because I'd spent a little time at boarding school and the discipline and conformity were familiar.

In 1980, Rhodesia ceased to exist. Elections, which for the first time were to include the Indigenous population, were brokered by Britain, and the now infamous Robert Mugabe became the prime minister. Things changed rapidly in the fledgling Zimbabwe and I decided it was time to leave. I went to Britain, as that was where my father came from, and besides, I had a girlfriend there! Once in Britain I was faced with the issue of how to sustain myself and with no tertiary education, I ended up in a variety of odd jobs. One day, I walked past an army recruiting office and decided to see if I could join. I thought it'd be a case of offering my services and being eagerly accepted. I stressed that I wanted to be an officer – no more being sent on dodgy operations by a nineteen-year-old subaltern for me, thank you very much. The recruiting sergeant was kind and explained that it wasn't quite as simple as that. Thus started an eighteen-month application and selection process before I was eventually accepted into training at the Royal Military Academy Sandhurst.

Despite a few setbacks, mainly due to my own belief that I knew everything and therefore didn't need training on ambush drills or how to behave in a convoy, I graduated in 1982 and was commissioned into the Royal Army Ordnance Corps. Just after commissioning, I got married and we moved to Gutersloh in Germany. After three years in Germany, I decided I wanted to pursue training in ammunition technology. This trade is aimed primarily at the management of ammunition and explosives, but has the side trade of Explosive Ordnance Disposal (EOD) attached to it. The course involved six months of formal education at the Royal Military College of Science at Shrivenham, a university exclusive to the military. During this period, my son William was born. After the scientific phase at Shrivenham, the course moved to the School of Ammunition in Kineton where we put the theory into practice. The final phase of the course was the introduction to the disposal of terrorist improvised explosive devices – bombs!

I had a natural aptitude for this discipline and felt I'd found my vocation in the army. I was picked up for a tour of duty as a bomb disposal officer with 321 Explosive Ordnance Disposal Company in Belfast, a tour that lasted six months, during which I was involved in 115 live incidents. It was a very busy time. I revelled in the excitement and responsibility of such a dangerous and testing profession. I was so hooked up in my own little world that I failed to recognise the effect this had on my family. I also neglected to pay attention to the effect it had on my own nervous system.

Shortly before the end of my tour, I was called to a van that'd been abandoned under a small bridge in a suburb of Belfast. The van had a poorly constructed hoax device in the rear and I assessed that the Irish Republican Army (IRA) had planted the van in order to draw the police away from another area – a frequently used tactic to allow activity to proceed uninterrupted elsewhere. After a few attempts to open the vehicle, I became a little impatient. It was our fifth job of ten that day. It was a busy time and fatigue became an issue for the whole team. We'd been on the ground for a number of hours and I was beginning to become concerned for the safety of the cordon troops who were keeping the public away from the area. I approached the vehicle with the intention of searching the passenger area by hand – something I'd done a number of times and which I felt was safe to do. I have no idea what stopped me but, when I opened the door of the van, I noticed a small cut in the fabric of the seat. I gently lifted the edge and discovered a device containing 1 kilogram of Semtex explosive that could be triggered by an improvised pressure plate. The idea was that anyone who sat in the driver's seat would be killed instantly. I managed to disarm the device, but slowly became aware that the device had been intended specifically for me. The more I thought about it the more I realised that the IRA had been taking careful note of the way I operated. It became personal. I simultaneously felt flattered that they would view me as a significant target, and very threatened and alone. Until that moment, I'd unconsciously seen myself as some sort of saviour. Suddenly, it was no longer a game. I was no longer an extra in someone else's movie. I resolved to be more suspicious and careful in the future.

My time in Belfast was formally recognised by the award of the Queen's Gallantry Medal. I was delighted to be given this award, but secretly felt a little shame when I acknowledged my own fears and trepidation I'd so often felt. I left Northern Ireland and was immediately put onto a series of compulsory courses required for promotion up to and beyond major. I found this six-month period almost intolerable. In hindsight, I'm now sure that this was the first sign of PTSD. The subject matter and the pompous officers teaching us seemed almost irrelevant in comparison to the role I'd just undertaken. I completed the courses, but was by no means considered star material. I was offered a job as the Weapons Intelligence Officer for 8 Brigade in Londonderry. The job primarily entailed the command of a section of military police investigators who would report on all terrorist incidents in our area. My job was to interpret trends in attacks and to recommend countermeasures whenever any new device or tactic was deployed. The job came with a darker side – covert work as a specialist advisor to the various intelligence-gathering agencies. Typically, this would involve deployment on covert operations to insert listening equipment or covert cameras. As a technical resource, I wasn't given the same degree of training as the agencies I supported; therefore, I frequently felt out of my depth, particularly when inserting into the more hostile areas of the Bogside or out in the country areas of Fermanagh and South Armagh. As normal, I just feigned confidence and went along with it, despite several narrow escapes, which left me quaking in my boots.

During the tour, a young soldier was shot and killed very near to my married quarter. He was deemed too young to be allowed to patrol the streets and was given the job of driving the soldiers' children to and from school. The IRA shot him on his way back from a drop off. This affected everyone in the brigade, as it demonstrated how vulnerable the families were. Quite understandably, my wife decided she'd had enough of Ireland and moved back to the mainland with our son. Perhaps I should've drawn a line under my career as a bomb disposal officer at that point, but bravado and the belief that I was bulletproof made me stay. I was posted to the Armagh Brigade to take over the Weapons Intelligence section in the south of the province.

South Armagh, traditionally known as Bandit Country, was a real departure for me. All of the work was carried out in rural areas and I felt more lacking in tactical know-how than ever. It was during this tour that I attended a bombing incident where a young corporal was killed. Corporal McGonnigal had been patrolling with his section along a road in South Armagh when a large device was detonated as he passed by. My investigators and I were asked to remove his remains from a swampy area, approximately 50 metres from the point where he'd been. He'd been decapitated by the blast and his shattered body was lying in amongst a bed of reeds. We pulled him out and placed his remains in a body bag for transport to hospital. This event affected me deeply for a number of reasons, some of which I don't wish to discuss. I only mention it as he regularly features to this day in intrusive thoughts and in my dreams at night. These are classic symptoms of PTSD, and had I had any real information on the condition, I may have sought some help at that point. Actually, in truth, I probably wouldn't have. I know enough of myself now to recognise that I would never have admitted to weakness.

My next tour of duty was probably the happiest of my career. I was sent to Sandhurst as a platoon instructor and entrusted with the training and development of officer cadets. This was a total change for me. Instead of dirty civilian clothes, long hair, a bushy beard, and never a minute without a pistol in my belt, I was in a world of starched uniforms, shiny shoes, gold braid, and exquisite occasions such as graduation balls and passing out parades. I loved every minute, and I like to think that my slightly unconventional approach to military life helped my cadets to be sound leaders who cared for their soldiers. I know this to be true in a few cases, as I've had exactly that feedback from one or two of my charges in later years. It was therefore with much sadness that I was released from my tour slightly early to be promoted to major and to deploy to Saudi Arabia with a newly formed company of soldiers to undertake EOD and ammunition disposal duties during Desert Storm. I was back in my element with a real task in unconventional circumstances. My wife was pregnant with my daughter at the time and she was keen for me not to go. It has taken me many years to acknowledge that it was purely my own selfishness that prevented me from asking to be excused on compassionate grounds. My wife's father had died not long before that time, and that, coupled with pregnancy and a husband away at war, must've been an enormous strain – something I should've been sympathetic to and supportive of. Instead, I deployed to the desert with a rag-tag bunch of officers and soldiers to play big boys' games in the sand.

The Gulf tour, whilst difficult in its day-to-day execution, was relatively incident and stress free. It was a very busy six months filled with large-scale demolitions of excess explosives and the repacking and recovery of all of the British ammunition and explosives that'd been on the fighting vehicles. I left Saudi slightly early, as my daughter's birth was imminent. I arrived home about twelve hours after she was born, and things were beginning to take on a semblance of normality.

My next posting was to Germany in command of a company of 155 men and women and we ran a small ammunition depot in Sennelager. This was a very peaceful period and I was able to be a 'family' father for a change.

After two years I was called back to Northern Ireland to command the Weapons Intelligence Unit, the headquarters of the Weapons Intelligence Sections with which I'd previously served. For me this was a great honour, but my acceptance of the appointment was a selfish decision. Once again, I was potentially putting my family in harm's way, and was committing myself to great risk.

This tour went on far longer than expected due to a terrible air crash that killed twenty-nine of my colleagues from the army, police and security service. We'd all been programmed to attend a conference in Scotland

and were to be flown over the Irish Sea in an air force Chinook helicopter. I was taken off the flight at the last minute because of a covert operation that was due to be executed that evening. I was terribly disappointed. This disappointment disappeared several hours later when I learned that the helicopter had crashed and all on board had been killed. In effect, this left a massive hole in the intelligence community and those of us left were required to pick up the slack and cover the missing people's duties. My tour was extended by a further eighteen months. I actually found this tour very difficult. I was a 'technical resource' for a number of the covert agencies working in Northern Ireland at the time and, to be honest, I was never totally clear who I was working for on these covert technical tasks, and was certainly not privy to the overall objective or agenda for most of the operations. Suffice to say, I was frequently severely tested, both technically (most of the work was in hostile areas and done in the dark) and in terms of my nerve. I was bloody terrified for a good proportion of the time. That was the trickiest thing to deal with. One just didn't admit to fear. *Is today the day?* I remember asking myself each morning. I should've recognised this as an unhealthy sign. Having been involved in so many incidents over the years, I now know that I was bouncing between feelings of horror, guilt and fear, whilst desperately trying to maintain an aura of confidence, competence and normality.

Towards the end of my time in Northern Ireland, I learned that my name had appeared on an IRA targeting list. It'd become personal and my family ran the risk of becoming 'collateral damage' should an attack be launched against me with them nearby. The army decided that I needed to get out of sight for a while and, as I had a brother living in Melbourne, I asked if I could do a two-year exchange with the Australian Army. Surprisingly, they accepted this suggestion and so started a wonderfully peaceful time. I wasn't expected to work too hard and the family had time to travel and just be a family. As a unit, we decided that Australia was the place to be and we started immigration proceedings. The British Army must've been fed up with anyone it sent to Australia resigning and staying on, so they enforced the policy that an officer could only resign from the UK; therefore, I was posted to 11 EOD Regiment in Didcot. I was responsible for contingency planning for the UK's response to terrorists utilising chemical, biological or nuclear devices. The work was potentially interesting but my heart wasn't in it. I realise now that I was beginning to feel the effects of PTSD. I'd become a bit 'removed' from the family and had trouble sleeping and concentrating. These I now know are classic symptoms, and whilst I had a little disquiet over how I was feeling, I didn't seek help, which is another classic trait of soldiers with PTSD.

Many years later, when I was living in Australia, I was lucky enough to be included in the program that was the original gathering of our fabulous group of veterans, and we learned about how this condition manifests itself and typically how people react to it. The group was very quiet during the introductory session, as I think we all recognised ourselves as falling into some or most of the categories. We heard that individuals may have anger issues, experience substance addiction, or they may just be unable to cope in 'normal' society. I recognised myself as being the 'bury my head in the sand guy'. I'd ignored all of the signs that something was wrong and put my aberrant behaviour down to 'getting old', 'pressure of work', or a thousand other excuses. I was sleeping less and suffered with terrible headaches every day. Things came to a head when I discovered that my wife had been having an affair for over twelve months, and we separated in the worst possible way. I thought I was coping, but realised I wasn't when a visit to my family doctor on an unrelated matter resulted in him committing me to a psychiatric clinic for treatment. This was a big deal. He made it very clear that if I chose not to go to the clinic that he'd call the police and have me formally committed, as he believed I was a danger to myself and potentially to others. I was gutted. I finally had evidence from someone else that I was definitely not right and that I'd, for the first time, lost control of my life. I spent the next twelve or so months intermittently attending work but mostly being on sick leave or moving between several clinics. The beginning of a suggestion of recovery was when I finally received some support from the British Army (they have a reciprocal arrangement with the Department of Veterans' Affairs – DVA) and was sent to Ward 17 at the Heidelberg Repatriation Hospital. This recovery was further assisted by the love and support I received from my dear friend Dymphna, who dragged me through some of the bleaker patches of this period.

Things were certainly not good. I was severely sleep-deprived, profoundly depressed and suicidal. The facilities at Ward 17 were rough, but being amongst other veterans who 'understood' was a massive comfort. I didn't feel alone in my confused state. Being placed on suicide watch was a salutary demonstration of how far out of kilter my life had become.

Ward 17, despite its lack of modern fittings, was my salvation. I had a couple of visits there over the following months and found the place to be both welcoming and supportive. The staff was firm with the inmates in that they wouldn't tolerate bad behaviour and were encouraging in the way they gently nudged us towards re-entering society through low-key, 'normal' activities, such as craft lessons and the occasional short visit to a nearby shopping centre.

Throughout all of my time in the various clinics, my son William, who visited every single day without fail, supported me brilliantly. His non-judgemental presence was a constant reminder of what I had, rather than what I'd lost. I'll always be grateful to him for his patience and love during that difficult period.

Eventually, I was invited to attend a month-long residential course on how to live with PTSD that was held in the neighbouring Ward 18 at Heidelberg. This is where the group first came together. The group comprised a bunch of veterans mainly from the Vietnam conflict, with the exceptions being a naval veteran who'd seen service in a number of theatres of operations, and myself, the token Brit. We were all a little tentative to begin with and some of the members weren't sure they were in the right place. It soon became evident that we were all in exactly the right place when we were taken through the symptoms and effects of PTSD and each one of us recognised our own personalities and traits as being a perfect match. Here we came across the angry guy, the drunk, the guy constantly on the move and unable to settle, the denier, and, in my case, the guy who buries his head in the sand. All of us, to one extent or another, had vehemently denied that anything was wrong, and convinced ourselves that we were coping just fine, thank you very much!

The program gently took us through a variety of exercises and lectures designed to assist us in recognising our condition and offered strategies to allow us to cope in our jobs, lives and relationships. Perhaps the most heartening thing I heard in the early part of the course was offered by one of the lady clinicians. She told us quite forcefully that we weren't sick – this insidious condition wasn't a disease or illness, it was a war-caused injury. The only difference between us and a gunshot wound sufferer was the absence of bandages or visible scars to tell those around us that something was wrong. I found this idea to be very helpful. Perhaps this wasn't my fault after all; maybe there was a reason for my collapse. Maybe, just maybe, I could tame the monsters enough to find some light in my life again.

To be honest, I remember very little of the specific content of the course. What I do know is that the cumulative effect of lectures, guidance, support, and the shared experiences with my colleagues was enormously positive. The process was brutally confronting and often very difficult. I found the telling of personal experiences difficult as the stories sounded too fantastical to be true. My military life was so far divorced from the peace and normality of life in Australia that the tales sounded like short stories from cheap novels. We all quite quickly recognised that the group had a lot to offer individually and we resolved to try to stick together.

Towards the end of the program, the wives and partners were included in some of the sessions and we were again confronted, this time by the effects of PTSD on the families. I remember being astounded at the fortitude and strength of these women who'd resolutely stood by their men through what must've been some hellish times.

The relationship between the members of the group has grown over the years, and I now believe we all act as the primary support point for one another in matters relating to PTSD. I'm pretty sure none of the men have called one another when they're in a crisis, but it's certainly a very comforting feeling knowing there are people out there who know one another down to the smallest detail, and who understand and empathise with the complexities and impacts of PTSD on our ability to function 'normally'. As our relationship has grown, so has the ability to spot when one of the gang is having difficulties, and for the group to band together to provide support.

Around this time, a fledgling relationship that was beginning to form with Susannah began to get more serious. We'd worked together on a project team when I first came to Australia. She was engaged then. One day, she rang to ask if I could be a referee for her as she was applying for a new job. I hadn't seen her for a number of years and suggested we should meet for a coffee so I could find out what she'd been up to. When we met, I found out that her engagement hadn't lasted and that she'd suffered with periodic bouts of depression. It seemed we were in similar boats. We started seeing one another and the early days weren't without their problems. Essentially, Susannah and I were at different points in our lives – I'd been married and she hadn't; I had children and she wanted to be a mother. The difference in our ages didn't help either. The poor girl was now confronted with becoming involved in a whole group of damaged veterans without the benefit of attending the program. To her everlasting credit, she immersed herself in the group, which developed into a mutual support group. I'll be forever grateful to Susannah for her love and support. As I've said, we've had our difficulties, a feature that, sadly, is all too common when one partner has PTSD, but I won't go into that. Suffice to say, she's displayed strength, resilience, grace in the face of difficult situations, and, above all, unfailing love and belief in 'us'.

I guess it'd be easy for me to reel out a long list of traumatic experiences that have stayed with me and continue to haunt me. To my mind, that's a given for all of us and isn't really suitable for this publication. Suffice to say, we all had a good look at our own mortality at some point and had all been irrevocably changed by the experience. We all have this condition in common, and we're all affected by it in different ways. It's taken a long time, hard work and soul-searching to get to a point where I can function reasonably normally. To me, that's the point of this book: to let those poor souls who are left to scream in the dark know that they're not alone and that it's possible to re-join the human race. I don't wish to be defined by this condition. I don't want to be known as that poor old bloke who can't let go of the past, however accurate that may be. Despite the terrible price we've all been asked to pay for our service, I managed to find a single positive thought with regard to my PTSD – to me, it means that I was tested and I survived. Sadly, I was injured at the time but I'm learning how to deal with my injuries and am working towards a life where PTSD is a minor irritation, rather than a big black dog that is constantly waiting to bite me. I may never get there, but it's a quest worth pursuing. Besides, what other option do we have?

I'm acutely aware that this hasn't been an entirely personal journey. Inevitably, those closest to the veteran suffer from the fallout. If the veterans affected by PTSD don't understand it, it must be impossibly difficult for those around us. In my case, this has been particularly true for my children William and Rebecca, who lived through my service years and witnessed first-hand their father gradually crumbling. Both have been brilliantly supportive, even when they had no real idea of what was happening. Bec was young when things got bad and I know she felt it a great deal. William was older and was able to cope a little better. It's also been especially difficult for my partner, Susannah, who stepped into this maelstrom without the benefit of knowing the root cause. Collectively, their love and support has been the main thing that has kept me going.

I recently returned to Northern Ireland. My hope was that I'd be able to settle some of the ghosts that visit me daily, but sadly the experiment was a failure. When visiting some of the sites of the incidents that worry me the most, I found that my eyes and brain were registering a perfectly peaceful and normal scene while my inner instincts were screaming, 'Run!'. It would appear I'm a little like Pavlov's dog and am hard-wired to react without logic. I remain disappointed that this experiment didn't have the positive effect I was hoping for – in fact, it's freshened up many of the troubling thoughts I frequently have and I'm left feeling a little forlorn that the notion that PTSD cannot be cured may be accurate. I know for a fact, however, that it can be managed effectively and that there is definitely a 'life after'. The quality of that life is dependent on accepting that the condition exists, on taking steps to control the ongoing symptoms and on allowing yourself to think positively whenever possible.

BEYOND THE BROKENNESS

Susannah Newman

For Chris, life-threatening operational duties over many years took a gradual and sustained toll. I've come to think of each incident he faced as a bit like seismic activity, and the aftermath as deep structural cracks. I realise this sounds dramatic, but the story of his life is a bit like that.

I see these cracks as the basis of my personal PTSD story, which I think explains the difficulty I've experienced in trying to find my own narrative. I never witnessed the overt aftermath of Chris's service as a bomb technician, only the more insidious and unclear impacts of the subsequent trauma.

My story is basically about the knock-on effects of Chris's former life, with our own fault line running through them. The scene is messy and hard to chronicle. There are a million stories in the depths of those cracks, many of which are not mine to tell.

To get around this, I've taken a more analytical approach to this story, inspired by my recollection of a church service Chris and I attended with his Perth-based family and his mum, Joan, in 2012. It was the festive season and, after a long period of geographical separation and unresolved conflict in our relationship, we weren't feeling very festive that Christmas morning.

In a service based on some well-known lyrics from Leonard Cohen's song 'Anthem', the female minister shared some moving thoughts about injuries like Chris's. The gist of her sermon was that you can focus on the brokenness or you can pay attention to how the light slips through the cracks.

The light, the minister explained, is the understanding that allows you to reconcile yourself to any wounds or sorrows and begin to see and celebrate all that you have.

After years that'd nearly broken us completely, I remember feeling that the minister was speaking directly to me. There was a huge rift between Chris and me that was seemingly insurmountable but, perhaps, with some perspective and hard work, we could find a way forward.

THE CRACKS

Tendering

I first met my international man of mystery, as I call him, in the late nineties, when we briefly worked together as contractors on Defence tenders. Chris was fresh out of the British Army and still sporting a rather impressive military moustache.

He's a handsome man and I was quite struck by him when he was introduced to me in the office as the guy who knows everything about explosive ordnance. Whatever that was.

Bombs! This guy was a recently retired bomb technician who'd earned some very impressive post-nominal letters during his military service: Christopher Hugo Hodder, MBE (Member of the British Empire), QGM (Queen's Gallantry Medal). He was interesting and charming.

In fact, in my shy way, I might've found Chris a little intimidating, if he hadn't been the friendliest, most approachable man I'd ever met. My mother reminded me once that I'd sometimes talk to her about Chris, describing him as 'so lovely'. I swear I wasn't smitten, but I did admire him.

One of the things I liked most about him was the way he spoke about his family. He was very happy for them to be starting a new life together in a much safer place than the likes of Northern Ireland. They were just about to move into their very own house in Park Orchards, which seemed to be a big deal for them after the transient life of the army.

Not that Chris and I had heart-to-hearts during our time working together. I had no idea what he'd done to become 'a highly-decorated man', as he once jokingly described himself. I can't recall hearing about his idyllic childhood in colonial Africa. I didn't even notice the Rhodesian lilt in his accent.

Our relationship was a professional one and I wouldn't have imagined that, years later, we'd end up together. I had other things to think about at the time, like nesting in my own newly purchased home with a fiancé-to-be, and the possibilities the year 2000 might bring; the Millennium bug, for example!

Sadly, as the clocks rolled on into the noughties, things closer to home would prove far more problematic than the Y2K bug. By the time we saw one another again five years later, our respective situations had changed enormously.

Harley rides and worn-out shoes

Fast forward to 2005, when I found myself looking for contract work and nervously rang Chris to ask for a reference. Those post-nominal letters I mentioned above look great on a CV.

One of the first things Chris said to me was, 'My wife left me'. I thought of the good-looking, outgoing family man who'd made such an impression on me six years earlier and wondered what'd happened in the intervening years.

I responded with, 'My fiancé and I broke up'. More than two years before that fateful phone call, I'd called off my engagement, sold my house in Surrey Hills and moved back in with my parents temporarily. In the surrounding details, I sensed there was common ground for us to explore – rejection, instability and more.

'I can't give you a reference without hearing what you've been up to in the past six years. Do you want to meet for a coffee?' Chris asked. That's where it all began. One coffee meeting led to a series of coffee dates where we would 'talk shit', as Chris put it, smoke cigarettes together, and 'bleat' about troubling events of our recent past.

My international man of mystery in winter 2005

I love this photo from that time, with the advertisement in the background that says, 'Warm up this winter'. When I think back to what those winter weeks were like for us, it makes me smile. But perhaps you see some sadness in those kind eyes? I knew it well, in my own way, and I'm sure this helped seal our bond.

It was during these initial, heady weeks hanging out in city cafés together that Chris, still getting over his separation, felt he needed to set some boundaries. I remember this moment well because it was a defining one in the scheme of my life.

Initially, the conversation was warm and full of anticipation, like the rays of winter sunlight peeking through the skyscrapers of Collins Street. As we sat with our hands hugging our steaming lattes, we finally admitted our attraction to one another.

It didn't take long for Chris also to admit that he wasn't ready for anything too serious, given his recent troubles. At that point, the tone of the conversation changed. He looked me squarely in the eyes and clearly stated, 'No marriage; no babies'.

As I recall it, this happened well before we were officially in a relationship, but long enough after I'd developed sufficient feelings for him for it to pose a dilemma. Though I can't recall exactly how I responded, I certainly didn't say, 'I'm okay with that'.

After all our caffeine-fuelled confidences, Chris knew my take on these things, and I reminded him of this. But following some difficult years for both of us on the relationship front, neither of us liked the idea of walking away from our strong attraction before we knew what it was exactly, or how long it was going to last.

Having said that, I do remember feeling very conflicted when, shortly after this conversation, Chris asked me out on a proper date. I hesitated, but, with the butterflies in my stomach overriding the remnants of any long-held girlish dreams of weddings and baby bumps, I threw caution to the wind and said yes.

I was still living with my parents as after my break-up I'd returned to full-time study in health sciences. I distinctly remember introducing Chris to Mum and Dad the night of our first official date. He turned up on his candy-apple red 1991 Harley Electra Glide with a spare helmet, a warm greeting for my parents and a great big hole in the toe of his boat shoe. Characteristically Chris.

My parents smiled reservedly at him. This was the Chris who was 'so lovely': a bikie type with worn-out shoes, a post-army paunch and salt and pepper hair. The guy who claimed he'd turned grey overnight after a close call with an IED in Northern Ireland. The guy who'd put a smile back on their daughter's face, but wasn't interested in marriage or children.

Chris often tells the story of my pillion ride that night. Just before we took off together on the Harley, he said to let him know along the way if I felt uncomfortable. 'We'll just go for a short ride and you can indicate to me at any time if you want to stop. We can easily go back,' he said.

Cruising up Hoddle Street, there was a point when I tapped him on the shoulder and, as he tells it, he thought to himself, *She hates it.* But instead, as we pulled up to a traffic light, I leaned in, put my arms tight around his belly and yelled enthusiastically, 'Can we go further?'.

My conflicted love

The answer at the time was a heartfelt yes and here we are. Together all these years down the road, I'd be lying if I said the ride was easy for either of us – we've hung on by the skin of our teeth – but at least it's never been boring! It's a miracle we've hung on at all, given the amount of oncoming traffic.

Thinking back to when our relationship was just starting, I remember fielding concerns from close friends and family members – those who were brave enough to speak plainly, in defence of my future self. This retired British Army officer was lovely, but what would be the price of going further?

Not knowing Chris at all, some offered feedback along the lines of, 'You could do better for yourself'. Initially, when it seemed I was having a fling, this was a bit of a joke. For example, I laughed uneasily with my boss at the time when Chris came to pick me up from work and, clocking his greying hair, she'd said to him, 'You must be Susannah's father'.

Some months later, after Chris dropped the bombshell of no marriage, no babies and his PTSD worsened – those well-earned grey hairs became no laughing matter. A number of people chastised me, given the difference in our ages and conflicting stages of life.

Chris was a forty-six-year-old baby boomer who, long before we met, had already experienced the milestones that'd so far eluded me. He'd married in his early twenties and had a family. Now, sadly, for a range of compelling reasons, he expressed no desire to reinvent the wheel.

I was thirteen years younger, of generation X, who, for reasons both within and beyond my control, had stalled on marriage and babies. Though my failed engagement had changed my trajectory sharply, I made it clear to Chris that I hadn't given up on these two life goals.

Our mutual decision to enter into a relationship regardless is really the central conflict of my story with Chris. Though this choice has brought us countless moments of happiness over many years, it also created a rift between us from the very beginning, when we were already on shaky ground.

So, what happened to my relationship wish list – those detailed specifications women should use to evaluate men as sensible and satisfactory prospects for the longer term? I guess you could say, if I ever had one at all, I discarded it for Chris. This worried some of my friends and family members.

If I'm honest, I could be impulsive when it came to romantic relationships. I'd been known to dive straight in and not think things through. This is precisely what I did with Chris. There was something about him, or us, that made me more impulsive than I'd ever been in my life!

At a 'tipping point' age, this was far from ideal. I ended up head over heels, in stark contrast to Chris's attitude, which was much more restrained. He was careening towards a divorce and more unwell with PTSD than I realised. The last thing on his mind was a future with someone else.

Ward 17

Long after the bombardment of prolonged active duty is over, some veterans continue to take cover. In worst-case scenarios, some feel they have no choice but to live the rest of their lives that way.

I'm thinking of the reclusive veterans sometimes seen up on Mount Macedon at the Anzac Day service. It's like they magically appear out of the bushland to stand beneath the Memorial Cross in the pre-dawn darkness. Once the sun's up, and they've paid their respects, they disappear as quickly as they came. Off they go into the morning fog, like grey ghosts; avoidance personified.

While I'm not saying Chris is this badly affected by PTSD, he'll be the first to say he can be like them at times. All it takes is a situation that exacerbates his trauma-related symptoms – those that elicit strong emotions, or create a perception of risk or 'danger'.[1] Not surprisingly, back in 2005, as the fun of coffees and Harley rides morphed into reasonable expectations on my part of spending more time together, this is exactly what our fledgling relationship came to represent to Chris. In the context of his life then, which I won't go into here, I was a risky proposition.

Following one heated telephone conversation, Chris did something to me that he'd never done in service of the British Empire. He went

AWOL (Absent Without Leave). All texts and phone calls ceased, and the Harley no longer rumbled up the street in front of my parents' flat.

Naturally, I found this ghosting bewildering and hurtful. As I thought about what'd gone wrong, I remember asking myself how a man who'd won a medal for gallantry in service could behave in such an ungallant way.

Chris had admitted to me that he didn't have the 'emotional wherewithal' for anything too taxing. I was beginning to see what he'd meant. This was the moment to heed those warnings and move on.

I may have succeeded if his behaviour had been as simple as rejection, and not the relapse it turned out to be. What I didn't realise is that it's not at all unusual for people with PTSD to withdraw from friends and family when the symptoms take hold. Or that it can be an early warning sign that the condition is escalating.

Just as I was starting to get on with my life, I got an unexpected text from Chris, saying he'd been admitted to the Heidelberg Repatriation Hospital after a spectacular sleepwalking event. Following weeks of depression and sleep deprivation, he'd taken a few too many Stilnox to help him sleep and woken up naked at the bottom of his garden with no memory of how he got there. Upset and worried, I rushed to his side.

There, in a little room on Ward 17, I met a version of my friend I rarely see: Chris after a few full nights of sleep. The doctors had taken him off the Stilnox and used a cocktail of new medication to help him get some rest. The difference in him was striking.

Whatever misgivings I had or any behaviour on his part that preceded this reunion, I knew I was in trouble. He was sweet, apologetic, attentive and, to me, heart-wrenchingly vulnerable. My resolve to move on fell away completely.

It may seem counter-intuitive to someone less besotted than I was, but in truth there was nothing I wanted more than to be with Chris from that point on. I'd missed him when he went AWOL. I'd felt bereft. There was no thought of something 'better', or more between us at that stage, just of how best to support his recovery.

The PTSD Program

Treatment began in earnest for Chris when he was promptly transferred into the PTSD Program. The course would be a turning point for him.

It would also introduce us to eight Vietnam veterans and their partners. Unfortunately, my relationship status with Chris at the time meant I was unable to join the partners' group on the program. I really could've done with the knowledge and skills the ladies gained in those eight weekly sessions together. Instead, it seemed I was learning about PTSD the hard way.

You can read about the symptoms of combat trauma and try to understand what your partner goes through, but it won't necessarily help you predict how their 'stress disorder' is going to play out as you negotiate the unique demands of your relationship. We needed education and a lot of counselling to understand that, and it remains a work in progress.

One thing I know for sure is that things would most likely have been better for us if Chris didn't have the heart of both a soldier and of a trauma survivor with PTSD. I'm not saying he would've changed his mind about marriage and children, just that working through our differences may not have been quite so volatile.

I often wonder where we'd be if it weren't for the example of the women in our PTSD group who have somehow managed to hold tight against the odds. This is no small feat when 'for worse' includes a complex condition like chronic PTSD with its problems of 'trust, closeness, communication, and problem-solving'.[2] So many of the associated behaviours and feelings can make it hard for partners and their veterans to connect in the way they want and/or need to.

Stuck on standby

I didn't understand how deep-seated the issues could be until, in 2007, one of the women from the group lent me a DVD produced by the Veterans and Veterans' Families Counselling Service (VVCS; now Open Arms) called *You're Not in the Forces Now: an informational video for Vietnam veterans and their families*, presented by Nic Fothergill.

I've held on to it all these years, with the sticky note on the front from Robyn that says, 'This is the DVD I told you about. It may or may not be useful'.

Nothing has helped me understand the subtleties of Chris's condition more than this 'debriefing session' from the VVCS's Residential Lifestyle Program about the potential effects of military life on the 'human stress response'.

According to psychologist and Vietnam veteran Nic Fothergill, the roots of the trauma don't necessarily stem from involvement in war. A lot of the issues veterans present with could really have more to do with their training.

As Fothergill explains, repetitive military drills and 'aggressive' simulations are designed to change the way a soldier operates – to shift the dial on his response to threat. With repetition, he becomes primed to fight 'without thought', no matter what the consequences, and not to cower. As I understood it from Fothergill, this process can be equated with programming a 'stand-by button' for 'automatic action' deep into a soldier's psyche.

If it weren't for this preparation, a soldier wouldn't be able to reliably 'assault through' an ambush. Or, in Chris's case, quietly and calmly walk towards an improvised grenade, pick it up, then proceed to dismantle it by hand. Instead, his instincts might tell him to freeze like a spot-lit rabbit would or hightail it to the hills; that is, after all, a more 'normal, natural thing to do'.[3]

If you Google 'bomb disposal', you'll probably bring up a Wikipedia page that features a picture of Chris in Belfast in 1987. There Chris is, in his blast suit, walking past a sign on Manor Street that says, 'Prepare to meet thy God'.[4]

When this photo turns up on social media, I've seen people refer to it as 'iconic', and it certainly is a powerful image from that time of conflict in Northern Ireland. But for me, it's also utterly evocative of the change Fothergill describes in *You're Not in the Forces Now*.

Chris was so good at overriding his natural stress response that he braved countless long walks and lived to tell many a tale of derring-do. These days, this makes him a fascinating dinner party guest, but also a bit hard to live with sometimes.

Something I also grasped from Fothergill is that if fighting mode has served a soldier this well, the 'inner tension' it requires can become stuck, or even hardwired. After service, family members may experience this as unhelpful or inappropriate responses to everyday stressors – irritability, for example, at seemingly minor things, or explosive outbursts of anger.[5]

As I see it, it's like a veteran continues to respond to perceived threat as if an ambush awaits him around every corner.

Breaking points

With a legacy like this, it makes sense that every traumatised soldier may eventually reach one or more points, post-war, where the tension breaks through. This can come long after service, and tends to happen when you combine ageing with a fair amount of pressure – a 'highly emotional' conflict almost equivalent to war.[6]

I've seen this twice with Chris. Both times he ended up at the Heidelberg Repatriation Hospital and needed anti-depressant medication to help get his symptoms under control. The first time was when his marriage was ending. If Chris had a point of reckoning, this was it. The break-up of his family unit completely blew the lid off his PTSD. It was as if that seismic intensity I referred to earlier suddenly hit eight or more on the Richter scale.

The day I rang Chris to ask for a reference, I had no real understanding of the magnitude of his statement. Separations are awful at the best of times, but separations when you have PTSD can be plain dangerous. When I eventually came into the picture, I was completely unprepared for the aftershocks.

The second breaking point was in 2011, when our life-stage conflict finally got out of hand. Two things led to this: the work stress Chris was under at the time and escalating strain between us around the baby issue as I approached forty.

By this time, 'no marriage, no babies' had become like a mantra for our relationship. Though intellectually I acknowledged that Chris had been upfront, when I observed him enjoying parenthood I began to feel increasingly ill at ease that his boundaries were so black and white, while I'd allowed my own to be erasable.

As I cried (joyfully) at several weddings and held the precious newborns of friends and family in my arms, it felt like I'd jumped out of a fishbowl and was looking in on all the colour and activity from the outside, gasping for air. Slowly but surely, the disquiet I inadvertently experienced began to give way to resentment, justified or not.

Inevitably, there came a point when the conflict between us spiralled out of control. After a series of gut-wrenching arguments, Chris stood his ground. 'I was clear from the beginning,' he said. 'I don't believe in the institution of marriage any more and I can't give you children of your own. What are you going to do about it?' And then he crumbled, fully aware that he'd given me an ultimatum.

Afterwards, he sat outside on the back verandah for hours, grey-faced and silent. He had a cigarette in one hand and his head in the other. 'I've ruined your life, haven't I?' he eventually asked, adding my childlessness to the burdens he already carried. I replied, 'I don't think that. We are both responsible for the choices we've made.'

'I'm going to lose you, aren't I?' Chris asked despondently. There was something about his demeanour that suggested he was in deep trouble. I rang VVCS the next morning to get us some help and he was back in Heidelberg Repatriation Hospital by mid-afternoon.

We saw a social worker there who reminded me that Chris's capacity for additional stress (beyond the residual stress of PTSD) was limited. If we wanted to continue our relationship, we'd have to simplify things. Less conflict, more goodwill.

A difficult month followed as we made an uneasy truce and shifted into recovery mode once again. At the end of each workday, I'd visit Chris and try to keep the conversation light. In the evenings, I found myself in an empty house, wrestling with the precariousness of our situation and the decision we both had to make. Deep down, neither of us wanted the relationship to end, but we also knew things couldn't carry on as they were.

I tried to remember my feelings six years earlier when I'd first visited Chris on Ward 17 at Heidelberg Repatriation – when all I wanted was for him to get well and to be more available to me. He asked something of me around that time. 'No expectations; no demands,' he said, in much the same way he'd come out with, 'No marriage; no babies'.

This was a big ask, even at the beginning of a relationship. But at that point, it seemed like a reasonable request, given he'd just spent several weeks in a psychiatric unit. I now understood how symptomatic it was.

When there isn't any more

If you've ever read the children's book *Madeline*, you may remember Ludwig Bemelmans' closing lines:

And she turned out the light—
and closed the door—
and that's all there is—
there isn't any more.[7]

I once had a counsellor quote them to me as I was trying to map out a way forward following Chris's time at Heidelberg.

I remember the counsellor and I were discussing the unusual complexities of my relationship and whether it might be best for me to bow out. I said I wanted to persevere, and he looked at me like I was a masochist. 'Is it enough? If it is, stay, but you will likely pay a price,' he said. This idea of a price was nothing new to me. I'd been hearing about it since 2005. I knew I'd pay a price from the very beginning. I just didn't know how much a condition like PTSD could inflate it.

It turns out that almost any need I have for 'more' sits right next to all the tension Chris still carries. What I mean is that when I express a need that challenges our status quo, Chris is likely to react irritably or angrily, depending on what's at stake. When I say more, I don't mean big-ticket items such as marriage and babies necessarily, but rather things that are a bit more foundational, such as being able to say freely, 'I love you', when that's how you feel. Or, as the years fly by, making long-term plans together. Such things have been surprisingly challenging for Chris.

I'm not being critical of him when I say this; rather, I'm trying to address the symptoms. It's no surprise for someone who has a chronic stress disorder. In the PTSD brain, there's so much going on already, it leaves very little buffer zone for more, particularly if it's seen as an added pressure.

Though Chris is very loving in his way, those structural cracks I referred to mean there's always a risk he might break. And because I love him back, I've learnt to respond accordingly. I've adjusted my own behaviours and expectations to help offset the damage.[8]

I speak from personal experience when I say you can lose a great deal in having to do this. If you're not careful, it's like you slowly become entrenched in your partner's condition, exerting every ounce of 'sensitivity' and 'self-control' you can muster, just to keep the peace.[9]

Our foreshortened future

In 2016, after more than a decade with Chris, I began to fear the long-term consequences of living on standby. While there was a range of reasons for this, the most pressing one was my need for a greater sense of security. This meant extending our domestic partnership into some more financial territory. As part of this, I wanted us both to think through and prepare for 'in the event of' scenarios. After Chris had a few health scares, I felt this was a vital thing for us both to do for each other.

While Chris agreed it was important, it was and remains a very challenging prospect for him. Why would you want to think consciously about the possibility of things going horribly wrong when your bad dreams are already a variation on this theme? A variation rooted in actual lived experience. A variation ingrained so deeply in your psyche that you have a diagnosed mental health condition.

Though we made headway with financial planning, it was an unnecessarily lengthy and combative process, so much so that we needed around forty sessions of counselling through the VVCS to help us work through it. Both Chris's military service and his divorce have influenced what we'll be as a couple, so we've had a bit to sort through.

In many ways, Chris is still the bomb disposal guy walking the streets of Belfast. He's armour-plated, self-contained and solitary. I don't know this guy well at all. I didn't meet him at this stage of his life. But, later, I know I was attracted to him, and that he's had an enormous impact on me. Now it sometimes feels like we both bear the weight of his blast suit. It's like our lives have been shaped by the spectre of that sign, far away on Manor Street. There's more to this than his military conditioning. Following a traumatic event or events, veterans can develop very 'exaggerated negative beliefs or expectations about … the world', and their place in it.[10]

In the psychiatric criteria for PTSD, this symptom used to be referred to as a 'sense of foreshortened future'.[11][12] In other words, as I understand it, many trauma survivors simply don't expect to have a normal life span, and all that could accompany this.[13] This occurs to such an extent that it can undermine their capacity for trust in relationships and their handle on future commitments.[14]

You can imagine this might be worse for a bomb technician who spent every day of his active service thinking he could disappear in a puff of smoke. You could say a portion of Chris's brain is still attuned to an armed bomb. He regularly retreats to his house at Phillip Island and silently regroups in front of the television. He spends whole weekends at a time dozing in his favourite armchair

Together in Belfast in 2018 with the Manor Street sign above us

by the wood heater. It seems as if he's snoozing with an internal alarm. Because of ongoing nightmares and sleep issues, he needs time to rest like this, and to be alone.

Sometimes, I imagine him heading off to the island and never coming back to me. He would spend his days whittling, handcrafting knives, feeding the cockatoos, and taking his tinnie down to the water for a spin. I wonder if he'd be better off living solo in this way. But then he video-calls me twice in one morning to show me a kookaburra on the verandah, and to tell me he's missing me.

Chris can be reclusive, but he can also be caring, funny, kind and still very loveable. I like to think that I've had something to do with this resilience, although I also know that relationships can make or break a veteran with PTSD.

THE LIGHT

Amazing friends

It's fitting that I've started writing this last part of my story after I've just returned from a girls' weekend with four of the ladies from our group. Together, we rented a gorgeous boutique cottage in Wangaratta and filled its rooms with our friendship and laughter. No topic was off the table, from food and orgasms, to death and grieving.

I love these women and their wounded men. As Chris did the PTSD Program with them in the first year of our relationship, they've been a feature of our relationship from the beginning. They're an amazing group. They help to bind Chris and me to one another.

On the Saturday afternoon we sit down together with a drink and the conversation shifts to our men. We start talking about some amusing habits they have, and then somehow end up comparing notes on their nightmares. It's quite a shift, which is par for the course when your man is a veteran and trauma survivor.

I tell them that writing this PTSD story has made me more curious about Chris's dreams. Each day, after we've said good morning to each other, I ask him, 'What did you dream about?' In the past, he'd simply replied, 'Oh, you know, stuff', but lately he's been talking more, and I'm very pleased about this. The only trouble is, this 'stuff' isn't at all easy to hear.

I steel myself and begin to recount one of Chris's recurring nightmares; the one in which a bomb's blown a woman through an iron railing. Her male companion had stepped on a pressure mat when he was entering a neighbour's flat ahead of her. All they were doing was checking on the neighbour and they became collateral damage. The man was blown to pieces and she was thrown back onto the balustrade.

Chris attended this scene many years ago in Londonderry and it remains etched in his brain. He's often revisited by this 'poor mangled creature' lying on the ground against the wall, her body shredded by the railing. He sees the corner of her floral sundress flapping in the wind. The colours of the dress are very vivid, and he can even smell the summer breeze. It's like all his senses are still heightened.

When I tell the women about this, I unexpectedly get a bit tearful. I feel for Chris when he opens up to me about such experiences. It's like he lets me in, then I express the emotions that he can't. Nightmares such as this one wake him up most nights at around 4 am. The scene in Londonderry is one of many that haunt him.

The women of the group empathise and share some of their own stories of their partners' bad dreams. Years ago, the PTSD Program gave them some knowledge, permission and skills to start voicing the costs for those who love someone with PTSD. Now, we 'tell it like it is' when we're together, which is something our veteran partners thankfully encourage.

Immediate family

The next topic to come up as we share a couple of drinks together is our families, in their many forms. We're terribly sad that we lost Glenda recently, so first we acknowledge this, and what Terry and his four adult children are going through. We're thankful he has their support.

When it's my turn to talk, I share some thoughts I've been having lately about Chris's family. They've been on my mind a lot because of my struggle in writing this story. I even sat down with his son Willy and spoke to him at length about the events that first led Chris to the Repatriation Hospital.

I can't talk about it all here, but I do want to acknowledge the untold stories among us. I believe the impact of Chris's extraordinary military experiences are a big part of who we all are today. I know Willy, for example, remembers Chris's absences well, but also the homecomings, and how proud and relieved he felt when his heroic dad would appear back on the doorstep in his battle fatigues.

That man in uniform is a far cry from the Chris I started seeing in 2005, when he was unwell. I'm told it fell on Willy to become the hero for a while in the year prior, and, at the age of nineteen, he did a sterling job of supporting his dad. Chris often says he might not have survived that time if it hadn't been for Willy's care and concern on the home front.

I've been trying to pinpoint when things settled down after the PTSD Program. The course was a turning point for Chris but the real change for us happened in 2006 when he finally moved out of the family home in Park Orchards. He rented a little cottage in Mitcham where we began to spend a lot more time together. In fact, it wasn't long before I moved in. After all the volatility of the preceding year, we suddenly found ourselves enjoying a very calm and happy time in each other's company. We became involved in each other's family and social lives. We began to build a life together.

At this point, we didn't just commit to each other, but to a number of things that came along with this change. For example, Bec and I had to forge a relationship with each other reasonably quickly, as she was regularly living with Chris at the time. Further, I found myself interacting regularly with Chris's soon-to-be ex-wife, Liz. In doing so, we were both amicable. Chris's ageing mum, Joan, also entered the picture that year. She left South Africa to live in Australia. None of this was anywhere near as challenging as it could've been. Bec was only fifteen years old in 2006 and showed incredible maturity in the way she adjusted to the changes in her life, which was a sign of the awesome, resilient adult she would become. We had fun together in that little cottage. It was what Chris needed after his long stay at Heidelberg Repatriation Hospital in 2005.

Relative to our situation on the home front, I'd say life as a blended family of sorts has been peaceful. We all rally together when we need or want to and, speaking for Chris, I believe this has been very healing for him.

My lovely man

Sunday morning arrives and I'm sitting with the ladies at the kitchen table in my courtesy bathrobe, having a cup of tea. One of them says something to me like, 'Okay, Susannah, it's time for you to debrief'. I hesitate and get a bit defensive. 'I have nothing new to report,' I deflect. 'Everything's fine.'

They know I'm lying. Ten minutes later, I'm telling them about something on the home front that's really pushed my buttons recently. It's not Chris's boundaries I'm wrestling with – I get that he was clear about them from the beginning – it's the ongoing and unexpected fallout from them that has surfaced as we've been working through our financial planning. 'No marriage' has begun to have a material impact that neither of us ever considered. Regardless, in counselling, Chris renewed his vow that he'll never remarry, and I renewed mine to work with this.

Maybe that's more romantic than wedding vows – that we agree to try to love each other as unconditionally as possible, without a contract. In that moment at the kitchen table though, I let the ladies know that I still struggle with Chris's terms from time to time. Though I've mostly reconciled myself to a life without matrimony and motherhood, I occasionally still need to acknowledge or honour the possibilities I relinquished back in 2005.

Then I remember changing the subject by saying something silly such as, 'I'm feeling a bit exposed in my fluffy bathrobe right now; I'd better go and make myself look a bit more presentable', and we all laugh. There's more than twenty years age difference between these ladies and me, but that doesn't matter one bit. We all get along so well.

As I'm about to get up from my chair, Robyn stops me. She says to me, 'If you could go back, do you think you would do things differently?' That's a big question. I decide to go with my first response and answer, 'Well, I'm sure Chris is the great love of my life, and I wouldn't change that, even if I couldn't be that for him'.

Perhaps the one thing I would do differently back in 2005 is banish the thought that our relationship might help Chris start afresh; that I might be 'the light' for him that would somehow change his view of things. Those structural cracks were way too big for me to play that role.

In May 2018, Chris and I went on a pilgrimage to Northern Ireland, accompanied by our close friend Dymphna, and revisited some of the experiences that shaped these cracks. I found this helpful because I gained more insight into the nature of his service, but it was also confronting at times.

When he was in the military, Chris saw and did things that I know violated his values and belief in the 'sanctity of life'. This has given his own life a unique flavour, one that's laced with a fair degree of guilt. It's an unfamiliar flavour to someone as protected as I've been.

When I hear him reminiscing, or when I ask him about his nightmares, it always makes me think of the term 'nostalgia', from one of the very early constructs of PTSD. I know it's not used now but it seems more personal and poetic to me than the PTSD acronym.

Nothing captures the nature of Chris's condition more to me than the notion that he has difficulty focusing on the present (and making plans for the future) due to remembrances of things past: his fractured homeland in Africa, the many incidents that haunt him and his heartbreak over the way his family unit was affected.

As Dymphna and I watched Chris stare regretfully at a certain poppy cross in Belfast, I had to acknowledge that he'd never release himself from the weight of his past. He wouldn't want to, lest he forgets. All I can do is give him the support and space we both need to live with it, as well as we can.

It has taken time and effort for me to accept this as our reality and to learn to turn my attention to the myriad ways the light does get in. Lucky for us, there's been a lot of light, as if it's proportional to the depth and breadth of the cracks. Though 'more' has been lacking for us on many fronts, the desire to understand one another and work at our relationship hasn't been.

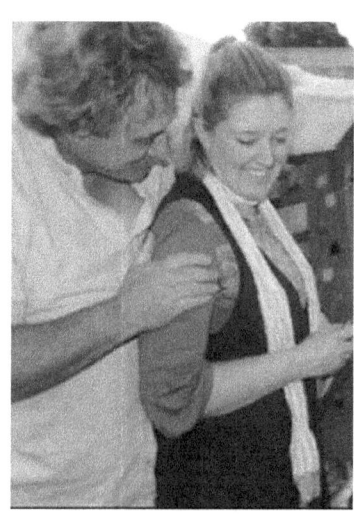

My man being lovely

We've supported each other through some defining experiences over the years. Things like my Honours year, health issues, work transitions, landmark birthdays, and the passing of some of our nearest and dearest, including my dad and Chris's mum, Joan. Throughout such events, we've been loving and loyal companions. Our partnership has stood the test of time, against great odds. I'm grateful for the bond that has sustained us so far, the family and friends who've supported us unconditionally, and all the skilled help we've had along the way.

CANDLE IN THE WINDOW
– THE STOKERMAN'S JOURNEY –

Garry Daly

The snippets herein are a very small part of a very full life – a life that, despite some bad times, I mostly managed to enjoy. I'd do it all again. The sad part about my life journey and its adventures is that there were casualties along the way; the worst of these was my family. The scars now are all but gone.

KATAMATITE 1958

My destiny and adventure began on a Wednesday night at the fortnightly picture show in the Katamatite town hall. Admission for kids was a shilling, a lot of money for Mum in those days, and we usually had only sixpence to spend at half-time. The trick was to sit next to our mates whose parents were farmers; they had more money to spend on lollies and would gladly share. Jaffas were the favourite; you could roll a couple down the floor at a suspenseful or spooky scene in the movie.

God Save the Queen blared from the speakers. On the screen, while our national anthem played, the Union Jack and our Australian flag were crossed and fluttering, and a Royal Australian Navy (RAN) destroyer burst between the flags. I was hooked. I wanted to be a sailor on those warships. In great excitement, I told Mum and Dad, who were both ex-WWII Australian Army. Dad was a gunner, having served in the Middle East, Greece, Crete and Ceylon, and Mum was a signalwoman based at Queenscliff and Portsea. My grandad was also an army man who served in the Middle East, Gallipoli and France in WWI. Mum and Dad agreed that the navy would be a good future job, but why not the army? Follow the tradition! No way – the army didn't have destroyers.

I am the eldest in my family, with one brother and two sisters. We've always been close. We were very lucky as we had wonderful parents and a happy childhood.

Four years after this inspirational night, I went along to the Armed Forces Recruiting Office in Queens Parade, Albert Park in Victoria. I was advised that if I passed the exams and medical, I could get into the adult intake as soon as I was seventeen years old, either a nine or twelve-year enlistment. I passed all the tests and on 3 June 1963 I became a recruit in the Royal Australian Navy. My journey into a life of adventure had begun.

THE ADVENTURE

I was at the RAN recruit school, HMAS *Cerberus*, and it sure was an awakening! As a teenager, I was undisciplined and thought I knew it all. I thought I was tough. Within 24 hours of my arrival at *Cerberus* my world changed. Discipline was imposed. The navy commenced to make a man out of a boy. I learnt how to march; how to handle and care for a .303 rifle; how to present, order and slope arms; how to shoot; all about naval history and tradition, basic seamanship, fire-fighting and damage control, physical fitness, housekeeping; and so many other things about the navy and what it expected from you.

After a gruelling three months, I was then categorised for branch training. Much to my disappointment, I was to be an underwater controller (UC), a seaman, not an engineer, which had been my choice. The navy had its quota of engineers at that time.

Our passing-out parade followed the completion of recruit training for the June intake divisional classes. We marched in formation to the RAN's wonderful brass band. It was a day when parents could come along and marvel at their changed sons. Following pass-out, it was time to pack my seabag and board the *Cerberus* Navy train to Melbourne for a weekend's leave before heading to Sydney. I was pretty proud to have fulfilled my boyhood dream and to be going home in my bell-bottoms as a RAN sailor.

On the Sunday night I took the Spirit of Progress to Sydney where I joined HMAS *Watson*, the Navy's Underwater Control and Weapons

Training School at Watsons Bay. I didn't want to be there; I wanted to be at the Engineering Training School at HMAS *Cerberus* that I'd just left.

Halfway through the UC training, I was called to the base gangway where the officer of the watch (OOW) advised me that my younger brother Ross had been involved in a very serious motorbike accident and wasn't expected to live. Mum wanted me to come home. Ross was in a coma. Just about all that could be broken was broken and his prognosis was dire. I was sent home with instructions to call the commander's office when I knew Ross's situation. I was granted fourteen days compassionate leave. At the end of this period, Ross was still in a coma and there was nothing I could do to help, so I returned to *Watson*. Ross's condition didn't improve in the weeks following. He was still in a coma three months later. I was very worried about him and the impact on Mum and Dad, although eventually he came out of the coma and after extensive rehabilitation he was able to work.

As a result of my leave, I'd missed too much of my UC training and was falling behind, so I requested a change of rate to the marine engineering division, as a marine engineer mechanic (ME), which I'd initially wanted to do.

HMAS *Sydney*

My timing was perfect, and my request was granted. I became part of an experimental new training regime where I'd go to sea for a year as an ordinary seaman. I'd do this sea time on HMAS *Sydney*, an aircraft carrier built at the end of WWII, mothballed for many years in Sydney Harbour. In 1963, she was brought back into RAN service and commissioned as a training and troop ship.

I drafted onto the *Sydney* at Garden Island Naval Dockyard in 1963 and reported to the officer of the watch. I saluted and told him I was Ord (ME) Daly drafted from *Watson*. 'A what? There is no such rate. Report to the Master at Arms office.' Same response. It seemed the Canberra Navy had failed to tell the powers that be on the *Sydney* about the new training scheme.

Next stop was HQ1 and the engineering office. Finding my way around a large ship while lumping my seabag up and down ladders was a daunting experience. Eventually, with some help from a bloke who was a stoker, I was introduced to the crusty old Chief Petty Officer ME. Same response: 'No such bloody thing, son. Do you know what a stoker does? Do you know what a boiler is, or a turbine, or a turbo generator, or a diesel generator, or refrigeration plant … ?' After some ridicule and him determining that I had very good mechanical aptitude, the chief stoker (whom I later learnt was regarded as close to God as you could get on a warship) advised me that I was to be an experimental ME3 until he found out more about the 'bloody new training scheme'. The most junior engineering rate at sea at that time was an ME2. I was to do all that an ME2 did and I was to learn 'f***ing fast' or I'd find myself back at recruit school or in civvy street.

I was allocated to a stokers' mess, issued with a hammock, two boiler suits, a pair of boiler boots and a locker. This was to be the beginning of my career as an engineer.

After a few weeks doing all the shitty, dirty and hard jobs that were part and parcel of being a junior engineering rate, HMAS *Sydney* was to go to sea on exercise and to support an amphibious landing exercise with the army at Hervey Bay. My first job was to learn how to 'punch sprayers' in one of the ship's two boiler rooms.

To get down into 'A' boiler room while the boiler was lit and operating was, for the first time, a scary, but exciting experience. First, you had to enter an airlock through the first hatch, close it and then open a second hatch, close it and enter hell, or that's what it seemed like. First the searing heat, then the noise, then the smell of steam and oil hit you, then down more ladders and you were on the bottom plates and the boiler fronts.

Two boilers faced each other with a petty officer marine engineer (POME) in charge and a stoker ME2 at each boiler front. The POME, by way of hand signals, directed the stokers to put on or take off the burners or 'sprayers' on the boiler. This task required a technique that involved turning on or off the heated furnace oil and then pulsing the extremely hot air flaps with both hands. This had to be performed at lightning speed in order to maintain sufficient fire in the boilers to produce sufficient steam to drive the ship's propulsion steam turbines and other machinery.

Working doubled-up, alongside the boiler front stoker ME2, along with some not-so-gentle verbal encouragement from the POME, one soon learnt how to punch sprayers. I was on my way to becoming a would-be stoker. This was more like it – machinery and mechanical stuff.

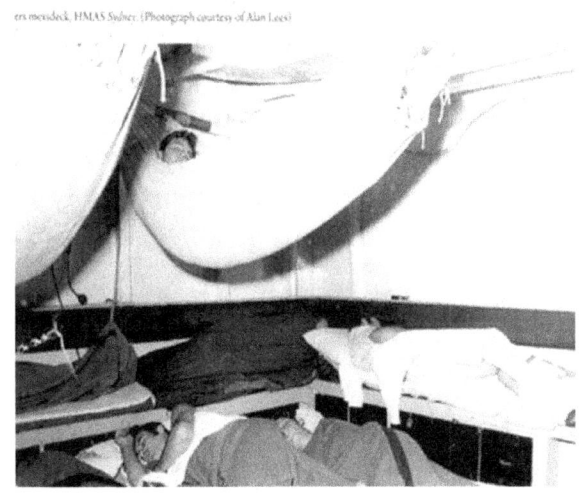

Stokers' Mess HMAS Sydney, 1964

It was hard and very hot work, 50°C, and four hours on, eight hours off, with theory training in off-watch time.

I soon had mates amongst HMAS *Sydney's* stokers, even though they used to take the piss out of me for being an ME3. There were four of us to take the piss out of; we were all change of rates. I became great mates with one of those stokers; he was a good mate to have, as he was a Commonwealth Games boxer and later became a professional champion light heavyweight during the time we both served on HMAS *Derwent*. He went on to star on *TV Ringside*. Sadly, he took his own life about twenty years after this. At his funeral, his ex-wife, whom I'd met in our navy time, told me that for many years he'd suffered depression, which she blamed for the breakdown of their marriage and for his suicide.

HMAS Sydney - *Royal Australian Navy, Sea Power Centre-Australia*

The sea time training on *Sydney* ended and I was posted to the HMAS *Cerberus* Marine Engineering Training School to undergo the first MEQ (Engineer Mechanic Qualifying) course under the new training scheme.

The course was demanding, with lots of marine engineering theory and workshop practice, study and exams. It was at this time that I was christened Delo by a stoker mate, Gunns, after the American comedy TV show *Delo and Daly*. Today, fifty-five years later, I'm still called Delo. I first met Gunns when we did our MEQ course at *Cerberus* in 1964. We remained mates up until his death in April 2019.

HMAS *Parramatta* and the stokerman

After the Marine Engineering Qualifying course in 1964, I was drafted to HMAS *Parramatta*, then a modern Type 12 anti-submarine frigate. I was on a real warship, a warship not unlike the one that blasted through the flags at the Katamatite pictures six years before. I was an ME2 (stoker), a real sailor. We proudly called ourselves the Elite of the Fleet and Custodians of the Golden Rivet.

HMAS *Parramatta* was a totally different ship from HMAS *Sydney*. It was significantly smaller and had air-conditioned living spaces with bunks and modern machinery. She was at the end of a maintenance cycle, refit at Sydney's Garden Island and about to commence work-up trials prior to a lengthy SEATO and FESR deployment.

My first work-up and sea trials experience exposed me to the life I could expect on a real warship: physically hard and hot work, endless training exercises/war games and a continuous state of war readiness that the navy and our government expected and demanded of us. I liked it. It was the real stuff. Full-speed trials and refuelling at sea from a tanker or aircraft carrier. Gunnery shoots, anti-submarine and mortar firing exercises, fire drills. Tannoy announcements such as 'Hands to Action Stations', 'Hands to Emergency Stations', 'Assume NBCD State 1 Condition Yankee', and 'Special Sea Duty Men Close Up', honed the crew's skills and the ship's capability for war.

I didn't have to wait long for this training to be put to the test. At the end of 1964, we were back at Garden Island when one morning a 'Clear lower deck' announcement was made and our captain advised the crew that we'd march to a naval facility at Woolloomooloo to be addressed about our SEATO and FESR deployment. Old hands told us younger hands that this wasn't normal.

A ten-minute march saw us at a navy store facility. We assembled inside and sat down to be addressed by two lieutenant commanders from Naval Intelligence. They advised that the then Indonesian President Sukarno had declared war against what was then Malaya. The Australian Government had made plain its resolve that if Malaya were subjected to invasion or subversive activity, then Australian military assistance would be added to that of Britain to defend the British colony Malaya. We were told of the Indonesian Confrontation and its history. Consequently, RAN warships in the Strategic Reserve (SEATO) based in Singapore were to be made available for naval patrol and escort operations to counter possible incursions by Indonesian warships, and to prevent movements of armed parties of communist Indonesians in sampans and local trading boats.

We were shown pictures of the types of Indonesian warships and aircraft that Indonesia had purchased from Russia; shown pictures of Indonesian troops; and we were told that we were going to this 'undeclared war' and would deploy in a few days to Singapore before commencing patrols and guard ship duties around the Malaya Peninsula, Malacca, Borneo, Singapore and Indonesia.

The closing advice was that if we were unfortunate enough to engage a hostile Indonesian MIG jet then we 'might kiss our arse goodbye', as our gunnery system probably couldn't track these fast-moving jets. He told us not to talk about what we'd just been told as it was considered a military secret, and to tell anybody who asked that we were just going 'Up Top' – what the SEATO and FESR deployments were called by sailors. Loose lips sink ships.

Far East and active service

We departed for Singapore and began patrol duties. Patrol was characterised by long periods of tedious routine, punctuated by moments of highly intense activity and occasional hazards, such as encountering Indonesian warships. Fortunately, none of these proved hostile, though I had no doubt we would've prevailed.

Our Confrontation patrols in the Malaysian Peninsula, Borneo, Kalimantan and Singapore waters were conducted during both day and night, so we stokers, stuck down below in the ship's engine or boiler room, were the proverbial 'mushrooms'. We didn't know what was happening above us. We'd often close up to defence stations or action stations. If you weren't on watch in the machinery spaces you'd be at your allotted damage control station, but if you were down below you could only assume what might be happening by the engine movements – *full ahead, half ahead, full astern, stop* and so forth – when the ship manoeuvred to encounter suspicious vessels for boarding or communication. When we came off watch we'd ask our mates and the seamen who'd been on the upper deck what had happened.

In addition to patrols, we carried out guard ship duties at Tawau, close to an Indonesian Nunukan Island Navy and Army facility. Guard ship duty enabled prompt naval gunfire support to Commonwealth troops ashore if required. Our patrols continued through 1965–1966. In 1965, a communist military coup in Indonesia was put down by the then Indonesian Army General, Suharto, and this saw President Sukarno deposed by Suharto, who then went on to become Indonesia's President.

While all this was going on with the Indonesian Confrontation, the USA and South Vietnam were asking Australia to support them in hostilities in Vietnam. On 25 May 1965, Prime Minister Menzies announced Australia's official involvement in Vietnam. With the retrospective allotment for duty of HMAS *Parramatta*, this marked Australia's first declared commitment to the war.[1]

We soon sailed, after a paint change and removal of recognition numbers. After some reconnaissance and surveillance work, we steamed south to rendezvous at Manus Island, Papua New Guinea with the troopship HMAS *Sydney* and the destroyer HMAS *Duchess* to begin the escort of *Sydney* on its first trip to Vung Tau, Vietnam. During the passage from PNG, our aircraft carrier HMAS *Melbourne* and destroyer HMAS *Vampire* joined us.

Parramatta and *Duchess* took *Sydney* into Vung Tau Harbour on 8 June 1965 and provided a protective screen while HMAS *Sydney* unloaded and then left Vung Tau. We didn't know what to expect of Vietnam's coast or Vung Tau, as this was a first. Subsequently, the ships were always in a high state of readiness. When at action stations in a Type 12 frigate, the boiler room and the engine room's hatches were padlocked closed on the outside! This was done so the ship wouldn't flood if hit in the machinery spaces. The first time I experienced this was surreal. With machinery noise as loud as a jumbo jet, I heard the hatch dropped and I swear I heard the lock click, and, 'Bad luck stokers, locked down!' We were locked in a machinery space with boilers, super-heated steam, fire and hot oil. It would be flooded if we were hit by a shell, torpedo, or had any other impact.

Because of the perceived threat from Chinese submarines while in transit to and from Vietnam, and from North Vietnamese swimmers with limpet mines and explosives in Vung Tau Harbour, at least one destroyer or destroyer escort/frigate always escorted HMAS *Sydney*. In transit, the escorts would carry out an anti-submarine surveillance screen while closed up at defence stations and while unloading and loading. In harbour, boats from *Sydney* and her escorts would patrol around the troopship while navy divers would regularly inspect the hull, propellers and anchor chains. In the early trips to Vung Tau there was always the threat of artillery attack against *Sydney* and its escorts.

Following this Vietnam deployment, HMAS *Parramatta* undertook more patrol and guard ship duty in the Indonesian Confrontation until its end in 1966 when *Parramatta's* crew participated in the 'Beat the Retreat' at Labuan, Malaya. Little is known in Australia of what's referred to as 'The Secret War' or 'Konfrontasi'. While Commonwealth casualties were relatively low, the toll of Indonesian civilians killed by Indonesians was horrendous. It's believed up to half a million civilians were killed and mutilated throughout Indonesia and more than one and a half million imprisoned. At the time, we weren't aware of the extent of the fighting in Indonesia between those Indonesians who supported the communist troops and civilians. In 1978, when I first went to work in Sulawesi, Indonesia, I saw total villages that'd been destroyed and I spoke with Indonesians who were there during the confrontation. What they told me was horrendous. They spoke of rivers running red with blood. They still harboured fear and some hate. It disturbed me that all this was going on while we, the Brits and the Malays, were patrolling and protecting on land and sea and in the air.

Once, while on patrol, I nearly drowned in the engine room bilges under machinery when the ship's bottom filled with hot oily water. I was a skinny ME2, working with an Engine Room Artificer (ERA) repairing an extraction pump when the ship made a very hard turn and tools and parts rolled into the bilges under the port condenser. The ERA told me to get in the bilges and retrieve the tools and an extraction pump part that had rolled there. I got stuck, with just my face out of the water. I could barely breathe and couldn't move backwards to get out. Stormy, the chief of the watch, had come down to help but he was too large and couldn't get to where I was. He told me to wriggle out of my overalls, which had snagged on a bolt. I managed to do this and my mate Algy dragged me out by my feet. I emerged from the bilge nude like an oily rat and said to him, 'Mate, I thought I was going to croak. Drowned at sea'. I headed straight up the ladder out of the engine room to the upper deck.

This incident didn't bother me too much at the time but in later years when I began to experience the same disturbing bad dream night after night, this claustrophobic incident featured. I dreamed that I was stuck in the bilge on a ship that never went into port – just sailed to nowhere. While I haven't said much about the serious stuff that we did during these times, HMAS *Parramatta* was awarded Battle Honours for service in the Indonesian–Malaysia Confrontation 1964–1966. Like many Australian military awards, recognition wasn't made for many years after the action or time.

Despite the endless hard work we did in HMAS *Parramatta* during the Indonesian Confrontation and Vietnam, we did get to enjoy ourselves. We 'showed the flag', visiting exotic countries and their cesspits that seemed to attract sailors. We visited Singapore, Hong Kong, Penang, Port Swettenham/Kuala Lumpur, Sandakan, Manila, Subic Bay, Bangkok, Japan's Kobe, Hiroshima, Nagasaki, Beppu, Tokyo and Yokohama, Fiji, Noumea, New Zealand and more. We also visited some Australian ports. It wasn't all hard work, although it was work hard, and when we hit port we played hard, let off steam and behaved badly. When home in Australia we saw family.

Sea-time training and experience in HMAS *Parramatta* saw me promoted from ME2 to ME1. After examination, I was awarded my Auxiliary Watch Keeping Certificate, the essential qualification for promotion to Leading ME. I'd gained significant marine engineering knowledge, qualifications and experience.

A couple of days before reaching Sydney from our 1966–1967 SEATO/FESR deployment, I was enjoying an evening beer, a large can of Abbots with my mates Algy, Boori and Doustie. Our lieutenant commander came up to us for a chat and to tell us we all had shore postings when we returned to Australia.

I was leaving HMAS *Parramatta* after an often hard but enjoyable three years. I then went home for some long overdue leave before drafting into HMAS *Lonsdale* at Port Melbourne. This only lasted three weeks before I was moved to the RAN's Victoria Naval Police Office.

At this point I should mention that despite the hectic navy sea-time life, I did find time to enjoy female company, a 'girl in every port'. I was engaged to a Melbourne girl, Sandy, whom I married not long after settling into the shore patrol in 1967. It was, as a lot of marriages were during that era, a 'shotgun wedding'. While Sandy's mum was insistent that I marry her, my parents weren't happy about the situation. In fact, Mum told me that I had to wait until I was twenty-one before tying the knot, so that I couldn't blame anybody for forcing me to get married.

HMAS Parramatta - *Royal Australian Navy, Sea Power Centre-Australia*

HMAS *Parramatta* was my home for three years. It was a great ship with a good, happy crew who were hardworking and proficient in everything that was expected of them. I had great mates in HMAS *Parramatta*. Today, I'm still great mates with a couple of stokers who I sailed with in *Parramatta*, but sadly some of my mates are no longer with us due to asbestos disease and post-wartime related medical issues. My great mate Algy succumbed to mesothelioma at fifty-nine years of age, the result of asbestos exposure. Our ships were 'steam ships', asbestos lagging by the mile. Only Boori and I from the picture below are left. Lest we forget.

Relaxing on Parramatta's quarter deck under the old White Ensign, 1965. From left: ME2s Algis (Algy), Skudutis, Garry (Delo) Daly, Ord ME Huck Haynes and ME1 Barry (Boori) Powell

HMAS *Derwent*, Far East and more

My twelve-month shore posting at HMAS *Lonsdale*, when I was learning to be a husband and a dad, flew by. In 1968, at twenty-two, I was back at sea on HMAS *Derwent* leaving behind a heavily pregnant wife and baby daughter.

I hardly had time to unpack my sea bag when we left Garden Island for deployment to the Far East and the SEATO/FESR, Up Top again. We hadn't long cleared Sydney Heads when I was called to the bridge and advised by the officer of the watch that a signal had been received advising that I had another daughter, born that morning. Kelly was born on the thirtieth of the month, as were her sisters, Tracy and Lisa. I don't quite know how we managed that, but it must have been a stoker achievement.

HMAS *Derwent's* deployment was very busy. We travelled to all the usual South-East Asian ports and to countries that I hadn't visited before: South Korea's Seoul and the 38[th,] parallel, Incheon and Pusan, Ceylon's Trincomalee, India's Madras and East Pakistan's Chittagong (now Bangladesh).

There'd been a typhoon and monsoonal flooding a week or so before we steamed up a very big river to Chittagong. The river was putrid with all sorts of debris, dead animals and lots of bodies. Our on-board lieutenant doctor was worried about the possibility of cholera in the river water that we stokers distilled into the ship's fresh water tanks. We hadn't made the adjustments to the evaporators before and weren't sure of its effectiveness in killing the cholera. The doctor had us put chlorine in the water tanks. The water tasted like a public swimming pool. To overcome the chlorine taste we all flocked to the canteen and bought soft drinks, but these soon ran out, so we bought Sal Vital, which was generally used to keep bowel movements regular, and soon we were all shitting through the eye of a needle, but the water tasted better.

It wasn't long before we were out to sea again and could fill our freshwater tanks with good distilled water. We then steamed to Singapore for a short maintenance cycle, and then escorted HMAS *Sydney* on its thirteenth trip to Vietnam's Vung Tau in February 1969. After this, we steamed to Bangkok and Hong Kong before turning towards home. We returned to Australia ten months later and I saw my second daughter Kelly for the first time. After a quick maintenance period and leave for the crew, HMAS *Derwent* was away again. This deployment took us first to Noumea, next to Pago Pago (the capital of American Samoa), then to Pearl Harbour to be welcomed by a United States Navy (USN) band and Hula Girls (USN wives). We were then fully involved in exercises and war games with the USN nuclear submarines and other warships. From Pearl Harbour, we continued our deployment, proceeding to Singapore via Kwajalein, Guam and Subic Bay. We escorted HMAS *Sydney* home in time for Christmas, having spent the previous Christmas in Hong Kong.

It was during my time away on HMAS *Derwent* that I became an angry man and first used violence to get a message across. I'd been promoted to LME (leading engineer mechanic) and one of my jobs was to maintain the ship's two water distillation units installed in the boiler room. These produced distilled water for the boilers and the ship's potable water. They'd been giving trouble for a few days and in order to get them operating correctly I spent fourteen hours solid in the boiler room maintaining and testing them until they worked. I knocked off, showered and lay down to rest when I was shaken by the third hand, who said, 'Delo, one of the vaps has shit itself'. 'Who's on watch?' I asked. He told me it was the guy who was known to be a 'menace to machinery', one who should never have been a stoker.

I looked at the troublesome evaporator, made some adjustments, and called the menace to machinery to where I was standing. I abused him for his incompetence. He made a stupid comment so I belted him in the face and landed him in front of the POME in charge of the watch, who was astounded. He yelled, 'F***ing hell Delo, what are you doing?' I replied, 'Shut up, mate, or you're f***ing next.' As the menace to machinery had to go to the sick bay with a broken nose, the incident was reported. I was charged with striking a junior rate and had to front the captain.

I should've been demoted to ME1, but the engineering officer spoke well in my defence, so no demotion. I lost my four-year good conduct record and badge, which effectively stopped my chance of promotion to POME for a couple of years. It was around this time that I began to feel that things weren't right. I was becoming very quick to anger and anxious and didn't understand why, but one didn't talk about things then, instead bottled it all up. If you were to talk about things, you were a wimp.

On return to Garden Island for a major refit, I had a very short posting from HMAS *Derwent* to HMAS *Sydney*. I didn't want to be there; I wasn't a big-ship man. On my first watch on the turbine throttles while sailing out of Sydney Harbour I got a kick in the arse from the senior engineer for operating the throttles too fast, like a 'destroyer cowboy'. I argued with him and was very close to belting him. One just didn't argue with a lieutenant commander. Later, he told me to leave if I didn't like it. I did, unofficially. As soon as HMAS *Sydney* berthed at Portland, I packed my seabag, walked down the gangway and hitchhiked to Melbourne. When I got home, Sandy said that the shore patrol had been there and as soon as I got home, I was to report to HMAS *Cerberus*. I was very lucky: no demotion or severe punishment was meted out and after being there for a couple of months I went back to sea again to HMAS *Yarra*.

I can't imagine how hard it must've been for Sandy and my two girls at this time. I'd been married about four years and hadn't spent much time at home. I'm sure Sandy was aware of the lifestyle of sailors in those days and must've been suspicious of me when I was away, but she never accused me of cheating. She just got on with her life as a sailor's wife and took good care of our girls. It was a big adjustment being at home with my family. I had to do most things differently. I had to be a husband and a dad, curtail my behaviour and be more responsible. But we were happy, we didn't argue or fight, and tried to make the most of the time we had together. Sandy was a good wife and mum, she kept an immaculate house, and the kids were well clothed and behaved. I expect my family would've preferred me to be home all the time, and I did miss them, but I always believed they managed pretty well without me.

HMAS Derwent - *Royal Australian Navy, Sea Power Centre-Australia*

HMAS *Yarra*, Far East and elsewhere

This deployment on HMAS *Yarra* saw the usual Up Top stuff that we'd done endless times before, but this was a shorter trip. On return to Australia, we exercised and trained for a short time before departing for Hawaii and Pearl Harbour via Noumea and Fiji to undertake anti-submarine work with the Yank nuclear subs, as we'd done on HMAS *Derwent* about twelve months before. These trips to Hawaii and Pearl Harbour weren't all hard war-game work; we got to relax in the great US Navy facilities and other places like Waikiki, Sunshine Beach and the infamous Hotel Street. When not 'relaxing' and responding to the American/Hawaiian girls' we even found time to play a bit of sport. However, I was away from my family again.

Australia calls

A couple of months later, HMAS *Yarra* was back in Garden Island for a long refit, during which time I came to the end of my nine-year enlistment in the RAN. At 0900 hours on the morning of my departure, I walked off HMAS *Yarra*, my last ship. I was a different person from the seventeen-year-old who'd joined the Royal Australian Navy nine years before. I'd gone from being a naïve teenager to a knowledgeable, well-travelled and often angry twenty-six-year-old man, who'd experienced service life that'd included active service in two war zones. I'd been well trained, and I was qualified in marine engineering. I'd seen and done things that only sailors had. I'd led a hard and sometimes dangerous life. In addition, working in very hot, noisy and asbestos-ridden engine and boiler rooms and machinery spaces took its toll on most stokers in one way or another. But it'd been a bloody adventure.

Prior to my discharge I'd discussed signing on for another stint with the engineering officer and I'd been offered promotion if I did, but Sandy was totally against it. I had two daughters and a wife who I'd barely been

HMAS Yarra - *Royal Australian Navy, Sea Power Centre-Australia*

with. She reminded me that I was a husband and a father. My options were navy life or family. I chose family.

I was uncertain how I'd adjust to this new chapter in my life. Having been in the navy for nine years, with a wife and two young girls for five of those years, the navy was like a family. Rigid routine, a place for everything and everything in its place, discipline, a pecking order, constant time at sea, continual exercise and war games and adventure. The longest continuous time I'd spent with my wife and child was twelve months. It'd been hard for me to adjust to living every day in a home with a wife and baby for company instead of a mess full of generally boisterous stokers. But adjust I did. I quickly learned to be a husband and dad and to lead a life totally alien to that which had become familiar. Is that not what I was in the navy for?

I'M A CIVILIAN

In May 1972, on a cold Sydney afternoon, I did the rounds of the pubs I'd frequented over the years, said my farewells, then took a taxi to Central Station and hopped onto the 'Red Rattler' night train home to Melbourne.

I was still in the navy but had a month's leave. I had a navy home in Frankston, but I was eligible to get a war service home loan of $9,500. I decided to buy our first home at a new estate on the edge of Dandenong. I paid $14,500 for a house and land. By this time my leave was over, and I was a civilian. We'd moved into our new home and, while still awaiting my navy discharge and qualification certificates, I applied for a job with a Dandenong engineering firm. I met with the manager for an interview, and was offered a job at HMAS Cerberus. I couldn't believe it; my first civilian job was to be back where my engineering career had commenced.

By the time the Cerberus and another construction job had finished, my service certificates had arrived. I could seek a better, permanent job. I secured a job as the services engineer at a pharmaceutical manufacturing plant. This was a good job – very close to my home and mostly good people employed there. I did my job well and got along with management. After two years in this job, I started to get anxious and moody. We were a happy family, now with three kids, Lisa having arrived in 1973. Why did I feel this way?

The mates I was working with and getting to know at the pub after work on Fridays and Saturdays weren't like those that I had in the navy. They lacked spirit, weren't adventurous and were too tame. Work was becoming boring with not enough challenge, no risks, and the same work, day in, day out. I was frustrated, impatient and I was getting angry more than I should. I was often feeling quite low and couldn't relax. I needed change – a job that I could lose myself in. I applied for a more challenging overseas job. I think Sandy realised that things were troubling me, but she never questioned me too much, just accepted what I told her when she asked.

My civilian adventure begins – 1974

Two months later we had tenants for our house, and my family and I were bound for Nauru. I had a two-year contract as a steam power station overseer with the Nauru Phosphate Company. I enjoyed the work, and the mates I worked with were more my type. They knew their stuff and had been around a bit. They liked a beer. They had a bit of larrikin in them, just like me.

Despite Nauru being a very isolated place, life was good. Our house on the hill was old but good and overlooked the harbour. We had a very social life. Sandy had good female company and Tracy and Kelly went to the local primary school; Lisa was still a toddler. It wasn't long before anger and mood swings bothered me, and sleep became a problem. After a big Sunday session at the staff club following a very busy couple of weeks at work, I had a very serious motorbike accident on the way home. I woke up 24 hours later in hospital and spent two weeks there.

Two months before my two-year contract was up, I was asked if I'd do another two-year term. I wanted to; Sandy didn't. Twice now I'd had to make a career decision to do what she wanted. I told my boss that I wouldn't be staying and why. He tried to talk me around, and even asked his wife to talk to Sandy. She said, 'No, either you leave with me and the kids or you can stay on your own'. I wasn't too happy about it; after all, I'd taken orders for nine years and had to do things that didn't please me. I was faced with a decision that I didn't want to make; however, I didn't want to lose my family for a job.

While this was all happening, I received a telex from the CEO of the pharmaceutical company I'd left to go to Nauru. He knew my contract was nearing its end and offered me my old job back. Sandy was over the moon. I wasn't, but I accepted the job offer, so we went back to Australia. I was back doing the same work, day in, day out with the same boring people whom I had left two years before. I was frustrated and troubled.

Twelve months later, I was feeling twitchy again. I wanted more: adventure, challenge, excitement and risk-taking. My family life was good; Sandy and I were happy with each other and the kids were enjoying family visits and holidays with Nan and Pop and we had a close group of friends, but it wasn't enough for me. I was a changed man. It was around this time that I began to believe something with me wasn't quite right. My navy time was still often at the forefront of my mind – the good and the bad. I was often in *navy mode* and it dictated how I worked, what I expected from those who worked with me, and how my home life and family functioned. I think because my work and lifestyle had changed, I began to expect more from people; I'd become a perfectionist and was often quick to anger. I didn't suffer fools lightly and when I wanted to get this message across I could bring a strong man down verbally.

I was always looking beyond the horizon. The navy had made me a traveller and had changed the way I thought. Maybe the travel bit was in my genes: my great-grandfather was a Swedish seaman in sailing ships; another great-great grandfather was an Irish sea captain; and another family member was a whaler, sealer and explorer.

My world and the way I was looking at it were different from how it was for me in 1963. Was this normal? Was this change to be expected if you were an ex-serviceman? I didn't know. I just knew I was a very different person, a bit confused and at times very low and anxious. When I couldn't relax, I'd often listen to my favourite song, Creedence Clearwater Revival's 'Long as I can see the light'.

The words in the song summed up how I was feeling a lot of the time and I'd often play the tape at home, at work, or in my car to lift my mood.

Despite all this, my relationship with Sandy was still good. We'd been married for nine years and I loved her and my three girls. I was a good provider, husband and dad. However, I felt like my life was slipping by me. The navy taught me that with discipline comes character; it'd trained me well technically, strengthened my resolve and taught me to be a leader. I needed to make use of my service and engineering training. I wanted some payback; I'd get on with my life, my way. One Saturday, soon after making this decision, I was reading the 'Situations Vacant' section of *The Age* and saw a job advertised for a power station maintenance supervisor position with Skilled Engineering's subsidiary Indonesian company, PT Tekniskil, the company I'd later manage. The job was at a nickel mine in Sulawesi Indonesia. I applied, was interviewed and offered the job.

It's rough in the jungle

I resigned my position at the pharmaceutical company and told Sandy and the kids. It was difficult trying to explain to them why I wanted to do this when I didn't know myself. I didn't want to leave them alone but I was driven to do things my way. Two weeks later, I was on my way to Indonesia and the Soroako nickel mine site on the edge of some lakes and in the jungle. The mine campsite had rough accommodation by today's standards. It had a cyclone fence around it with armed Indonesian security guards at its entrance, a wet mess and a rough village with bars. This was more like it!

My first job was to put the power station's two steam boilers and turbines into preservation. With my team of thirteen Indonesian workers, of whom only two had any real experience as a fitter, and only three who could speak any English, we set to work. We had completed one boiler and started on the second. All was going well, but then the Hydro Station shut down. Twenty-four hours later, one boiler and turbine were in operation and the station was up and running, but not before I'd abused the Indonesians who were conking out on me; it was Ramadan and they hadn't eaten and weren't strong at the best of times.

The results of this work did me lots of favour with the power station and mine management, although I did get a dressing down for racism and verbally abusing my Indonesian workers. One of the English speakers had dobbed me in. This wasn't the first time for me; I had a similar scenario soon after arriving at the mine with a Korean worker. We confronted each other. He did a karate dance around me. I grabbed a 24-inch Stillson wrench and he saw the folly of his action. It's unnerving to think that I could've killed the bloke.

Had I spent too much time in Asian countries? I asked myself. Regrettably, at the time I justified that they were weak bastards. On reflection, I think that it was my mental state that made me think this way. I was a perfectionist and wouldn't accept failure or poor work from my workers.

Despite these indiscretions, I was still in the good books. I was asked if I'd be interested in the power station maintenance superintendent's job, working directly with the mining company. The position was going to be vacant in a few months, and of course I said yes.

My contract with Tekniskil finished and I returned home to Melbourne and told Sandy the good news. 'We're not going. Go on your own if you want it so much,' was her response. For the third time, I had to decide between my family or my career and my desire to challenge myself more. I was very angry and disappointed. This was a great opportunity. It was good money, good married status accommodation, and kids' private/boarding secondary school education paid for by the company in Australia or elsewhere. I humbly had to advise that I couldn't accept their employment offer. I had a couple of weeks off before getting another job. Being home with my family was great but I generally would feel very low. I'd been feeling this way for several years. It wasn't my family life, and I liked my work, so I thought, *It must be me.*

Given a challenge

Soon after my return to Australia, I made an appointment to speak with people at Skilled and was soon working in a supervisory role on various client sites. I moved on to a supervisory role in their South Melbourne head office. After three months in this role, another door opened with the offer to manage the Indonesian contract work.

I thrived in this new opportunity. I learned quickly and soon got to know my way around the Indonesian Embassy in Sydney and the Melbourne Passport Office. I reported to the two managing directors and ran my own race. Next, I began working as a project manager at petrochemical refinery and paper mill maintenance shutdowns in Victoria, South Australia and Tasmania.

It wasn't long before PT Tekniskil won another contract in Indonesia and I was back in head office managing the Indonesian work, this time in Irian Jaya at a huge copper and gold mine at Tembagapura.

It was 1980. I was thirty-four, earning big dollars, flitting all over the country, wheeling and dealing, and socialising a lot. One night, I met Vivienne, ten years younger, vivacious, very pretty, and separated with two kids. My dick took charge and what I expected to be a one night stand developed and I made a very hurtful mistake. I walked out on my family. Sandy and I had been very happily married for thirteen years. We had three lovely young daughters, our own home, and we lived pretty well. I hadn't strayed during my married life. Today, I still wonder if I'd been mentally stable and well at the time, would I have done it? I don't think so. I had everything a man could want. It was almost like I had a brain snap.

During my turbulent 1979, Skilled had set up an office in Singapore, but it wasn't working. One of Skilled's owners called me in for a chat and said that he wanted me to go to Singapore the following week to sort out the troubled project and the operations business. This was on a Friday afternoon. So, off I went to Singapore.

I stayed on in Singapore for two months to get some semblance of an operations department in place. As agreed with my boss, I returned to Melbourne, gave my report, and had a week off. Then Skilled's MD asked if I'd go to Singapore, full-time, as operations manager. I agreed without hesitation. This was good news to me – a new challenge that I hoped would occupy my mind and allow me to function without invasive thoughts affecting my life.

South-east Asia calls again

I was promoted to Tekniskil's South-East Asia regional manager based in Singapore. I began commuting to Jakarta every couple of weeks.

One of my local partners was an ex-Indonesian Army Brigadier General who saw service during the Indonesian Confrontation. He was one of President Suharto's men, a bit of a hero during the coup and one of the good guys. He knew of my navy service from my CV and we'd briefly spoken of the Confrontation, a subject discussed with caution in Indonesia. At a party one night in Jakarta at his very nice house, he pulled me aside to show me something. He went to his bookshelf and pulled out a photo album and asked, 'Was this your ship?' It was a photograph of HMAS *Parramatta* in the cross hairs of a tank's gun that the Indonesians had embedded as shore defence at an Indonesian Confrontation Army and Navy base at Nunukan Island close to the border with Tawau. At one time during patrols on *Parramatta*, we ventured up an inlet close to the Indonesian base. The presence of the tanks was known to the captain, as he stopped the ship just out of the tank's range and, as a taunting gesture, sounded the ship's siren. Then we turned around and continued patrol. This is when the photograph was taken. Small world!

By this time, Vivienne and her kids had moved to Singapore and settled in well. Tracy, my eldest daughter, was at school in Singapore. I hadn't yet divorced Sandy.

I continued running the Indonesian operation from Singapore and at the same time establishing operations into Brunei and Malaysia. I seemed to operate better when under pressure. It hadn't taken me long to work out that work was a diversion for me. Knowing what I know now, I believe that I was fighting depression and had been for several years. While I was generally well and tried to keep fit, I was drinking socially to lift my mood.

Things continued this way over the next two or more years. I returned from a business trip to the Middle East very unwell. I called my MD to report on my trip and I think he picked up that something wasn't right as he asked if I was okay. I told him I was tired and was feeling crook. 'Doctors up there are no good. I want you to come to Melbourne and see your old doctor,' he said. I flew down and saw my doctor who diagnosed depression and advised me to see a doctor as soon as I returned to Singapore. Following this visit, my boss asked what the doctor had said. 'He reckons I'm suffering depression. Bullshit,' I said. I was ashamed to accept that it might've been true. However, I knew something wasn't right with me.

My MD knew a bit about depression, having experienced family trauma as a result of a tragic car accident. 'Get help,' he advised. I didn't. He convinced me to bring in another expat to give me some help. For the first six months, he shadowed me to learn the ropes. I made him operations manager and slowly introduced him to the Indonesian operation. After eighteen months, I transferred him to Indonesia as operations manager, reducing my need to go there regularly. I could concentrate more on Singapore and other places.

But life wasn't meant to be easy

In 1983, I was thirty-nine and running a company spread over South-East Asia. Due to business growth, I'd employed a Scottish engineer and based him in my Kuala Belait, Brunei office, and another Scottish engineer whom I based in my Kuala Lumpur, Malaysia office. I was flogging myself hard, but it was keeping the demons away.

I ventured further afield. I had the Middle East in mind. This project was with a Swedish manufacturing company for the construction of a particle board plant in Aqaba, Jordan. As there were no trees in the desert, timber was shipped from Malaysia.

This project was carried out at the time of the Iran-Iraqi war and was a pretty interesting and unstable location. Because of this situation, I carried two current passports when I travelled to the project to enable me to get out of the country via Israel if I had to.

I was still spending a lot of time between Malaysia, Brunei and Indonesia and marketing and tendering the bigger contracts. Things were really coming together, but I wasn't. I was working gruelling and inflexible hours to deflect my mental health issues. We were even doing maintenance work on Australian Navy warships at the old Royal Naval dockyard at Sembawang. I was often invited to wardroom and chief petty officer and petty officer mess cocktail parties on the ships.

Business was good, but I wasn't. I was easily irritable, experiencing highs and lows, and had very frequent mood swings. I couldn't relax unless I was water skiing or having a quiet drink. I was starting to not trust people, even Vivienne. Despite this, we were enjoying living in Singapore. However, one night, before I was to fly out to Jakarta, we argued. I told her I wanted to be alone and didn't need her in my life and that I'd fly her and her kids home to Australia. When she pleaded with me to stay I couldn't give her a reason as to why I'd made this decision.

I was now a single man in Singapore with my eldest daughter, Tracy. When she finished school and went back home to her mum, I was alone again. Things continued work-wise, but I was personally not right with the same issues. A good female friend said I was like Jekyll and Hyde.

Eventually, Vivienne and I began to communicate. I returned to Australia on business and we patched things up. Six months later, I returned to Melbourne and we married. She and her daughter moved back to Singapore. Soon after, my youngest daughter, Lisa, moved up. Sandy and I had obviously divorced; however, she'd never stood in the way of our kids spending time with me and she wanted the kids to be happy.

Who dares wins

In the mid 1980s, I was still mentally troubled. I'd purchased a house in Essendon, as I was spending half my time in Australia setting up a National Maintenance division. We had some early success when I bid for and was awarded the maintenance contract at the Brisbane Expo.

I negotiated sponsorship of the firework and laser show that would promote Skilled and Tekniskil every night for the 180-day duration of Expo. Together with the firework and laser technicians, we put together the visuals and soundtrack for the nightly show. It was amazing to watch and I felt great satisfaction and pride for being involved in Australia's second Expo.

Soon after this, as my national maintenance plans became known through marketing, I was asked to present a paper at a National Maintenance Management Conference in Sydney and Melbourne. Firstly, I had to write the paper, which was titled 'Contract Maintenance: The Future Direction'. I'd never spoken in front of an audience full of maintenance managers, engineers and senior management people, but I wasn't nervous about doing it. Despite my mental health issues, I'd become a very confident man. I presented my paper and had some serious questions thrown at me from the floor, but I received strong applause afterwards. Following these two presentations, I was invited to present my paper to the Institute of Engineers at the Wollongong University and then at Caulfield Institute of Technology to the Society of Tribologists and Lubrication Engineers. Skilled went on to use my paper in its marketing years after I'd left.

I continued with my multiple roles and by 1989 I'd been in Singapore/South-East Asia for nearly ten years and was now MD of the Tekniskil group's six companies. It was a busy but enjoyable time. We lived in very good apartments/condominiums and the kids went to a private international school and enjoyed shopping in Orchard Road with lunches at our favourite Italian and Mexican restaurants. When at home, things were very social. We had many friends, expat and local, and we had a ski boat that we took out on Sundays. I'd joined the Masonic Lodge, Sir Stamford Raffles' chapter. My dad, who was a mason, visited Singapore with Mum and he was at the lodge ceremony when I did my first degree. To keep fit I used to run with the Hash House Harriers. We went to Europe on holidays.

Things, however, were changing within Skilled, and these changes were going to affect me.

For the first time in their history, Skilled appointed a General Manager, whom I'd have to report to. Within six months of this change, I no longer wanted to work at Skilled.

We went back to Australia during Christmas 1989. While on leave, Vivienne and I travelled to Benalla to catch up with friends. I said I was considering resigning and coming back to Australia. One of them told me about an engineering job at the Wangaratta District Base Hospital. I was sure I could do it.

The closing date for applications had passed; nevertheless, I phoned the deputy CEO at the hospital and asked if the position had been filled. It hadn't. He was hesitant to accept my late application, however, he agreed after I told him of my career and experience.

On the flight back to Singapore, Vivienne and I discussed what I was going to do. She wasn't happy about it, as she loved the lifestyle in Singapore. I wasn't going to bend a fourth time. Three weeks later, while I was in Indonesia, I was advised that I'd been short-listed and asked if I was still interested. Within two weeks, I was at the hospital for my interview. This was my introduction to public service bureaucracy. The interview went very well and I was offered the position of chief engineer.

A NEW BEGINNING

Vivienne and I flew back to Australia and first met with a friend who had a real estate business at Benalla who showed us a farm at Warrenbayne. We both said yes. It was perfect, a lovely mud brick house, with a huge garden, big shed and a workshop for me to play in. I purchased a hundred ewes and a couple of rams, some chooks and Guinea fowls. Eventually, I was able to manage the place on weekends and after work with Vivienne's help. We really loved it all.

My work was going well, but the mental issues that'd been troubling me over previous years were still there. They hadn't been too bad in the first year at Wangaratta. However, I was becoming an angry, belligerent man, often very down when not busy at work and I was arguing a lot with Vivienne. She said that living with me was like walking on eggshells all the time, that I was a bit crazy and she thought that I'd become distant at times.

Often, I'd climb the hills on my farm and sit on my favourite rock amongst my blue gum plantation, sometimes for a couple of hours. I was beginning to enjoy solace. I also found myself weeping when I was alone for no reason. It was time to talk to a doctor about my issues. I'd never done this. Vivienne and I both had the same lady doctor who I felt comfortable with and I suspect Vivienne had told her about my mental health issues. The doctor diagnosed me with major depression and prescribed anti-depressants. The medication started, and it would continue for over twenty-five years.

It wasn't long after this that Vivienne had a very bad accident while horse riding. A kangaroo spooked the horse and, despite being a competent rider, Vivienne was thrown from the saddle and dragged until the horse came down on top of her. She broke her back, some ribs and a knee, and had a smashed-up ankle.

She spent a lot of time in Wangaratta hospital. She came out in a wheelchair and then spent time in rehab in Melbourne. It was a long haul and some of her injuries are still with her today.

I continued at the hospital for another twelve months; however, I wasn't mentally good. I was pissed off with stifling bureaucracy and getting twitchy again. Solution? I thought it was time to move, to raise the stakes and to make the challenge more exciting. I'd do as I'd done before when in this state of mind.

I applied for a position as chief engineer at a still-under-construction casino resort at Christmas Island that was managed by Casinos Austria. I got the job. I resigned my position at Wangaratta, leased my farm and went to Christmas Island. Vivienne joined me a couple of months later and ran the wardrobe department, although she had restricted mobility and much pain in her back and left ankle.

On a business flight to Perth one day, after we'd been in the air a little while, a passenger walked past me heading for the toilet and his wallet fell from his pocket. I gave it to him on his way back. He thanked me and we started to chat. He was well dressed. I noticed his gold tie bar was a silhouette of a warship. I said to him, 'That's the *Parramatta*.' I told him I was a stoker from '64–'67. 'Do you remember me? I was the captain,' he said and introduced himself. 'Yes, I do. You were a bit of a cowboy, but a good skipper, but you did put us on a rock.' No comment. He then invited me to join him at his seat. He announced loudly to the other passengers, 'This is one of my *Parramatta* boys. Champagne for all, please, steward'.

We hooked into the champagne and he asked me if I remembered the song of the stokers. I did and sang: 'Roll along, you rusty bastard, roll along. To the turning of your screws, we sing this song. Oh, your shipside is not fine and the pigs drink Penfold wine. Roll along, you rusty bastard, roll along'. He was over the moon. He'd retired an admiral and now had a charter boat at Cocos Island. Big come down. Such is life.

At the end of my contract I resigned. I wasn't mentally well and the island had only very basic medical facilities. We left Christmas Island to return to mainland Australia. We took a travelling holiday before I started my next position as General Manager of Invenio, a German-owned automotive design and development company.

I knew nothing about automotive design, but my role was to set up an office and administration in North Melbourne, then set about marketing and developing the company in Australia. After two years, the company was well established and going well, but I wasn't. Again, I needed to do something to distract me from my worsening depressive state. Medication wasn't doing it for me.

Vivienne was mobile again. I'd purchased a business for her that she could operate from our farm. Called Horse Drawn Holidays, it had five beautiful Clydesdales and five gypsy caravans. We also began operating a B&B, Vivienne's Retreat, at our farm. Vivienne loved working with the horses and the B&B, and both went well, but our marriage wasn't good.

My personal situation was worsening. My mood swings were longer and more frequent. When alone, I'd weep. I couldn't sleep without medication, as my brain would be in overdrive. I was on a cocktail of strong anti-depressants. I was twitchy again; diversion would fix me!

Sandland calls

As luck would have it, an old friend had tracked me down and phoned me from Singapore to ask if I'd set up and operate his company in the Middle East. I said yes, but it would cost him.

Three weeks later, I was off to Dubai. Soon I was all over the place: Abu Dhabi, Oman, Bahrain, Qatar, Saudi Arabia and Azerbaijan. Lovely, friendly, Islamic places! Not on many travel itineraries. But the work suited me; it was very interesting and often very challenging.

After I'd been working out of Dubai in Sandland for eight months I went home for ten days leave, which didn't go well. I suggested to Vivienne that she come to Dubai, but she didn't want to. I went back to Sandland for another twelve months, finished my contract and quit. I was troubled. I flew home and I knew the day I arrived that my marriage would be a struggle and that it was going to be difficult for me to manage in my state of mind. I had trouble coming to grips with the way I was, and I wondered why I couldn't maintain a relationship with a woman I loved.

Back down to earth

While I was having some time off, I set up my own company, Healthtek, and started to work as an engineering and project consultant on a part-time basis. I was soon consulting for my old hospital and several other hospitals; this was the year of Y2K. They were all scared of system failure with machinery and other hospital equipment.

At the same time, a good ex-work mate whom I'd employed previously at the hospital asked me if I'd help his mate out by temporarily managing his engineering business in Melbourne, as his mate was ill. *What about me?* I thought.

I agreed to work only two days a week, as I had hospital commitments. Soon, I was full-time managing the engineering business in Melbourne and subcontracting some of my Healthtek projects. I was seeing less of Vivienne and really having problems with anger, mistrust and major sleep issues. I'd told Vivienne that I couldn't stay with her. Just like that! No consultation. I'd made yet another bad decision that would hurt another good woman. Why was I wrecking others' lives and my own?

A couple of months after this, I met Joan at a business function. I wasn't seeking romance, but it happened over the following weeks. We lived close to one another. She had a senior position at a university, was very intelligent, and was studying for a Masters degree. We had interesting conversations, which was all I was looking for. After twelve months together, things were getting bad.

I was like an over-stretched wire waiting to snap. I had a blow-up at work and walked out on a guy who'd paid me very well and was most generous in other ways. For the first time in my working life, I had no plan or job to move straight into and I was a mental mess. I didn't want to be here anymore; I contemplated suicide and Joan and the police stopped me.

I knew I needed help. Joan convinced me to see a doctor. I was diagnosed with major depression and a couple of other conditions. My anti-depressant medication was changed, and the dosage increased again. I began to see a psychiatrist and a psychologist, which took the edge off a little. After a couple of months of stewing in my own misery, I picked myself up. I needed to work and soon secured a position as the business development manager with an international project management company.

Around this time, I began the process of lodging claims with the DVA, supported by letters from my GP.

MY STRUGGLE BEGINS

In 2001, I had a new work challenge. My life got better and I was at it again with very interesting work in China, Philippines, Fiji, Turkey, Kazakhstan, Kyrgyzstan, and Uzbekistan. It wasn't long before I became belligerent. Travelling helped me to cope. Work was my best medication, but after two years I quit yet again. During this time, Vivienne and I divorced.

Change of direction

It was time for a something different. After doing some reverse engineering for a company, it was suggested that I should consider becoming a valuer. I did, and I adapted to it, soon qualifying to register as a Certified Plant, Equipment and Machinery and Equipment (PM&E) valuer. I set up my own company, DVS. I started arguing with the owner of the company I initially contracted with and with other staff. I threatened one guy with violence.

I had to move on despite the very good money. I started with another company, but the same issues arose: lots of anger and no sleep. I could never relax unless I was immersed in my work. Fortunately, people who did this work were in very short supply in Australia and subsequently very well paid, and I'd become known as a good PM&E valuer because of my engineering background.

Although I still had my Warrenbayne property, Joan and I were living in Melbourne. We had a villa unit at Port Douglas, so I went up there for a break. I was my own boss. Joan had established her own consultancy company in Melbourne, so she was able to pick and choose assignments. She came to Port Douglas for a break and secured a position at the Cairns TAFE. After six months, the drive each day was too much for her and she went back to Victoria. I continued my consultancy work until I needed a break.

I went back to my farm to try to get myself together. Joan went back and forth to Melbourne, where she was lecturing at two universities. We had a place at Williamstown and she'd come back to the farm on weekends, or I'd often go there for a few days. When I began to get better, I became bored and at Joan's suggestion I applied for a position as chief engineer at a Queensland island resort and was successful. Joan was appointed as the resort's human resources manager.

I lasted less than a year. I was moody, and stuck into some staff. In addition to my chief engineer role, I was also the workplace health and safety officer. I raised some serious workplace health and safety issues, and I eventually blew my top. It all came to a head at a company function when I argued publicly with a senior staff member and I got physical. The next day I was asked to resign.

We had a resident nurse at the resort, so I spoke to her about my issues. She told me I needed to see a doctor pronto so I saw a doctor on the mainland. I told him that I'd been treated for depression for many years and was on medication for it. He told me that I needed more help than he was able to give, and I shouldn't work until I had things under control.

He phoned the psychologist who'd treated me in Melbourne. She asked if I'd go into the Heidelberg Repatriation Hospital if she could arrange it. I agreed. The next day she advised me that I could see a repat psychiatrist as soon as I returned to Melbourne. Joan didn't want to leave her job until she'd completed her contract. I was fine with that. I'd go back to Victoria. I didn't want anybody in my life with the way I felt. I flew back to Melbourne and saw a psychiatrist at Heidelberg. He diagnosed PTSD and I was soon on the intensive PTSD Program.

MEET THE BOYS

I was one of eight vets on the PTSD Program. All are Vietnam vets except a British Army guy who'd seen service in Northern Ireland and Rhodesia. We were a mixed bunch; however, we all got on very well with each other and still do.

I don't think any of us quite knew what to expect on the program or how it would help us. At first, I was apprehensive. How could I be fixed if I didn't know what was wrong with me?

Over the next month, we interacted in group meetings with the psychiatrists and other medical people. We lived Monday to Friday at the same off-hospital-site accommodation, and we had some laughs.

I think we all benefitted in some way from the program and learnt more about ourselves. We all had similar issues and we talked openly about them with each other and the psychiatrists and psychologists. After the in-house program ended, we all made regular visits to the Repat to talk with the psychiatrists or psychologists who'd treated us on the PTSD Program.

During this time, Joan returned home and we were living at my farm at Warrenbayne. I'd been advised by my treating psychiatrists and GP not to work, so I stayed on the farm and tried to keep busy.

I'd go to Williamstown some weeks to be with Joan or she'd come to the farm for the weekend. I think we both needed our own space for a bit and this arrangement seemed to work. I decided to have a crack at breeding boar goats. I could see a big future for goat meat, so I purchased some purebred boar goats and kids. This gave me a bit of an interest and kept me active.

Meanwhile, the PTSD group was still together, thanks in a big way to the guys' wives who organised monthly get-togethers. They'd really become involved. They attended sessions arranged by the Repat and were strongly behind their men. Joan didn't show a lot of interest; she was 'too busy'. Despite Joan's lack of interest, we were getting on well. I was on anti-depressants and behaving myself when I was with her.

Joan had her own farm at Merrijig and I had plenty of time on my hands, so I started going over there and working on the small run-down old family home. Joan had an interest in using her property for tourism. To do this, and to please Joan, I foolishly sold my farm, my herd of purebred boar breeding stock goats, my Clydesdales and my wagons.

This was one of the biggest mistakes to make. I moved over to Merrijig. Despite my many faults, I was never a selfish man.

I made many friends in the community, so it all seemed right. One night Joan told me she'd accepted a job in Alice Springs, and we'd talk about it on the weekend. Having no prior discussion, it seemed that she expected me to be happy that she'd accepted this high-power position.

In the twinkle of an eye, our plans were out the window. Joan moved to Alice Springs, along with my furniture from the flat in Williamstown. She'd only been there a couple of weeks when, on a nightly phone chat, she excitedly told me she'd bought a unit in Alice Springs and that I could come there. I flew up to spend some time with her. The unit was nice but I couldn't live there.

I made another trip to Alice Springs a few weeks after this and stayed for a couple of weeks. I told Joan I didn't think I could live there. We'd keep commuting. All through this time, I wasn't good. At home, I went to the pub some evenings to try to lift my mood. Again, I dragged myself out of the shit and decided to see a bit of Australia. I had a 4x4, so why not? I bought an off-road camper trailer and headed for Alice Springs via lots of places, including the Birdsville track. My brother and my Jack Russel, Buddy, came along for the ride. When we got to Alice Springs, my brother flew home. I think he'd had enough of me. Buddy stayed.

I'd only been there a week or two when Joan went for work to a Northern Territory Aboriginal community. While she was away, I hooked up the trailer and explored some of the MacDonnell Ranges. I even relaxed a little. Joan then had to rush to Mansfield as her mum was very ill.

I continued with my planned trip to Cairns to visit Lisa, then on to Townsville to attend a three-year navy engineers' reunion. I was in Charters Towers when Joan rang to tell me her mum wasn't expected to live and could I please come home to Merrijig. I quickly drove to Cairns, left my Jeep and trailer at Lisa's place and flew to Melbourne; however, by the time I got to Merrijig her mum had passed away.

Family members were considered local legends, so a very big funeral was followed by a huge wake at the Merrijig pub. I got very drunk. Joan drove us home. As she reversed, she clipped another car and kept going. I verbally abused her all the way home. When we got home, I started again. I don't know what I was saying, but it must've been bad, as her adult son, who'd gone home earlier, woke up and came to support his Mum. I turned on him.

Joan and her son left and went to her brother's place. After a while, her brother and ex cop cousin came and dragged me off the couch where I'd passed out and they proceeded to kick the shit out of me. I got to my feet and retaliated as best I could, but I wasn't in real good shape. I called the cops, but they said they were busy.

The next morning, police were at my door. They told me to get out of the house and not come back. I protested about having to leave the house I lived in; however, he told me it wasn't my house, so I had no option.

They took me into Mansfield, and then the senior constable took me to hospital. A doctor patched me up and said I should lay assault charges. The senior constable took me back to the police station to make a statement. While I was doing this, Joan and her cousin issued me with a restraining order citing verbal abuse and violent threats against Joan's son. I didn't know what I'd done. For twelve months, I couldn't talk to Joan and I couldn't go on the property. I had a lot of stuff there, including a tractor, farm machinery, tools and personal effects.

I'd messed up yet again. I had a vague memory of what'd happened and I was shattered.

The senior constable drove me back to Merrijig to pack my bag and get my ute. We had a chat about it all and he gave me his card and asked me to call him as soon as I had myself sorted.

I didn't know what to do, so I drove to Melbourne to Mum's place. She nearly collapsed when she saw me. I stayed with Mum for a couple of days, but she kept crying. She was very fond of Joan, and the feeling was mutual, so she chastised me for what I'd done, but she couldn't believe what Joan had done to me. She wanted to call Joan, but I couldn't let her because of the conditions of the order.

I flew back to Cairns to be with Lisa and her family. I stayed with her until I sorted myself out.

I'd been in Cairns a couple of months when the senior constable from Mansfield called. He said I should lay charges of assault against Joan's cousin and brother. I was reluctant, but he pushed and I agreed. A court date was set but I decided to withdraw charges. I didn't want to drag Joan through a court case that would hurt her.

Unlucky for some

I'd lodged a couple of claims with DVA before the PTSD Program. The one for hearing loss was accepted and the one for Chronic Obstructive

Pulmonary Disease (COPD), although I'd never smoked, was knocked back. I also claimed for depression and peripheral neuropathy. A couple of years ago, when I eventually did speak with an advocate, he called what I'd done a shotgun approach that was doomed to fail.

Following the PTSD Program, I decided to make another claim for mental illness that was supported by reports from my GP. I also had statements from my two ex-wives and Joan, and a guy I'd served with on HMAS *Parramatta* in my navy days.

Foolishly, I did it all again myself, without advice or guidance. I was in no mental state to be doing any of this; I was angry, confused and not thinking rationally. I was rejected by DVA when Writeway, the DVA research service, became involved. I appealed and was knocked back again on the claim for mental illness despite DVA's psychiatrist stating that I was, in his written words, 'TPI [Totally and Permanently Incapacitated] and would never work again'. However, he stated in his report that my mental condition wasn't caused by my war or RAN service, despite a history of mental illness that began soon after my discharge. My claim for depression was again rejected and I was belittled and humiliated by the review panel. COPD was accepted, and I was begrudgingly granted a 100% disability pension, 60% for COPD and 40% for hearing. Three psychiatrists and a psychologist had diagnosed PTSD, depression, and anxiety over a long period, but this was disregarded.

I read a book called *Hands to Boarding Stations: The Story of Minesweeper HMAS Hawk: Confrontation with Indonesia 1965–1966* by John Foster. John was the Commander of HMAS *Hawk*, 1965–1966, one of our RAN minesweepers that was involved in the Indonesian Confrontation at the same time I was there on *Parramatta*. His records of places, events and things that occurred confirmed things that I'd written about in my application to DVA that Writeway had stated weren't factual.[2]

I accept that I made mistakes in my claims, particularly in making them without guidance; however, being knocked back in this manner almost did it for me. Why go on? Suicide crossed my mind again. I was still on medication and seeing a psychologist and a psychiatrist, but the anti-depressants weren't working. I was mentally ill and had been that way for close to thirty years. There was no history of mental illness in my family. I had a stable upbringing thanks to very good parents. I'd never experienced any trauma or danger prior to joining the navy. What'd happened to me and why? I didn't know. Despite all this, I was still very close to my family and tried to be a good dad and pa.

The final straw

Throughout this time, I had great support from the PTSD group and their wonderful wives. Laurel and Marney offered to speak with Joan. Laurel did this, but from what she told me I gather Joan said, 'Some bad decisions were made the night it all went wrong'. To this day, I don't know whose bad decisions they were.

I was still in Cairns. I was soon referred to a psychiatrist and admitted into The Cairns Clinic, a mental health facility. I was on another cocktail of anti-depressants, which made things a little better for a while, but my problems soon swelled again. I went back to the psychiatrist, who happened to be one who'd treated me while I was on the PTSD Program. I went back into The Cairns Clinic for a second spell and my medication was changed yet again.

I had more downs than ups in the first couple years in Cairns. Depression and bad dreams were hammering me. Sometimes I'd drink to be happy and to escape whatever was wrong with me. After a while, with the cocktail of anti-depressants and the medication to help me sleep, I began to feel a bit better, but I knew I had to do something to distract my mind. I got into a bit of strife one night at a local bar and had an altercation with a guy who had nothing good to say about ex-servicemen and vets. As a result, I spent the night locked up in the Cairns jail. I was sixty-four years old. I'm not a criminal, so why was I behaving like this?

I bought a Jeep and a caravan and headed north-west. In the early part of my travels, I met up with Nikko and Marney and spent a few great days with them at a remote fishing camp north of Darwin. I continued my travel through the Northern Territory, Western Australia and South Australia. By Broken Hill, I'd had enough so continued back to Cairns.

I had another crack at the DVA claims that went nowhere. I called the lady who was the signatory to the knock-back letter I'd received, but didn't get to speak with her; instead I spoke with another lady who advised me that I'd 'never get the Intermediate Rate, EDA [Extreme Disablement Adjustment] or TPI'.

To say that I'm bitter is an understatement. Mates with the same issues as me who I served with on the same ships, same dates, same active service and doing the same work, are now in receipt of TPI, EDA or Intermediate pensions and benefits. Writeway screwed me over, as they'd done to numerous others. For me, it's not all about the financial issues. It's more about the feeling and belief that I was deemed not worthy.

In addition to my accepted disabilities, I have another, very long-term medical condition, peripheral neuropathy, for which a claim has been rejected. I'd suffered foot pain since the 1970s but did nothing about it. I eventually spoke about it with a GP. I've been on medication to treat pain associated with peripheral neuropathy for close to sixteen years. I lodged a claim for this disability; however, it was knocked back because the neurologist that I saw through DVA wrote in his report that 'no toxic exposure or other cause could be properly identified'; therefore, he determined that my disability was caused by alcohol consumption while in the navy and, because it was my choice to drink, the neuropathy wasn't caused by my service. When the neurologist examined me, he asked if I'd been exposed to toxins while in the navy. In our work we used several toxic types of chemicals and I named those that I could recall. I wasn't aware at that time about the possible exposure to Agent Orange. As this condition worsened and I was on the maximum medication dosage to ease pain, my GP in Cairns referred me to a neurologist at Townsville. He conducted a series of tests and confirmed the peripheral neuropathy. He asked about my service time and Vietnam.

Because of the high mortality rate of navy personnel suffering neuropathy, cancers and other diseases, compared with that of army and RAAF personnel with Vietnam service, the DVA commissioned a study to be conducted on Agent Orange.[3] The study, conducted by The National Research Centre for Environmental Toxicology, Queensland Health Scientific Services, concluded that the high rate of mortality of naval personnel was because all potable water on our warships at that time was distilled from sea water, and ships' potable water had been contaminated by Agent Orange, washed by rain and other water into Vietnam's coastal and Vung Tau Harbour waters. It was found that the distillation process significantly worsened the toxic effect of Agent Orange. Sailors, and perhaps soldiers and air force personnel, on the warships in these waters drank the water and bathed in it. Cooks cooked with it. The US Navy made the same findings.

The Townsville neurologist's report back to my GP states that the most likely cause of my peripheral neuropathy was exposure to the Agent Orange toxin in the ship's water. I spoke to a pension officer in Cairns who advised me that a claim related to Agent Orange would be a wasted exercise. I haven't pursued this matter further. In 2004, I had to have all toes fused; in 2018 I had a toe amputated due to infection; and I also broke a grand toe that became infected requiring IV and oral antibiotic treatment. After three months treatment, it eventually healed; however, my treating orthopaedic surgeon said, 'Healed but the joint is stuffed'. Some months after this I had an infection on my left grand toe and a neuropathic ulcer formed that wouldn't heal, even after seventeen months treatment.

I've suffered depression or mental illness since the mid-1970s. I've been on anti-depressants continually since 1992. But according to DVA my war and other navy service didn't cause or contribute to my mental illness. Despite my rewarding and successful post-navy career, the depression, insomnia, deafness and neuropathy that I've contended with have wrecked my life and damaged those that I loved.

I don't have many possessions left today. My farm, farm stock and all my farming machinery and equipment were sold. My horse-drawn holiday business was sold, and I no longer have my household furniture, a great collection of tools and my lifetime collection of antiquities from around the world.

But not all is bad. I do still have my three girls and five grandkids. My three daughters are now all in their mid-forties and early fifties and they're all very good mums and partners. They've all had their ups and downs in their lives. One has suffered mental health, peripheral neuropathy and other medical issues for a big part of her life. I wonder if what she lived with and witnessed of me during her formative years contributed to this. I have a very good and close relationship with Lisa who lives in Cairns and Kelly who lives in Melbourne. I have no contact with Tracy apart from when I saw her and her family at my Mums funeral. I have four grandkids in Melbourne and have a very good relationship with Kelly`s Rebecca and Lachlan. I was close to Lisa`s Madison for all her life but sadly that relationship has deteriorated.

My mental health issues have eased in the past twelve months. I'm still being treated for insomnia and take a small dose of an anti-depressant and other medication to help with this; however, after a psychiatrist managed an eight-month medication withdrawal, at my request, I'm off the cocktail of anti-depressants. I still take the maximum dose of medication to control my peripheral neuropathy pain.

I blame my military service for all those medical issues; so do the doctors, psychiatrists and psychologists who've treated me. I've messed up two marriages and a long-term relationship and hurt my kids. DVA claims these issues have caused or contributed to my long-term mental health conditions. I maintain that these conditions had manifested before

I began the destruction of my family life. Am I, and my treating doctors, right?

In 2017, I took a cruise to Papua New Guinea and the Solomon Islands. Before I commenced writing my story in 2016, I spoke about it with my treating psychiatrist. She was a little concerned that doing so may stir up old issues. Old issues were stirred up, but not entirely in a negative way. It did encourage me to have another crack at DVA. I was then in a much better frame of mind mentally than I'd been in the past. In early 2017, I got smart. I got advice from an ex-navy retired advocate. I did what he advised and in June 2017 I was awarded EDA. As I was past sixty-five, DVA advised me that I was too old to get TPI. My struggle with DVA spanned some fifteen years.

I'm still a single man and despite my long relationships, I was on my own a lot of the time. I've learnt to enjoy my own company. I loved three good women in my life: Sandy, the mum of my three girls, Vivienne and Joan. Three different women with three different personalities, yet I still managed to wreck things. Why?

In closing, I'm reminded of a song, Frank Sinatra's *My Way*. Yes, I sure did it my way: the good, bad, happy and sad.

My compressed version of my journey over fifty-four years will probably bore most who read it, but for those who do, I hope you can see the links and progression and the damage a mental health condition can cause if left too long before getting help. So, that's my story. I'm Delo the Stokerman who, for most of his life, kept losing sight of THE CANDLE IN THE WINDOW.

THE ENEMY WITHIN

John Marks

Early one evening, I received an unexpected, long distance phone call from my elderly mother. She would normally rely on me to phone (to save the cost), but on this particular day she had a question, which had clearly worried her for years. With courage, she came straight to it. 'Mum here. We weren't too hard on you, were we?' Somewhat taken aback by this question, I lied. I suspected she saw through my lie by the tone of her voice in reply. 'Oh, good,' she said, and hung up, happy to accept and share in our inabilities to face the truth. So the lies kept the peace, as they always had done. My answer should have been, 'You both were', and she knew it. It was a question Mum should have confronted while I was growing up, but indirectly she'd given me permission to tell my story.

My parents were well thought of in the local community and worked hard on their farm to make ends meet. Father did the bulk of the work, growing glasshouse tomatoes, acres of onions and milking cows, while Mother kept the house in order. My father's sporting days were his glory days, but they ended due to injuries and being played-out. He rarely spoke of his considerable achievements, football and cycling in particular, and so it was left to my mother to tell her version of his sporting prowess, proudly exclaiming, 'Your father played to win!' The Mount Gambier Brass Band and fishing were my parents' passions. Holidays by the sea, brass band concerts in the cool of summer evenings, sport and living in the country were the best of times and the worst, as my life slowly unravelled.

My father and I shared some good working days where conversations were limited. I was keen to impress him, but he was always the critic, rarely explaining anything. He would say, 'Clear off and don't come back', if he felt my work wasn't good enough. If my questions were too challenging or persistent, I would be sent to ask Mum. To any serious question she would say, 'Go and ask your father'. We never got on well as he saw me as 'fairly useless' and I often bore the brunt of his frustration and anger. Mum had a keen sense of what she saw as right and wrong and stubbornly refused to admit that her view was ever wrong. As a consequence of her intransigence, I would argue to the point of upsetting her. My father would be told and I would cop it. Wariness of punishment took its toll. I endured burdens of isolation, loneliness and uncertainty for most of my life.

THE EARLY YEARS

In 1951, aged six, on a bleak, wintry evening, we were all seated around a large wooden table in an old boundary rider's house that used to be part of the Moorak Station. My grandfather had purchased the house with an eleven-acre allotment, within a few miles of Mount Gambier. In that small, dark kitchen with its low ceiling, uneven floor boards, small windows set in thick limestone walls, and with the heat from the wood stove warming the room, the mantle lamp lit and placed on the table, we began dinner.

Boundary rider's house, photographed about 1900

Renovated with extensive garden

I was warned not to eat peas off my knife; nevertheless, I did. With my knife raised and the peas well balanced on the blade, I received a hefty whack on the back of my head. The knife flew across the kitchen, the plate skidded across the table and my dinner lay on the floor. Everyone laughed, but not me. My father said, 'You'd better clean it up, and you can go to bed without dinner.' Discipline began at an early age. I remember being sent to bed on numerous occasions with very little dinner for all manner of minor indiscretions, to remain there, in the dark, with the door shut. This punishment was onerous. My father meted out the discipline while my mother either condoned it or failed to intervene. Afterwards, Mum would nearly always say, 'It's for your own good', meaning it was for her own good.

On occasions, the leather razor strap was wielded, but more often I had my ears boxed, which was a backhander, with another for good measure.

There were periods of peace, at least for a few years, when Sundays were considered days of rest. Sunday School for my brothers and I, brass band practice for Father, and Mum stuck with cooking the Sunday roast. On winter evenings, we would all retire to the sitting room to warm ourselves by the open fire. The wireless would be tuned to ABC Radio for the Sunday night serials of *Deadly Night Shade* and *Two Roads to Samoa*. All the while my great-grandfather's sixty-three glass-eyed, stuffed native birds perched high on twig and branch were watching us from the display cabinet above the fireplace. Despite the good times, I was always alert, waiting for the next outrage. It would come soon enough.

From time to time, my two brothers and I caused trouble and a fair amount of chaos. My mother would cry, 'Enough!' and summon my father to deal with the situation. To even the score, all three of us had to share the blame. The procedure: we would stand at the door of the bathroom (a lean-to under the back verandah) and were called in, told to shut the door and bend over. Then came a few hard whacks with the razor strap and a warning.

I would always protest out of fear of being hurt. I would refuse to bend and so it became a fight, with my father trying to lay the strap on me. For that I received extra hits around my legs.

One day, after a week of receiving more than my share of punishment, I decided to make a run for it. My father ordered me back, but up the garden path I went. He followed with strap in hand. Terrified of being thrashed, I turned and ran with my father close behind. My mother and brothers cheered me on. They were amused by the escapade, but I wasn't. I could hear the thump of his rubber boots as he tried to catch me, all the while saying, 'I'm gaining'. I outran him and kept running further. He came looking for me to call me in for lunch, but gave up as I kept hiding inside the glasshouses to keep my distance. I made my way back home for dinner. Father, keen sportsman that he was and impressed with my burst of speed, suggested I should take up running. The idea appealed to me because I could now run away if I chose to.

As a teen, I was humiliated when, accused of lying or arguing to make my point, my father would backhand me in the presence of visitors, friends and relations.

As the years passed and friends were few, growing up became a flight into imagination, invention and storytelling, an emotional retreat to avoid my parents' displeasure. Arguments began when told I was too clever for my own good, or when reprimanded for reading while there was work to be done. Answering back, which I was inclined to do, usually ended with a backhander or harsh words. I earned the title of 'black sheep of the family'. Couple this with a lack of meaningful conversation and a barrage of criticism over the years and I withdrew further into self-absorbed loneliness.

I was about eleven and enjoying reading my first adventure novel when the angry voice of my father broke the spell. 'Where is he?' he demanded of my mother. He found me in the sitting room, dragged me by the collar from the armchair, and promptly marched me outside to help him weed the onion crop. I took my chance, slipped away, and returned to the house to continue reading. It was a good read. My father thought otherwise. He came looking for me. Seizing me by the scruff of the neck, he pulled me from the lounge chair, hit me with a swerving backhander and grabbed the book, which I tried to claim back, only to be met with a second clout. The book was placed out of reach to gather dust. I remember rushing from the house and into the garden in floods of tears.

To counter the dark days and to help resolve emotional issues, I still seek the sanctuary of a garden for peace and comfort, with its trees, flowers, open spaces, sunshine and rain. The freedom of roaming the country and walking for long hours is satisfying and calming, a chance to be lost in thought, to escape the constrictions and memories of a house once called home, and all that it stood for.

Reading was limited in my early years, as it was something you did if you had time. My mother's exact words still hold sway. 'Why aren't you outside doing things, helping your father? You can read that later. There is work to be done.' These naggings still continue to interfere with my concentration when I wish to read or write.

At school, home life pervaded. Anxiety, loneliness, and fear of punishment for making a mistake were constant companions. Inevitably, these continuous pressures meant doing well at sport or academia was beyond reach. To make matters worse, the Mount Gambier High School had arranged a penny vote talent night where students could perform with music and song. I was 'fingered' as someone who could play a flugelhorn. Reluctantly, I agreed to try. After a number of practice sessions with my Uncle Jack, the local bandmaster, in his blacksmith shop where I played out of tune with the clang of iron and the roar of the furnace, I then fronted the audience. It was a mess. Nerves got the better of me. I blew three or four decent notes and the rest was all wind and squawks. The audience was stunned into silence; I was mortified. I stood alone on the stage as the penny vote tins were passed around. I can still hear the clunk of the one penny from my friend in the third row. It wasn't over yet. All performers were asked to line up on stage while the results were read out: John Marks, one vote. I was humiliated. My brass-playing days were over. My parents never found out.

By chance, I was given an opportunity to play the part of Sir Toby Belch in a high school production of Shakespeare's *Twelfth Night*. My performance was greeted with much acclaim. This brought an important change and a new direction for me. It still wasn't enough and so on my final day at school, having taken two years to achieve an Intermediate Certificate, I packed my bag and walked the long country miles home.

1962

I had full-time work at seventeen, but no car and very little social life so, at my mother's insistence, I was allowed to borrow my father's car for an evening with the proviso to be home by ten-thirty. As it turned out, it was the last time. Arriving home about half an hour late, I was surprised by my father waiting for me in the shadows of the dark, cold kitchen, in no mood to listen to why I was late. He called me useless, among other insults, and if that wasn't enough torment, he then belted me with a vicious backhander, sending me to my knees. He stepped past me and went to bed. Distraught, I was alone in a very dark place. Shaken, dazed and confused, I walked into the darkness of the passageway with revenge on my mind. Then from the bedroom came Mother's voice: 'John, are you all right?' I froze and, after what seemed an eternity, I replied, 'Yes'. I retraced my steps, and in the half-light of the kitchen I quietly replaced the knife, closed the drawer, and braced myself at the kitchen sink as the enormity of my action, and the deep hurt inflicted by my father, took hold. In a moment of anger and violence he'd destroyed any modicum of trust I had in him. There was no apology. I never forgave him or myself and so we became strangers to each other. It was a tragedy – no conversations to remember him by.

Over the years, Mum often mentioned, with much satisfaction, how she convinced my father to allow me to borrow the car. Did she really know what had happened? What could I have done to save myself from the destructive thoughts of the incident that has bled consistently into my life, feeding my anxiety, abhorrence of violence and my dark, persistent memory of what might have occurred? All my life this has been a burden and with much apprehension I began conversations with my counsellor to put to rest this regrettable episode.

Sweet revenge

A very large Kreisler Radiogram was delivered to the farm, to take pride of place in the sitting room with its ceiling of hand sawn timber planks, thick damp limestone walls and hideous dark brown carpet. My brother and I chose it on a summer day and our father went pale and paid for it. This was, for me at least, sweet revenge. As I was working, it fell to me to purchase the records. The first two were Beethoven's *Fifth Symphony* and Tchaikovsky's *Sixth Symphony*.

The enjoyment of playing these LPs at full volume annoyed my parents considerably. Mother would protest, Father would turn off the gram and declare that there were better things to be doing. But there weren't. When alone, with the house quiet, the stylus was lowered, the volume turned up, and I would proceed to conduct the entire orchestra, watching myself in the butterfly-shaped, scallop-edged mirror above the mantle of the fireplace where once a menagerie of glass-eyed birds kept watch. With my hands waving in all directions, leaning in and away from the imaginary orchestra, I followed the score. On occasions, in the dark corners of the sitting room, I would indulge in the music of the Sixth Symphony, the *Pathétique*, for an emotional ride of epic proportions. It meant so much at a time when winter in the south-east had isolated the farm, and where the four walls of the old colonial house held all the secrets of my life. I had no wish to revisit the awful lies and guarded secrets so I would wheel the volume to ten on the Kreisler and collapse into the arms of a deep chair to be consumed by music. I needed to feel the bitter loneliness of rejection from those I wanted to love but couldn't. I wallowed in the darkness of the first movement, the allegro non troppo, until a violent change woke me and I entered into the full glory of my youthful misery. Then the third movement, the allegro molto vivace, was the music that resonated and saved me. It was a worrying time. I had nowhere to go and nothing on offer so out of necessity I had to create my own entertainment – a flight into an imaginary world where I played these symphonies, creating an aching loneliness that never abated.

Music was to become a passion and an important means of overcoming stressful situations. I particularly enjoyed the exhilaration of intense, dramatic music to overcome unwelcome thoughts, or a lullaby when nothing was making sense. I could slow down, sit still, breathe and allow the music to work its magic when all seemed lost.

1964

I purchased a second-hand EH Holden car in 1963. In the summer of 1964 I headed to Melbourne for theatre school. It was everything I wanted. In the summer of 1965, I was back there. I had found my voice. I was heard. I participated in numerous local theatre productions and my confidence grew.

10 March 1965

On a warm autumn day, my parents and I gathered in the gloom of our small kitchen with its uneven, lino-covered floor of green and beige, chartreuse walls and a nice red Laminex and chrome table with matching chairs. As bad as that was, our attention was focused on the slow, formal voice emanating from the turquoise and cream HMV mantle radio, set among the tea, flour and sugar tins above the stove. We stood motionless, listening to the rumble of a spinning government lottery barrel and the clatter of numbered wooden marbles. A measured pause, the announcement of the relevant month; pause again as a marble was fished from the barrel, then the number read in slow time.

'April … Number … Four.'

At nineteen, I had won a lottery that I hadn't entered. We listened on until the penny dropped. A heartfelt, 'Oh no!' came from my mother as she remembered the consequences of a past war. 'Turn it off, Dad,' she said. My parents sat close together, two shadows with covered eyes. Tips, our faithful dog lying near the kitchen door, felt the unease and slipped outside. I followed in utter disbelief.

At my mother's insistence, my father and my employer secured a two-year deferment for me from the first intake of National Service, with little expectation of being required in the future.

1966

I had a very dull twenty-first birthday in April, with my aunts and uncles and a few others. Standing room only in the old colonial kitchen with cups of tea, a few nibbles and the smell of mothballs. Standing with his back to the kitchen sink, my father made a vague speech, something about the keys to the house and for the first time I shook his hand. Not long after, everyone left for home.

Chris 1966   Those halcyon months we shared

Christine

1966 was the year of all years. My independence came one wintry evening in April at an art exhibition in Mount Gambier where I first met Christine Holt, an art teacher from Adelaide. She was beautiful, wrapped against the cold in her fur-collared coat, interested in talking and being close. Our relationship was tentative at first. Her twenty-first birthday in July was a big affair in Adelaide to which I wasn't invited, as Christine was unsure about our relationship. My disappointment was short-lived and some months later we were back together.

I was swept away. To share in Christine's art world was a wonderful departure from my own. It was the company she kept and her willingness to discuss and challenge my ideas and assumptions. With her, my education began.

In 1967, Christine was transferred to the Whyalla Technical School, some 800 kilometres away, to teach for a year while I stayed and worked in Mount Gambier.

We kept in touch with regular correspondence and planned weekends together in Adelaide. We were engaged on 18 March 1967. The visual and performing arts were central to those halcyon days of our blue sapphire engagement.

Plans were in place for our future, only to be undone with the arrival of an official letter requiring that I report for National Service on 13 July. Given the news coverage and reports of the war in Vietnam, I wrote to Chris of my concern regarding the possibility of going to Vietnam. She replied:

8th June 1967

Dear John,

Could not watch television tonight. There was a lot of fighting including Vietnam warfare. I felt sick at the thought. I feel so helpless and frustrated because I cannot do anything, not a thing to stop you from going away from me.

You will probably not even go to Vietnam, but the army takes you away enough. Remember you said that your whole life had been spent on the fence – neither one way nor the other. Well darling keep it that way. Neither go to Vietnam and miss call up.

The time between meeting Chris and the intervention of National Service was the happiest and most romantic time for both of us. National Service and the Vietnam War ruined hope and happiness. Our relationship was tested to the extreme, but through the hardships we endured and, as trite as it may sound, those halcyon months we shared proved to be the spark that kept us together.

NATIONAL SERVICE 1967

I packed up my possessions, sold the car, left work and departed by overnight train from Mount Gambier to be at Keswick Barracks, Adelaide on 13 July 1967.

Wednesday 12th July 1967

Darling Chris,

Here begins an epic, this is how I feel: war seems to be my only thought. Have been travelling by train now for half an hour: a cold, conservative carriage, wood panelled, fit for holiday crowds to journey to the beach in at the height of summer but not at the height of winter.

Left home in the cold & rain, the station cold and rather oddly quiet. Both Mum & Dad felt my departure very deeply. Mum was quite upset, as it was for me very sad, but at the same time a sense of excitement overcame to some degree.

Spent most of the day shopping for your birthday. Traded the car, now have considerably raised the amount in the bank. Rough calculations show a considerable fortune of just below $500. Have decided to increase my army allotment from wages (all being well) to $24 instead of $20 per week. Everything is finalized [sic] at home except I have lost my bank pass-book (have arranged for a new one) …

Hope you like all the gifts for your birthday, which I will leave at your place tomorrow. Hope the card fits the post. You can collect your gifts when you come down from Whyalla.

This bloody train! Hard to write in these swaying dog boxes. At the moment, my thoughts are very calculated, so the reason for short sentences on all subjects that come to mind. I will continue this letter a little later when the train stops; which it has now. So, I go on.

There isn't a lot I can say right now as I am very thoughtful about departing … [thinking] about our future world made me determined to live to see it all. These are but morbid thoughts which prevail at the moment …

Well after a lousy journey I am at your place resting … Have about an hour to go before signing [on] the dotted line, right now I feel like running away from it all, but what can I do. All I can think of is you at the moment. It would be nice if you could hold my hand right now. Never mind, 'she'll be right', as far as that saying goes. Must have some rest now and dream of you. Until the next letter my darling. I love you very much. Please be careful and look after yourself, always thinking of you.

Hugs and kisses.

Love, John xxx

I began National Service medically fit, under protest, unprepared and unsure of the future. Distance proved a formidable barrier, so in the two years of service, Chris and I were together on no more than six occasions. Our regular correspondence to some extent eased the feeling of loneliness and love we had for one another. Chris wrote often of her feelings.

Puckapunyal, Victoria, Recruit training

Dear John,

How wonderful it was to read your letter after not hearing from you for so long. I shall be all ears when I see you next, and boy I cannot wait for that weekend. I might fly down to Adelaide and be there quicker and maybe see more of you. Don't worry about Vietnam for the moment, I'm feeling very lucky at the moment; especially about that topic … everything will be alright [*sic*].
It shall be sad going home this weekend and not seeing you. Missing you very much darling.

All my love, Chris.

Singleton, New South Wales, Corp training

Letter from Chris:

> I think I have accepted the fact that it will be Christmas before I see you, but underneath I still keep hoping that it will be sooner. Every night I look for a letter, hoping this shall be the night. Letters have taken on an extra special meaning now that you are so far away and cannot write regularly. I could suggest something here but I think I'm frustrated enough.
>
> Before letters filled the gap between meetings, now they are our only means of communicating so in one way I loathe them. They have to say so much, they have to tell what each of us would have experienced, felt, seen and touched, had we been together.

Holsworthy, New South Wales

On 12 January 1968 I joined the 5th Battalion, Royal Australian Regiment (5RAR). Chris would send bright red envelopes and illustrated letters, perfumed of course. This would cause a deal of humorous comment on the parade ground when letters and parcels were handed out. Her illustrated letters became keepsakes, a memento of the time when we were young:

5th March 1968

> Do you know what the lines and flowers represent? The lines denote wind or breeze (communication) and it is carrying the flowers, a token of love, devotion, of memories, of dreams and anything you wish to be, all to you from me.
>
> Hope you feel the strength of the breeze.
>
> Love, Chris.

As a recruit and a private in the Australian Army, I found it exhilarating, brutish and alienating, but it was also an opportunity to test my endurance, both emotionally and physically. Unfortunately, growing up with a strong emphasis on fear of punishment, this fear flowed easily into an active army life. Small episodes of inconsequential failures caused me much anxiety and self-incrimination, along with a heavy dose of rebuke, army style. It was a most unwelcome burden and one I was unable to resolve. Regardless of the company of other conscripts, most days, for me at least, were couched in romantic loneliness. Music, such as the Beatles 1967 hit 'All You Need is Love', gave poignancy to my many weekends of solitude.

It was impossible to get to Adelaide for even a few days leave as the distance of 1,500 km was too much and so was the airfare. On one memorable occasion, I had extended leave and so with another conscript we decided to hitchhike from Sydney to Adelaide. We slept rough for two nights and arrived late on the third day. After a few days with Chris, I had to fly to Sydney on borrowed money to be back at Holsworthy Army Barracks on time.

Weekend leave in Sydney was usually spent at the Old Tote Theatre watching plays, or taking in shows to try to keep my theatrical aspirations alive. It soon ended, as 5RAR was making ready for deployment to Vietnam.

In late March, A Company 5RAR was sent to the Jungle Training Centre, Canungra, Queensland, as a demonstration platoon, returning to Holsworthy on 2 July. Chris responded to my news:

March 1968

> It doesn't seem a very bright future for us at the moment, does it, John? I hope that by the time you receive this that you have heard something more pleasant (other than) you will be going to Queensland (Canungra). This news sort of takes the bottom out of some of my hopes. Easter was going to be very likely. Since then the future has darkened. Kiss me – cos I love it.
>
> Yours, Chris.

In October 1968, A Company returned with the 5th Battalion to Canungra for intense jungle training. This was followed soon after by our deployment on 24 November to Shoalwater Bay, out from Rockhampton, where we would be eaten by sand flies and evaporated to chalk bones by the sun, for Exercise Nulla Nulla in preparation for Vietnam.

As my National Service was drawing to a close there was a good chance that I wouldn't be going to Vietnam because six months was generally the time required for overseas service. However, I was informed that, with no less than four months residual service, I would be flying out to South Vietnam in January with the advance party of the 5th Battalion. This was frustrating and very stressful news for Chris and me. Once again, our plans and aspirations were put aside as we contemplated the perils of war and our future relationship.

Leaving for Vietnam

The Christmas break in Mount Gambier was difficult, mainly because of the silence and lack of conversation with my parents. They had no wish to discuss my departure to Vietnam, or couldn't. They were intent on keeping their feelings very close. On a hot summer evening, before the 1969 New Year, my parents and I arrived early at the railway station. The evening had a peculiar sadness. Except for a few passengers and their 'farewellers' the platform was deserted. We stood together in the shadows at the far end of the platform; Mum, dressed in summer floral, and my Dad, in his usual suit trousers, cotton shirt and felt hat. It must have been hard for them. My father had no experience of war, but my mother did. She was remembering her brother who had also left for war and didn't return. We said very little, as sadness had overcome us. We shook hands and my parents wished me good luck. The train pulled out and they faded in a pillow of steam. I was on my way.

With Christmas leave and the Ceremonial Parade over, Chris and I then spent a few days together in Sydney before the time came to say goodbye. On that balmy evening at Sydney Airport, 27 January 1969, I prayed that this wouldn't be our last hug and kiss. Our wedding had been arranged for 30 August that year. If I made it, I wouldn't be back until June. Every moment was precious. That evening, with our arms around each other, we could barely watch distraught children hugging their dads, parents wishing their sons good fortune and to come back safely, and girlfriends in loving embraces. It was too much. I held her close, saying, 'Don't worry. I'll be back'. We kissed goodbye, letting our hands slip, feeling the last touch. A brief wave and we parted.

Chris sent a postcard to my parents:

> John was proud of me for not crying, but outside the airport I cried.

THE VIETNAM EXPERIENCE 1969

After a short stop in Darwin, breakfast at Singapore Airport, and a few hours the advance party of the 5th Battalion landed at Saigon. From there we flew to the Australian Task Force Base, Nui Dat.

Tent lines at the Australian Task Force Base, Nui Dat,
Vietnam 1969

As a rifleman in 5RAR, A Company, Company Headquarters (CHQ), I participated in these six operations in 1969:

Quintus Thrust: 1 March–9 March

Federal Overlander: 10 March–8 April

Surfside: 12 April–2 May

Twickenham I: 2 May–13 May

Roadside: 13 May–22 May

Twickenham II: 22 May–1 June

The Vietnam War was an exhilarating hell of endurance, sleeplessness, mines, fire-fights, never-ending patrols and every day the last. This is not to mention scorpions, snakes, other angry wildlife, ration packs, beer, cigarettes and a host of inflictions detrimental to good health.

Correspondence became the diary of my participation in the Vietnam conflict. What follows are my reflections and extracts from selected letters sent to Christine while on operations 'out bush'. As far as I know my letters were uncensored, just as well.

Operation Quintus Thrust: 1 March–9 March

29 February: Nui Dat the night before our first op. Under a green mosquito net in a four-man tent near the perimeter wire, hot and sweltering, half-naked on my stretcher bed with the Self Loading Rifle (SLR) near my pillow and the bayonet hidden in the sand bag wall, assailed by thoughts of, *Will I make it back?* With only hours before the move, sleep was impossible, at best a kip for an hour or two.

Early morning, the smell of damp sandbags, tarpaulin and smoke. A low fog rested on the distant line of bamboo jungle. Dressed at first light, shaved, pack ready, rations, water, rifle and ammunition, and then to the mess. No lights, cereal and coffee in the gloom, no words, the slowness of eating the only sound. Time to go; the tension and apprehension hang and bite. Will this be my last breakfast? We assemble, and in a cloud of damp summer dust we file out beyond the wire.

A Company 5RAR, getting ready to go on operations

I think today is the 1st Tuesday (4th) in March 1969

Darling Chris,

Have been out bush for 3 days – hot dirty war-like days. Every day the temperature has been well in the 90's [*sic*]. The ground is dry and baked hard by the sun, trees are brittle and the thorns vicious. Everyone wallows in dust and sweat. The evenings and nights bring some relief. Every night out here has been brilliant moonlight, quite hot, with very few stars.

Saturday night we walked till late at night over open ground and through a stinking creek waist deep. Finally, we stopped to sleep in the dust near an ominous range of mountains.

Sunday, we crashed through the bamboo to finally stop on a hill, dug in and rested in the blazing sun. We moved again that night. That night mortars and shells whistled overhead exploding over the hill to our front. Also, an enemy report kept our eyes open, the ground being hard, slept very little. The next day proved repetition [*sic*] of the previous with one difference. I erected my tent to form a sunshade, and with Vance Packard, a pair of binoculars, numerous brews of saline, cocoa and H2O the day progressed.

Last night excitement began. Late that night a murderous applause of machine gun and rifle fire resounded through the hills. Enemy were killed … and again more contacts. Last night was a no sleep occasion with such intense action. So, in a leaf-filled creek, under the thick bamboos under the moon, we hid and slept fearful the enemy may run our way ... You can send lots of lovely perfumed letters, everyone likes them, the perfume that is – the thing I hear most when I receive a letter from you is, 'Give us a whiff, Marksy'.

All my love, darling.

John xxx xx xxx xx xxx xx xxx xx xxx xx.
Over here they call these barbwire.

Chris replied:

I think there is a lot of difference between kisses and barb wire. Thank you, darling. Good night.

Operation Federal Overlander: 10 March–8 April

Tuesday March 18th Long Binh, 0100hrs

Dear Chris,

Two years to the day we have been engaged, it's been a long time and very soon this will all be finished ...

Special thoughts for today are about all I can offer you Chris for such a wonderful occasion ... 72 days till the beginning of June.

... p.s. the war continues with an increase in bombing.

Resupply: A Company at Long Binh north of Saigon

Saturday March 29th

My love,

At the moment I am sitting in the damp jungle in Bien Hoa Province. Last night and yesterday afternoon, rain slashed down as we moved through the 'J'. Consequently, we are wet, muddy and tired soldiers. On March 27 we travelled to this area by truck but not all the way. Just outside of Long Phanh village, some distance from our last location, the truck behind us blew up after hitting a mine. Our truck sped up because we thought we were under attack. No sooner had we done this when our truck hit a mine blowing half the engine out, disintegrating a complete axle and tyre. Parts of our truck were spread over 50 metres. With two trucks blown up in the space of two minutes and the wounded lying everywhere was a pretty rotten feeling ... When the explosion went off everyone was hurled forward crashing into me and those in front.

All I remember was dust, brilliant yellow and a head splitting bang ... Even today, 2 days later, I can still feel my aches and only slight headaches now and then. I'm alright [sic] though – but was lucky not to wear more injuries ... Some hours after the mine incident all I wanted to do was cry – just shock, but what a shock. Must hurry as we are moving again soon in search of the enemy ... I wish I could talk to you about thousands of different things – but is sufficient to know (for the moment) that I love you always.

All my love, John.

Twenty-two men were wounded: twelve were evacuated and ten remained on duty

The Bien Hoa Province mine blast

The violent blast on March 27, its effect and consequences, have remained. Being only a few metres from the explosion, my chest and head were severely impacted; crushed and suffocating I disappeared into a world of nothing. How can I forget the profound silence that followed while waking up on the floor of the truck with rifles and heavy bodies entangled, pressing down, one on top of the other? Through the choking dust came the low moaning chorus of the injured. Then the panic to breathe and the scramble to get up, expecting more enemy action. The sweep and search of the area, the held tears, the headache and shock as we sat down in an abandoned cemetery, on the headstones of the forgotten dead. Half-hidden in dry summer grass was a skeletal church with its collapsed terracotta roof, windowless walls, and a white cross at the apex of the portico. I elected to stay in the field while the more seriously injured were airlifted out. I made a poor decision that day, the ramifications of which became apparent soon after. We were in contact again the next day. I was on the edge of panic, seeing the unseen, still in shock and fearful that any moment could be my last. My promise made to Chris was now in jeopardy.

Some days after my lucky escape from the mine blast, and still in shock, we were again in contact with the enemy. We held a blocking position while D company was in direct contact and had casualties. Jets were finally brought in to bomb the bunkers and as A Company was at risk from the air strikes, orders were given to move out.

The narrow track we followed away from the bunkers suddenly turned right and I looked left into the jungle; it was extraordinarily black. I remember being captured, stung by the intense darkness and the threat it posed. Overtaken by fear, I panicked for the first time. Without hesitation, I began rambling loudly, much to the concern of others on that patrol. I knew exactly what I was doing, but for a short time I was unable to control my fear of the dark. I always felt ashamed of my inability to cope and so remained silent on that incident until now.

Much later, back home, there was no let-up; panic attacks and intrusive memories of that incident hurt too much, so I became someone else. It was like a strange final darkness that day of the mine blast. I made it back but I wasn't all right. As my hearing was affected, conversations became fragmented. Many words were lost, misunderstandings were commonplace, and on many occasions entire conversations became a babble. Feelings of acute isolation from others have lasted for years.

March 31st 1969

My darling,

I dream often of our wedding day now and life afterwards. Like me, you too have had a gut full of army life. The next two months can't go quick enough. Last night was rather frightening as artillery shells landed not more than 300 metres from our position, sending shrapnel and clods of earth through the jungle above our heads. Believe it or not, Australian artillery made an error in their calculations; consequently; we had approximately 12 shells explode dangerously near us. It had me worried, including every other soldier. Last night, two or three soldiers on gun picquet were confronted with a tiger – another hair-raiser. The night before, a number of us in CHQ area were awake most of the night as two cobras decided to go for a nightly slither. I quickly shifted my bed and worried all night. Lack of water is our main problem out here and a good deal of time is taken up with water resupply, which is rather good as it offers a chance to rest. Nothing much has happened and the sooner this is over the better. Haven't washed for days and sleep doesn't come easy where the enemy are active. Will continue later as we are moving again soon. It is now late afternoon and at the moment we are occupying an old but still used VC bunker system. Took some photographs of dead VC who had been dead for a month or two. They were wrapped in bag and tied. The stink was colossal. We had to dig up the three graves. Apart from that we have been walking most of the day. That is Vietnam up to the moment. I'm not enjoying it much.

Just made a big cup of cocoa for the OC [Officer Commanding] and myself, read a Playboy magazine and feel a little better. Sixty-four days and about then I hope to be on the way home to you.

All my love, John xxx

Unsettled spirits

Having gassed the bunkers to prevent re-use by the Viet Cong and the subsequent discovery of graves nearby, a decision was made to dig up the bodies and leave them exposed. With trenching tools in hand our small party set off along the hot, dusty track to do the job. The local Vietnamese were very mindful of unsettled spirits, so the idea was to haunt the area by setting free the spirits of the unburied dead. This was to act as a deterrent, thereby avoiding the toxic gas in the nearby bunkers. We could only hope.

Wrapped, tied, dug up and left exposed

Going bananas

While on patrol and cutting through an overgrown banana plantation, I lost sight of the lead soldier. Moving quickly to pick him up, I lost him down one of the many rows of the plantation. The person following then lost sight of me. Stranded, I had a severe rush of panic with the realisation that I was lost in a war zone. Assailed with a thousand disparate thoughts and in the stultifying heat of midday, all I could do was wait and watch from the shadows of the banana palms. I have never been so alert to every movement and leaf rustle. The situation became complicated but was finally sorted. This episode bothered me a great deal and was one I refused to acknowledge.

This incident still causes me considerable anxiety, with disturbing dreams and memories, each one almost the same, of being lost or abandoned in an unfamiliar place with no way out, going bananas.

April 3rd and 4th 1969

A bad day will write again as situation settles love John.

… Been a while since my last letter. Haven't had any more close calls but nerves are starting to become very jumpy … Yesterday we all walked solidly for 5½ hours with a 10 min rest, cutting through jungle. Arriving at our destination we were out again within the hour. We made a hot insertion (a helicopter landing of troops in suspected enemy territory) by chopper, after artillery and gunships had pounded the area previous to our arrival. From there we walked solidly again till dusk and this morning we were in contact with the enemy. After a brief fight, we occupied their bunker position … Apart from plain hard work, it's a life of brews and biscuits with peanut butter.

Tomorrow, my birthday. I will celebrate with big cigars, in a big hot jungle, with big snakes, big elephants and big explosions – boy, what a day every-day … must go … shots …

Today is my birthday – we have been in contact with the enemy all day and am now completing the letter before the mail goes out. I am alright [sic] just bad nerves. One of our elements suffered casualties, some fatal. Don't worry, we go back to Nui Dat soon. I love you darling, and boy! This is the worst birthday I have spent. All my love and kisses, Chris.

John xx

Lift-off. Going back to Nui Dat

Agent Orange defoliation

While on patrol, not long after our helicopter landing on 3 April, we chanced upon a large area of jungle completely defoliated with the chemical Agent Orange. By crossing this area our patrol became an easy target. But through it we went without incident. It was a surreal landscape, a desert of deep yellow clay sand from which a forest of dead tree trunks erupted skywards.

With the searing heat of the sun on our backs, we pushed on through a tangle of blackened branches to reach the cool, dark, green jungle on the far side of the devastation. The prolonged aerial spraying (1962–1971) of the defoliant Agent Orange throughout Vietnam decimated vast areas of forests and food crops. As a consequence of this blanket spraying, many Vietnamese people and servicemen exposed to dioxin continue to suffer from the insidious health effects of Agent Orange.

Operation Surfside: 12 April–2 May

April 25th 1969

Darling Chris,

Just a short note from the heart of the hottest place I have been in in Vietnam. In one day managed to drink a 'gallon' of water and loose [sic] it all in sweat during the day, and at night I think mostly of going home.

Today, one of our blokes stepped on a mine, which blew his foot off – two others received shrapnel wounds. In another company, two were evacuated as a result of a similar incident. Not a happy day at all. The jungle at night here is very noisy and alive with insects and very high pitched, loud, fire-siren-type crickets.

It is nearly dark now so must really write fast. Nothing much has happened yet here but the way things are going anything could. One of our group is at the sea tonight and look like having a go at some sampans. Must close now.

Love, John xxx

On patrol to the South China Sea

My back to a slim tree, in scant shade, midday South Vietnam. Smoke drifting from my last Alpine menthol. From the flickering shade, I looked out and saw threats from pale and deep shadows everywhere. A slight hot breeze rolled dust across hard, parched paddy fields, stretching to the impenetrable bamboo jungles on the far horizon. I was somewhat glad to have some shade. Then, the clack of stone on stone: a soldier deep in thought was picking up small stones and tossing them at a bigger one. The clack of stones resounded in the midday heat. I kept watch as I opened a new packet of Camels, lit up, felt the extra heat of the lighter flame, practised making smoke rings, but through my sweat-dulled eyes followed the drift of light blue smoke instead. Gave some thought to back home, hummed a tune and stubbed the Camel. Our wedding was a few months away and Christine was waiting.

The rest over, our patrol moved on to the South China Sea. Mid-afternoon, on a ridge leading down to flat, cooler terrain, we halted quickly to fill our water bottles from a punctured collapsible water container. Spotted riding high on my pack was a scorpion. Patrol stopped, pack dropped, searched, repacked and on our way.

April 27th 1969, Monday, 37 days to go

Darling Chris,

We were at the coast of Vietnam yesterday waiting for the enemy that didn't come. The South China Sea, blue and dangerous, offered us refreshment and elation. To swim with blue bottles, sea snakes and Sampans on the horizon was indeed glorious! Naked soldiers gurgled and soaked to wash a week's dirt from their tanned, white-bottomed bodies. Sleeping beneath battered pines in the sand hills, with the murmur and thunder of the South China wind and sea as a companion, was ecstasy. So, I found it, but it didn't last long.

Last night, previous to the dip in the sea and just getting comfortable in a hammock between the she-oaks … to the dunes we deployed. Small boats were coming in from a Junk moored out in the South China Sea to bring supplies to VC in the south. A warning light from shore warned them off and consequently the small boats on the dark sea returned to the mother ship. The ambush abandoned.

May 1st Thursday

... Still out bush ... Yesterday we went into an ambush position and later that afternoon we killed three 'Nogs'. I saw one with his brains blown out – not a pretty sight I can assure you. This morning, just after breakfast, two more enemy were fired on – they weren't killed. Apart from 'marching' (straggling!) through very thick jungle with temperatures well over 100 [°F] we have done very little else. A number of our crew have suffered the effects of the heat and other bowel troubles, which nearly always occur on operations. I wasn't feeling very well yesterday, but after taking an amount of salt and water I am beginning to pick up. When shots are fired, everyone forgets complaints – the best cure there is.

Wet with red stain, his brain
Lay in his shattered skull
The shard of missing part
Lay some yards away

Operation Twickenham I: 2 May–13 May

This operation was in the Nui Thi Vai Mountains in Phouc Tuy Province.

May 3rd Saturday 1969

Dear Chris,

Just a short note as we leave soon for the next stage of the operation in the mountains. My last op. This one should last till about to the 27th of May.

... Don't send any more parcels as I will be home soon.

I love you very much and miss you greatly – please pray for time to go quickly. I'm lonely without you. Love always, John

Monday 5th May

Dear Chris,

Well here I am out bush again with plenty of action taking place. Three more enemy were killed this morning and one of our elements contacted at least ten more. However, there is no confirmation as to how many were killed or wounded … We haven't suffered any casualties … Artillery and helicopters with rockets pounded the area just a while ago. At the moment things are quiet again, but for how long is very unsure. Personally, I hope we don't see any more Nogs but this operation will most certainly see a lot more action. It's still early morning, about 9 o'clock now, and even though I'm sitting still in the shade, sweat is pouring off me.

The condensed milk you sent over in the parcel is good gear in the bush. Only wished I could have brought all the other goodies with me but the weight and room factor unfortunately ruled the luxuries out.

The wet season looks like starting any day but as yet it hasn't broken – hope it doesn't while I am out bush (until the 27th that is). That approximately is Vietnam to date.

Received a letter from you this morning. With a big butterfly on it … Again! 5RAR are in enemy contact.

Later that day, I continued with this letter, feeling quite hungry after Chris wrote that she'd made a great cake:

> Don't eat all that fabulous cake yourself. Share it around liberally so that you can have one or two slices. My diet is two brews a day (lots of water), 1 small tin of fruit (6 half apricots), 4 dry biscuits and a small tin of cheese for breakfast and perhaps a small tin of meat (chicken & noodles or spiced beef) for tea. Try that one darling for at least 3 weeks and you will have some idea how living in the bush is in Vietnam – please! Don't eat too much. Anyway, Chris, look after yourself. I love you very much and each day makes Adelaide that much closer and you that much nearer.
>
> All my love, darling.
>
> John xxx

Ambush

One day, we had time for a brew-up before the ambush was set. When last light began to fall, a myriad of crickets screamed like fire sirens, monkeys chattered and birds carolled. In the canopy of the dark trees, thousands of fireflies glowed and extinguished. Suddenly, it was pitch-black. The shroud of night silence was profound, only to be broken by a hot breeze, acrid with charcoal smoke, scraping a vast army of dry swamp reeds nearby. In the intense black of that night and while on picquet duty all I could do, as the long jungle night held and threatened, was listen. An hour or two before dawn, a late rising moon shone like cold silver on a landscape clouded in drifts of low fog. The jungle, grasslands, swamps and low hills in the far distance were awash with drifting blue and dark blue shadows. It was easy to imagine enemy movement in that landscape of illusion. As the first light of dawn streaked dull through the chill mist, the cold moon faded into the lilac sky. In the breathless silence of that calm morning, nothing moved, as the monumental dome of the red sun rose to a murderous applause of machine gun and rifle fire, and three men lay dead.

Dawn South Vietnam.

This letter refers to the seven-hour battle in the northern valley of the Nui Thi Vai.

Tuesday May 13th 1969

(Twenty-one days and a sleep)

Darling Chris,

The last 4 days or so have been rather hectic. On Sunday, nearly all our company were in contact with the enemy. From about 11 o'clock until last light we were held down by enemy fire. Our platoon commander was killed (May 11th) and one of our in-take was wounded by a bullet through his cheek and out through his neck. He RTAs [Returns to Australia] on Monday. With a hand-full [sic] of A coy I stayed back to secure our company area and LZ (landing zone). Rounds from the contact were coming into our area. As I headed for a large tree for cover at one stage of the game about six rounds ploughed into the area of my feet. Was a close call but the guys in close contact certainly had a rough time; the enemy were well dug in and were using RPGs [rocket-propelled grenades] and Claymore mines against us. I took over from another sentry and spent a few hours alone on the far side of the LZ to cover the track leading to the main fight. We moved out of the area of contact early next morning and in came the jets with napalm and then artillery to demolish the VC camp. As one of the last out I could feel the heat of the napalm on my back.

The wet season has begun with tremendous gusto; lightning, thunder and rain that lasts for hours. Consequently, people were floating out of tents and paddling about to all hours finding a dry area. We were back at the FSB (fire support base) at this time and consequently the situation tended to be rather humorous. However, this is only the beginning of the wet. (Why haven't I got my camera?) Now for the surprise, I am at Long Binh again.

Operation Roadside: 13 May–22 May

13th May

Apparently, they are expecting a large enemy assault in the area and we are up here to play our part. This could be a bit hairy, but then again it may not eventuate too much. Ho Chi Minh's birthday on the 19th. (Hope he has a rotten birthday.) That is the day for trouble or thereabouts. Basically, that is the news from Vietnam with 21 days to go.

Received a letter from you and will endeavour to answer it in the time available ... You always look the best ever so, in 21 days or rather the 5th of June, I will tell you all sorts of wonderful things. Enjoy the tour. It's your holiday and have a good rest. Must return to the war and the forthcoming 13 days or so in the bush.

All my love, Chris.

John xxx

Life and Death in a Rubber Plantation

A wounded VC was dragged, dropped and left in the dirt at our CHQ position. He lay in his sweat and final dust, a putty man. While the medics were bandaging his wound our eyes met and in that moment of recognition, the fear of dying and the depth of sadness was overwhelming and unexpected. The armoured personnel carrier (APC) arrived to collect him.
The steel ramp was lowered and the dying man carried to the open door. Then the scrape of combat boots on dry leaves and a one, a two and a three and he was thrown into the APC. I saw and heard his head and shoulders smack the steel wall before he dropped.

I turned my back that day, moved on, but could never forget our shared grief and the manner of his death.

Eighteen days to go

May 16th 1969 *Friday* (Long Binh the thickest jungle you have ever seen)

My Darling Chris,

Just another short note from leech, tick and lice country. Since moving to Long Binh at the beginning of the week we have seen very little of the enemy. However, there are massive troop encampments of both enemy and friendly forces. Up here, north of Saigon, jet and artillery assaults seem to be in operation 24 hours a day. From the map our AO [Area of Operation] has the thickest jungle and therefore possibly the safest we have had for a while. Still one can never be sure of that. It is safe because the enemy nearly always move along tracks or roads while we scrub-bash our way round.

Have ten more days out bush and believe me, to have such a short time and still be on operations isn't exactly easy to take. Consequently, caution and playing it safe as possible is always a daily companion.

The first night out in the rubber we killed one enemy leader, the other ten or so enemy quickly dispersed. Apart from that we had rubber tappers in our area for half a day. I hope we go around in circles for the next ten days and do nothing hairy, that is all there is to tell you about Vietnam from my point of view. I hope you are well and I hope time is flying as much for you as it is for me.

Haven't had much opportunity to think about our wedding, honeymoon or anything for that matter. However, I am pleased with the state of my mind considering the amount of time we have spent out bush.

I might mention that don't send any more parcels over seeing that eighteen days is the time left over here. I might add I still have the cheese and toffee peanuts to consume at the Dat.

Honestly can't think of much more to write about Chris so, will save my thoughts that have evaded me in this letter for the next … Lots of hugs and kisses when I see you again darling in Adelaide on June 5th.

Operation Twickenham II: 22 May–1 June

May 26th Monday 1969

Dear Mum & Dad,

Just a short letter to let you know I am fit and well and am back in Nui Dat. Have been back since last Sunday night. The rest of the company arrive back on June the 3rd and we leave for Aust on June the 4th. Should be back in Aust on June the 4th that night and hope to be in Adelaide before or after midnight. However, a connecting flight may not have been arranged until the 5th. We will find out in the next few days. It is only 8 days and one sleep. I don't exactly like the situation around the different world trouble spots. Particularly Malaya and most of Asia.

On our last operation, we went to Long Binh for a week then back to the Nui Thi Vai Mountains for a few days, then back to Nui Dat. Apart from walking a very long way, getting wet, sleeping soaking wet, and hardly seeing any enemy for days, nothing much happened. Just very tiring and tense work ... By the way, this wet season is pretty soddy and it should start for real about the 1st of June – it rains with lightning and thunder that has to be seen and heard to believe. No need to write again as the letter would not reach me in time. By the time you receive this one I should be nearly on my way home. Anyway, keep fit, will see you soon and tell you all the war stories and show you the slides.

All the best to you both.

John

COMING HOME THE ROAD TO NOWHERE

Two of us were left, more or less stranded, on a wet cold night at Sydney Airport. We had just flown direct from the war in Vietnam and now we had to make our own way home. It was 4 June 1969; our tour of duty and National Service was over. The airport lights were going out as we caught the last taxi to the only place I knew, the Sailors' Rest Home near the docks – cheap, hard beds and no breakfast. Early next morning, in the drizzling rain, we caught separate taxis. I hadn't nearly enough money for the fare but the taxi driver was considerate, given my situation. A free flight from Sydney to Adelaide and I was on the way home.

It was a warm winter morning as I walked across the tarmac in Adelaide looking out for her with nervous anticipation. Chris was alone when she found me in the almost deserted terminal, and we stared at each other as strangers. It was a wonderful, warm, intoxicating embrace. Her perfume was perfect, the same she used on her letters to me in Vietnam. Having been apart for so long we had much to talk about but instead we fell silent. To break the silence, Chris told me she'd had to threaten to resign from teaching, as the school head had declined her request for time off to meet me. She was given time off without pay. It was a strange, romantic feeling, as we began again to know each other for the first time. Our letters promised so much love and happiness, but in reality the war and the long time apart had darkened our future.

Welcome home and a kick in the guts

After a few weeks rest in Adelaide, I made the train trip back home to Mount Gambier, where I expected a reasonable welcome from friends and relatives. Instead I met a wall of silence, indifference and barely disguised hostility. My parents took one look and said, 'You're back', and that was it.

Following those disappointments, I reported to Keswick Barracks Adelaide to be discharged from the army, expecting a welcome of some sort. Having reported to reception, I was sent to a corridor to wait for a medical check. I waited until an officer asked what I was doing there. Apparently, the receptionist had forgotten to inform anyone. Some hours later, after a brief medical, I eventually found the Stores Department to hand in relevant army issue. I introduced myself. The army corporal grunted and went rummaging for the paperwork while I began to unpack my army bag. 'Keep it, don't need it,' he said. With two quick thumps of a rubber stamp, he cancelled the paperwork. Bending down to push my combat boots and uniforms back into my army bag, I asked, 'Is that all?' There was no reply. Looking up, I saw that the army staff had left for afternoon tea. The process seemed unfinished, so moving to the entrance of their tearoom I asked again. There was no reply; I was simply ignored. I was dumbstruck. It was a kick in the guts. Not even a handshake, a conversation, a cup of tea or a biscuit. *Nothing*. This was my welcome home; left alone to make my way out, through the barrack gates, where two years ago I entered as a conscript.

I felt worthless and lost, sitting on my army bag, my feet in the gutter on the Anzac Highway, my head in my hands to hide the bitter resentment of being ignored and unappreciated. Then the ever-present feeling of having failed again resurfaced with a vengeance. Tired and spent, I wept. This was to be one of the darkest hours of my life while I waited for Chris to pick me up. She came, after she'd finished teaching for the day. Together in her Mini Minor, we drove away to begin our lives anew.

Army leave was over. I resumed work in Mount Gambier on July 13 to pick up where I left off two years ago. Everything for me had changed but everywhere was the same. 'How was your holiday'? I clearly remember being asked. 'I was in Vietnam,' I said. The persistent feeling of not being welcome lasted.

Aftermath

30 August 1969 was when our wedding took place at Holy Trinity Church, Adelaide, eleven weeks after my return from Vietnam. It was a fog of delight and pride. At the reception, with our hands together, we plunged the knife into the wedding cake, then they all sang and proposed a toast to us. Love was in the air, but so were the traumas of my Vietnam conflict.

From Rose Bay, Sydney, we flew to Lord Howe Island in a Sunderland Flying Boat to begin our honeymoon. Chris and I had a wonderful time of peace and quiet but it was to be short lived. On our return to everyday work and our new home, our relationship began to fracture.

Our correspondence promised so much affection for each other, but not this!

I was shouting and talking in my sleep, awake at the slightest sound or the faint smell of smoke, and going on *patrol* to check that doors and windows were secure at all hours of the night. Chris would find me sleepwalking and guide me back to bed. Then the night that completely unnerved Chris was when loud knocking inside the house woke her. She found me wandering up and down the dark passage, agitated and lost, tapping the walls with my knuckles and a spoon, trying to find a way out. I had no recollection of that episode, only Chris's account. As a consequence of my traumatic experiences in Vietnam, and the intrusive memories of violence, life became unbearable. It was the stuff of nightmares, dangerous thoughts and long sleepless nights. If I was in the garden, any loud noise usually found me on the ground taking cover, as I had done in Vietnam. At least those events were amusing. However, I experienced bouts of unexpected anger and verbal abuse. These were followed by feelings of remorse, but forgiveness from Chris was too much to ask.

A couple of years into our relationship, Chris threatened divorce if circumstances didn't improve. It was a difficult time but our love held. Then, four years into our marriage, our lives changed with the arrival of our son, Ben, in 1973, and then Bianca in 1975. It was a time of happiness with many trials and challenges; however, as the years progressed the recurrence and persistence of my war traumas caused much unhappiness.

Some years later, Chris took our children to Adelaide for a holiday. She'd had enough of my Vietnam blues, drinking and outrages. My mood swings frightened her and she was very unhappy. She packed up and left. I didn't hear from her for more than a week, and then she phoned to check if I was coping. I wasn't, so they returned home. It was time for me to take stock and make amends. I was to learn, much later, that she'd been planning to leave me for good because I was becoming unpredictable.

It wasn't until 2006 when I learned how unpredictable I had become. All was revealed at a counselling session I attended with Chris. I learned that she would go to bed fully dressed to escape quickly with the children should it be necessary. Apparently, I was verbally aggressive, drinking, and talking rubbish. I had no recollection of what was happening – what was I thinking? I was shocked and felt sick at the thought of how close we had come to disaster.

I played my part in war
Saw violent death first-hand
I explained with fervour my desires
But failed to see the tears in her eyes
And I closed the door to mine.

Through counselling, I learnt that PTSD had dogged me since coming home from the Vietnam War in 1969, but there was no label then for my depression, angry outbursts, high anxiety, booze and suicidal intentions. I loved words, so in the hours of intense loneliness, and having one too many, I wrote poetry and other ramblings to give a voice to the chaos in my head. Invariably, it ended in weeping anger. I often felt trapped and needed to be alone to taste the bitterness of being a victim. It was relentless. I felt ashamed and guilty about being a failure at nearly everything. But I would always declare, 'There is nothing wrong with me.' I worked extra hard to forget the war and the dark days of my early years. My supreme efforts in maintaining a show of happy normality worked for our family.

I worried excessively about how others saw me and took criticism very badly. Being overlooked or ignored hurt deeply. Between episodes of self-doubt and feelings of worthlessness, I threw myself into local theatre, directing plays such as *Waiting for Godot* and *The Crucible*. Apart from acting in many plays, such as *Oh! What a Lovely War* and *The Legend of King O'Malley*, I had part-time casual work on ABC regional radio. I needed to make a difference, to stand out, but my illusions and unmet expectations were causing much distress as I began to realise that what I desired and had dreamt of for so long wasn't possible. I was always awash with ideas, plans and enthusiasm, but once these ideas and plans were played out, my depression and sense of having failed sent me into the darkness time and time again.

On many evenings when the shadows were long, I would take the dog for a walk to the edge of a volcanic crater and watch the sun set over the dark lake far below.

It would be
Over by now
Except for
The dog
It was a
Long way
Down
But the dog knew that

Valley Lake, Mount Gambier, South Australia

I seemed to have confused my imaginative world with everyday normal living, which I disliked because of its dullness and entrenched habits. So, I found my internal world under threat and my delusions of grandeur were just illusions. When we were young before the war in Vietnam, Chris and I dreamt of a life so different from the reality facing us.

When angry and confused, I barely considered Christine and the children; however, it was a relief to everyone when I managed to be my 'old self'.

I was having panic attacks that were persistent and getting worse. Work and my social life unravelled as my Vietnam war continued. I needed to get away and so, after forty-one years, I decided to leave Mount Gambier for good. I had stayed too long.

MELBOURNE 1987 - TIME TO GO

The time had come to leave everything behind and begin anew, to put the family first and to give Ben and Bianca a better educational experience. I accepted a job offer in Melbourne and, in January 1987, we packed up and left Mount Gambier. We were all hard pushed by the change, and sad to leave friends and security. With less than $200 dollars in the bank, we settled into our new home, worked together, held on, and success came with university degrees for Chris, Ben and Bianca.

Panic attacks

I continued working hard in Melbourne but the change did little to lessen my bouts of depression. Panic attacks became more frequent and there was no relief from the persistent memories of my Vietnam experience. I had hoped for a new start, to leave my troubles and illusions behind. But I was wrong and I paid the price. For me to lose the ability to act and think rationally was, and still is, very concerning. There are many triggers: crowds, noise, confined spaces, loneliness, fear of failure, and, above all, intrusive memories of the Vietnam War and coming home.

The first time I zoned out wouldn't be the last. A few weeks before being discharged from the army in 1969, I was walking out of Westpac Bank when the pavement and my entire surroundings vanished. All was dead quiet; I wasn't there! Then a voice from a passer-by enquiring of my wellbeing brought me back. I have no recollection of how long I stood there, except for the moment I set foot on the pavement. That's all …

At a conference dinner in Hobart, with a large noisy crowd in attendance, all was seemingly well. Within a short time, I was overwhelmed by the noise of the crowd; conversations blended and grew louder. It was like listening underwater, awash with noise. Unable to comprehend anything, chaos and anxiety soared. I had to go. I began rolling up my rain jacket slowly, tighter and tighter so no one could see me leave. I knew this was bizarre, but such was my panic. When I thought nobody was watching, I bolted for the door. Outside in the fine rain, I put on my rain jacket and walked as fast as possible down a narrow dark road leading to the hotel, all the while talking loudly, fearful of the intense shadows experienced in Vietnam, and alarming pedestrians. I found the hotel, went to my room, locked the door and immediately hid behind a large armchair. I sat on the floor, my hands over my head, and talked and shouted to kill the fear and chaos. Finally it stopped, and there I slept until sunrise. This was a particularly bad episode.

At Perth Airport in 2007, while waiting to board a plane to Melbourne, I paced around the terminal continuously, conscious of other passengers watching me. My anxiety catapulted. Near to panic, I began to feel unwell, sweating profusely, not daring to put down my bag. Passengers posed a danger; threats were everywhere. I felt very uneasy, but I also knew it was untrue. Finally strapped in, I held on for the next few hours and slept on the flight back to Melbourne. The surprise was that nobody seemed to notice or care, as I was sure they would.

Sometimes I found it impossible to board a train or tram when alone. On a few occasions while waiting at Montmorency Station, I would become quite anxious. When the train arrived, I was unable to move. I would watch it leave, completely overcome with fear of what could happen on the journey in such a restricted space with no escape. So, I would return home with anxiety uppermost, dressed for the city, to spend many hours sitting in a dark corner. When she could, Christine would accompany me on trams or trains.

Recognition

In 1991 I saw for the first time the publication *Vietnam Remembered: Includes the names of all those who served.* It was a seminal moment. If my name was there, it would be the first public recognition of having served in Vietnam. With trepidation, I took the book down and began the search. Under the heading 5th Battalion Royal Australian Regiment, I found my name. Somewhat overcome, and with shaking hands, I put the book back and left the shop. I attempted to tell Christine the news but I was speechless. A month later, still in a state of disbelief, I finally found the courage to purchase *Vietnam Remembered.*

In conversation with another Vietnam veteran, I was told, to my disbelief, that I had to apply for my Vietnam medal. I applied for my Vietnam Campaign Medal in December 1988. It arrived in a cardboard box on 20 February 1989, twenty years after my return from the war zone. Many years later, I was made aware of my eligibility for the Infantry Combat Badge (ICB) for which I applied on 10 July 2006. Eventually my badge came with a letter dated 14 June 2007 and an apology for the 'unacceptable delay in response in this matter'. Further to this, the Royal Australian Infantry Corps and Australian Army awarded the ICB in 'recognition and appreciation' for my active service in South Vietnam with 5 RAR in 1969. Other medals soon followed, thirty-eight years after my homecoming.

A sense of worthlessness

Some time ago, feeling worthless and like a failure, I couldn't see the point of going on. Alone and despondent, and looking out at the garden from my kitchen window, I had the answer. Perhaps I might hang myself. On that day, in early spring 2003, the acacia tree presented the perfect branch, dead centre, over the back step of our timber deck. A place where I would be seen and found. It was fanciful, but the idea began to bother me and take hold. It became an obsession. Some days later, unable to let go of the desire, I wrote:

I am going to hang myself out to dry
To become like leather in the blazing heat
To swing in the hot breeze
Until the night turns to frost
To stiffen the bones and flesh rigid
To gather dreams like flypaper
And wait for the night gales
To break the hanging arm
To fall to the dead earth
Amongst the ashes

In twenty minutes, the poem was finished. I was feeling happier, but still troubled by the hanging arm. The branch had to go from my sight. With bow saw in hand, the temptation was removed. It wasn't enough. A few more 'hanging arms' in the garden needed to be pruned. Christine asked about the reason for pruning. I said it was necessary. She never read the poem but when alone I would read it, never tiring of the words.

THE LONG ROAD BACK CLOSING THE GAP

Returning home from the Vietnam conflict and trying to assimilate into the everydayness of civilian life created a wide gap for me. As a consequence of living in the 'gap', my life became intolerable, going nowhere, sliding between biting memories of the war on the one hand and illusory normality on the other. With no help available and my war service ignored for years, layers of complications piled up. This was mentally destructive and thirty-five years after Vietnam, I was admitted, exhausted and unable to cope with living a normal existence. The 'gap' had to be closed. Ward 17 and the PTSD Program were to be my ticket home.

Despair

For a long time, I had been overworking and in despair of going nowhere. For months, I made up bogus appointments, drove to a quiet, isolated street or park, locked the car and stayed there for hours. I knew, but still denied, that I wasn't well. Then in August 2005, my last day at work came as a result of a severe panic attack. In an instant, I became disoriented and confused. I could hardly breathe, doorframes and walls moved in and out. I ran to the car to escape the threat, and drove home in a catatonic state. Agitated and frightened, I arrived home to an empty house and locked the doors, as the Vietnam War experiences came roaring back. It was impossible; I knew I needed help, so began another journey of consequence.

Ward 17

I remember that day, the beginning of my collapse and capitulation. In my study, a room of dark and threatening memories, with the door shut so no one could see my distress, I summoned all my courage to dial a number Chris had pushed into my hand years before. The counsellor's voice was warm, consoling and serious. I was hardly coherent but managed to say, 'I think I need help'. We spoke for a while and arrangements were made. A few days later, I sat in my locked car, near the security entrance to the Repatriation Hospital, numb with fear, unable to think clearly. I saw the counsellor walk past from the corner of my eye, and ask the security guard my whereabouts. A tap on the window and I was found. That day when I was found and taken in will always be remembered with gratitude.

Why had it taken so long and why hadn't I sought help earlier? I had no answers. For me, the Vietnam conflict ended in June 1969, but continued for the next thirty-five years.

I march with blind eyes
Through cheering crowds of darkness
No hymns, no music
Only the whispering chatter,
The chorus, of the dead and the dying

Ward 17, Repatriation Hospital, Melbourne, Victoria, 2005

Ward 17 at the Repatriation Hospital became my home. Four weeks on anti-depressants, maximum three a day. Suicide watch for the first week. Nothing to do but hold tight, listen and respond, detail after detail, story after story, conversations with and without others. Nights ran into days. A strange time. My world was vast and empty with no sense of time passing.

I remember staring at the thin edge of yellow light that shone full length of the door left ajar, just in case …

There I was with others who were living their pasts, their nightmares and their mental traumas. These were the *me too* moments of conversations and group therapy. It was a big family from whom I remained a stranger, but from their stories I was not.

I began to understand that there was a path away from my delusions, anxiety, feelings of worthlessness, and my constant fear of failure. After four weeks in Ward 17, and with these thoughts as fleeting as they were, I embraced the PTSD Program.

Christine would come to visit from time to time. She was so gentle and genuinely happy that I had at last made my own decision to get help. Without Chris's steadfastness and love through all those trying years after Vietnam, our relationship would have surely collapsed; her visits and involvement in these difficult times cannot be overestimated.

Ward 18

I was invited to participate in a residential intensive PTSD treatment program at the Heidelberg Repatriation Hospital. The program started on 17 October 2005, which was also the beginning of our group of eight veterans and partners. For the veterans, it was a four-week residential with a further eight full-day sessions, once a week, until completion on 11 January 2006. Our partners participated in a separate program, but we came together on occasions to strengthen relationships.

The PTSD treatment program was intense and immensely rewarding. The individual and group therapy sessions were, for me, a godsend. The making of a collage to depict our lives has become a treasured memory for most of us in the program. We had all created something tangible, and by the act of doing, achieved a sense of fulfilment and a better understanding of ourselves – for me a happy experience.

We were all asked to talk about our collages. In trying to explain the vast array of pictures on my collage of memories, I was asked why I had blackened the windows of a small colonial house. I didn't have a reasonable answer then, but the question remained.

The answer: the house I grew up in was a store of dark and bitter memories and I was making sure they would stay there. However, in the writing of this story, and considering the question that remained from the program, I threw open the windows so I could to tell my story, as difficult as it was.

Our group of eight veterans and partners has, since the program, met regularly over the years, shared our lives and supported each other when required. We also maintain an individuality that leaves us free to pursue our own activities away from the group, but we also know that we are there for each other should we need support in times of crisis or celebration. To have shared our lives, our stories, and found genuine support and empathy for each other is reward enough; it was a wonderful beginning with no end in sight.

Christine and I attended a week-long, residential Lifestyle Management Course follow-up program at the Jumbunna Lodge Retreat on 19 February 2006. We found each other again, held hands, kissed and made up. It was the year of our sixtieth birthdays and we were happy. Chris made a welcome-back card for me, reflecting on the love we shared when we were so young. This was the spark that kept us together.

> Dear John
> When we wrote
> to each other, when
> you were in
> Vietnam, the
> letters reflected
> a love that
> can now be
> rekindled
> Love Chris
> xxx

Written 2006 Christine 1967

Christine: 20/7/1945–19/4/2007

Nothing, however, had prepared us for the catastrophe about to strike.

Chris was diagnosed with terminal pancreatic cancer a few weeks later. Throughout her illness, she focused on what was to be her last art exhibition.

For weeks and months before the February 2007 exhibition, the two of us would sit up nearly all night while she wrote, with difficulty, her poetry into the artwork. I would read the words to her and chat about this and that until she finished.

The doctors and staff at the Austin Hospital did all they could to get Chris to the opening night but she was too ill. We managed to visit the exhibition a few days later. The exhibition was a success and she was happy. After a long twelve months of love, hope and struggle Christine said goodbye at 11 pm on 19th April 2007. It was traumatic. Words were meaningless. All I could do was look on in dismay and disbelief and try to confront a unique sadness; an emptiness, a cruel hunger that requires no food. Her life was a precious gift and one I was happy to share with her. Counselling continued. That was the one commitment I kept. I needed to talk.

The following extract is from a long letter written during one of those long-distracted days and was meant to give voice to our time together and ease the anguish of her passing.

Dearest Chris

So much has happened after you left on April 19th 2007.

Where to begin?

I can only begin with you, day and night you are my companion and wish, if only, I could have held you close in those last days and hours. But you were so ill and frail. Do you remember the moment when all seemed lost, those last few weeks at home, when I had my back to you, you said, 'I love you' with such conviction that to this day those few words are well remembered? I regret not turning back but such was the emotional impact of your declaration that I was overcome with too many soft tears. Given your desperate situation, I tried as best I could to make the last days as light as possible.

Those letters we sent to each other while I was in Vietnam. Vietnam. Those days, how sad and lovely the letters were sometimes. Wedding plans, what our futures might be and the love we expressed to each other – but as we know the war put paid to many of our plans and the alienation we endured as a result of my participation in that war. I'm so sorry you were put through so much misery on my return. Thank you for hanging in; it couldn't have been easy.

Our PTSD group still meet and you are sorely missed. We are now writing our stories with our partners to whom we owe so much. I hope you don't mind but I'm quoting from your letters. It is a bit selective, dear, but I hope you will approve.

Love, John

With all the machinations, Christine's passing, panic attacks, loneliness, fear of failure, the Vietnam War, and depression, my way through was to take ownership of it all. I decided to start talking. For ten years, regular conversations with my wonderful counsellor, Dr Tarni Jennings, soared and plummeted, were sad and expansive, but always with hope for a better time to come.

Vietnam revisited

In 2008, I was unable to decide whether I should return for a holiday to Vietnam, the source of so much misery. Out of exasperation or kindness and a deal of directness, Tarni said, 'Just do it!' It was all I needed to hear. She gave me the confidence to go. Within a month or two, I was on my way.

I arrived alone, distraught and bewildered at Kuala Lumpur International Airport Hotel. In my hotel room I collapsed on the bed and buried my face in a pillow, my body heaving with hot tears never experienced. Then I heard my voice resonate within me and flow out to a loud audible declaration, 'I've made it. I've made it'. I worried for a moment that I was overheard. It didn't matter. Not now. For the first time in my life, I began to believe in myself. My journey had come this far. Tomorrow, Vietnam. Thirty-nine years earlier, I left the war zone, now I was returning.

Ba Ria market South Vietnam 1969

Holidaying in Vung Tau, Vietnam 2008

Not only was I going back, but also I had accepted that my life was what it was. I've made it. Those simple words meant so much and I was obliged to follow. I remember with pride that exalted moment with my arms outstretched, in need of a hug, so I gave myself one.

When my days are dark, those simple words inspire hope and a willingness to give it a go.

The three-week Battle Tour of Vietnam was an engrossing challenge. Everything had changed; it was no longer the war zone that I remembered. No danger or threat. In fact, I was happy to be back in that bustling country of friendly Vietnamese people.

Reminders of the war were few, but the government-run, sheltered workshops where young children, teenagers and young adults lived or attended were sad places. To see children with no legs or arms, deformed bodies and many with mental illness either as a result of chemical warfare, mines or poverty was depressing. I returned to Australia with empathy for the Vietnamese, and questioning why.

There are many days when my feelings are stretched and over-stretched and tormented with thoughts unwelcome, as it was on a particular day in the summer of 2014. Alone, I took two steps beyond the kitchen door, with garden secateurs in hand. Looking about and down, I found nature too vast, too bright, and unpleasant. Having failed to observe the garden or take in anything outside, I retreated the two steps and locked the door. I was forced to admit that all wasn't well, at least for the time being.

With the secateurs safely hidden just in case (a consequence of my persistent memory of that terrible evening when I was seventeen), and feeling quite anxious, I sat in my chair of wood and greyness and looked at another horizon, of events past, in the wilds of my imagination.

All this on what had promised to be a good day, when the garden beckoned and the world seemed at peace. But in that shut down house with its drawn blinds and locked doors, silence pervaded every corner. In the half-light, sitting motionless, all I could hear was the regular tick of the pendulum and the high-pitched singing in my ears, and then the mine exploded in my memory. It was all over and I slept.

Participation – giving it a go

In 2008, after revisiting Vietnam, my dear friend and next-door neighbour, Lisa, suggested that I might like to attend the East Doncaster Baptist Church. That wasn't for me, but, reflecting on the peaceful Sundays of long ago, I decided to place one foot and the next over the doorstep of the church. The sermons were philosophically challenging; the parishioners were generous in conversation and kindness. So, Sundays became my day of rest and reflection. I also sing 'F flat', if there ever was such a note, in the church choir.

On another occasion, the Vietnam veterans were given the honour of leading the 2016 Anzac Day March in Melbourne. This was to be my first Anzac Day March. The 5th Battalion led the parade, and as we neared the official party we were given (in no short measure) 'by the left' and 'eyes right'. I was back in step with 5RAR; a proud shared moment to remember.

These two events were particularly challenging, as my long held negative views and assumptions needed to be put aside. Eventually, after much deliberation, I decided to throw caution to the wind and just do it. It worked.

A JOURNEY INCOMPLETE

I cannot forget, cannot correct my mistakes, undo my failures, change the aftermath of the Vietnam War, or bring Christine back. I can, with conversations and storytelling, accept that my life is colourful, miserable, happy, depressing and, at times, full of remorse and tears. I'll always feel lonely and distracted with deep emotional thoughts. My past is bountiful and problematic. My life is what it is; the war was what it was. In the retelling, I found my way.

Love, I suspect, is all I need, but it was also essential for me to have a range of strategies to be able to cope with the bad days.

Sitting it out is not easy for me, but to sit still for hours (as long as it takes) in a quiet place to calm the noise and chatter in my brain is a strategy that helps, as it usually results in a welcome sleep.

Music is integral to my wellbeing: an escape from the torment of thoughts uninvited, and a reprieve from the spectre of violence that has hung over me for most of my life.

When the going is tough, into the garden I go. This has always been my escape through which work, achievement, reflection and happiness come.

Re-reading the correspondence that passed between Chris and myself from 1966 to 1969 was rewarding and difficult because we shared our intimate feelings, but also our prejudices. For thirty-eight years of our marriage we cherished the memory of those halcyon days that we shared before the Vietnam War. Our hopes and expectations were severely tested after my return.

With deference to Christine, my story became a love story, a never-ending adventure.

The decision to write our stories couldn't have occurred without the collective encouragement of the group of eight veterans and their partners. The years of support and togetherness are a blessing that couldn't have been envisaged when starting out on the PTSD Program in 2005. For me, a door had opened and I stepped in.

I have no stamina
To continue.
But I can dream.
Soar like an eagle
Over landscapes
Of my making
The beautiful chaos
Of memory
The exquisite agony
Of loneliness
The untrammelled vastness
Of thought
No horizon within reach
I've said it all
I am free

THERE'S NOTHING WRONG WITH ME ... OR IS THERE

Marty Miles

I'm a returned Vietnam veteran. I was conscripted into the army in mid-1968, Intake Number 13 (lucky for some, or not) at the age of twenty, an uneducated person with little life experience.

When I look into the mirror, I see a person who looks normal, has no scars, no lost limbs, is just a normal person, but inside feels different at times. Some days, I'm depressed and angry; some days, I'm good. Some days, I don't want to be here and don't know why. When I'm down I want to keep to myself, talk to nobody, want to be in a world of my own. I feel better until something goes wrong, then all hell starts up and I get angry and aggressive again. If someone is near, they cop it and most times it's the ones I love the most. That makes me feel worse, then I'll get depressed and it starts all over again.

Some days all I want is to be on my own; other days I need company, which I suppose most people want. Does that mean there's nothing wrong with me? I really don't know.

To help get through most of my days, I work, try to keep my mind active, which some days makes me tired. So, when resting, all I want to do is sleep, dreaming shocking things that, at times, wake me up. Then, when awake, I feel guilty for sleeping. Is this because I'm doing too much or am I getting old, or is it the medication I'm taking? Who knows?

I'm finding writing this piece very hard. At this moment, I feel I'm whingeing about myself and there are people out there worse off than me. That's another way I get through my day: by saying to myself how lucky I am. At least I can do things and have a great family around me.

After I left the army in 1970, I had that many jobs it's not funny. You name it, I've done it. I moved from job to job, not lasting very long at one place. I don't know how my wife put up with me, though I must say I was never out of work. Most of these jobs were physical and sometimes hard labouring work, which has kept me physically fit. So far, health-wise, I've been lucky in that I haven't had any serious physical illnesses.

Now that I'm retired I still seem to work as hard, but it's a different type of work: fixing up things around the farm and running around after my kids and grandkids. That keeps me busy most of the time.

With the farm, kids and grandkids, and catching up with other vets, life seems to be a bit better, but not all the time. I still have my days, as my wife can tell you. Having seven grandchildren helps a lot. When with them at school functions or watching them play sport or swimming or dancing, I feel so proud, and when the whole family is together: WOW! All the noise and fun – I feel so good. My three children have had to put up with some hard times in their lives: not much money and lots of yelling and screaming from me. That's when I was at home. Most of the time, I was at work, but they've all turned out all right. I'm so proud of them. I hope they don't turn out like me. All three are better off than I was at the same age and they're all very hard workers and deserve what they have.

After seeing so many psychs and telling them the same stories, I still don't know how to feel different inside. I know when I'm talking to them, I feel better for a while. Just talking and getting things out seems to release a lot of pressure, but things just go back to the way they were before the talks, for me that is.

I've got a very good wife who understands me and helps me a lot. After forty-five years of putting up with me, she knows how to defuse most situations.

Now, forty-five years after Vietnam, I look back to ask myself, 'Is there something wrong?' I never thought or talked about Vietnam for years because I wanted to forget about it. I wanted to get back to the normal life I had before being called up to the army. At that stage of my life, I wasn't married and all I wanted was to get married, to get back to my old job and to my old sporting activities.

Life had its ups and downs. Then about fifteen years ago, there were more downs than ups. Unknown to me, my wife looked for help for both of us. She arranged for a visit to a welfare officer who I didn't want to see because I just didn't want to talk about Vietnam. After a lot of persuasion, and about two years later, I got a pension. Since then, I've caught up with a lot of mates and now I go to a reunion every two years.

During the two years trying to get my pension, I went to a PTSD conference at Jumbunna in Healesville, which was run by Open Arms, a counselling service for veterans and families. I didn't want to go, but my wife enrolled us for a whole week. I still remember driving there, thinking at least I'd get to see all these sick people and also have a week's holiday. Upon arriving there, I was astounded to see they all looked normal. My wife still says I was rude because I didn't take part, just sat and said nothing. After three days, they showed a film called *You're Not in The Forces Now.* At times while watching the film, I felt very uneasy. I started thinking, *Is there something wrong with me?* When driving home after the course, I thought to myself, *I wish I'd taken part more.*

So, my wife booked me into another course. This time it was at Heidelberg Repatriation Hospital and went for four weeks, live-in. There were eight of us.

The first day in class, we were sitting in a half-circle and were asked about our pasts, including jobs. Whilst listening to the other boys' jobs, I froze, because they were ex-CEOs of companies, engineers, financial advisors and so on. I was thinking to myself, *You're out of your depth here.* I thought this especially because I'd had so many jobs in the past since leaving the army. I'd make a fool of myself. But things went okay.

The course helped a lot. I found out that I had depression, which made some sense. I remember one day during the course, we were asked about our memory. The facilitator asked, 'Is there anything you can't remember?' Because I'm a little shy I said nothing and listened to the others answering different things. All I wanted was someone to mention that they couldn't remember people's names but no one did. So, near the end of the class I found enough guts to ask the question myself. Well, all hell broke loose; the rest of the class joined in saying the same thing. That made me feel good and part of the class. I remember one of the boys saying to me later, 'There are no silly questions in this class, so speak up.'

The facilitators were excellent. All had different ideas on how to cope with each problem, but it was still up to me to work the problem out myself. Sometimes I don't think there is a problem when there is one and there lies the problem I have. After the four-week course, I came away feeling that I'd learnt something and made seven great mates and met their lovely wives and partners.

We still see each other about once a month for lunch at each person's home, which is good, especially with the ladies. They get together on their own in a room so we men can't hear what they're talking about, but we have a pretty good idea, although sometimes we do talk to each other, as a group, if we have a problem. This sometimes helps, but it depends on how much we've had to drink at the time.

In ending, is there anything wrong with me or not? I have to keep trying to get through each day at a time and when things get too hard, I need to talk to someone, mates, friends, family or anyone, to get it out there.

If you feel the same way, don't hold back. Go and see someone. It's not easy and it's not silly.

LOVE YOU! LOVE YOU MORE!

Laurel Miles

I met Marty when I was seventeen years old. I was very young and quite immature, but I knew from the moment we first met that he was someone special. We met at a local ballroom dancing school. I went on Friday nights and Marty went on Thursdays, but after a short while both of us were going to the Friday classes. Ballroom dances at local town halls became a favourite Saturday night outing for us, usually after he'd been playing cricket or football. Afterwards, we would have a hot chocolate at the local bowling alley as neither of us drank tea or coffee in those days. There were always lots of friends who joined us for these weekend outings. I had an 11.30 pm curfew that I broke at times, but not often. Usually we went to Box Hill Town Hall where there was ballroom dancing upstairs and downstairs was the supper room. I can also remember attending dances at Springvale Town Hall where there was both ballroom and rock and roll dancing. Sometimes we would go to the Pancake Parlour in Hawthorn, which was the first in Melbourne, but most often it was back to the Ringwood Bowling Alley.

We'd been dating for six weeks when he gave me a friendship ring, which was a really big deal in the 1960s. I still wear this ring every day; in fact, it's difficult to remove. That was 1967: miniskirts, conscription, the Beatles and so much more. There were no seat belts in cars and very few cars had bucket seats; most sedans had a full bench seat and

Laurel, 1969

column gearshift – great for sitting close together whilst driving and for making out! We were madly in love, but our parents weren't all that happy with our relationship. I guess they thought that we were far too young, but this didn't stop us. In fact, it made me more determined to be with Marty.

Then he was conscripted in 1968. Out of all our friends, only two were called up. It was really hard not to be able to ring him whenever I wanted, but we were able to keep in touch when he had free time at Puckapunyal. I remember that we'd get into trouble from our parents for tying up the phone for long periods. While he was at recruit training, I was lucky enough to have friends who'd drive me there on days when the recruits were allowed visitors. We had a picnic lunch, a little time together, then a long drive back home.

I was working full time with the ANZ bank in the city administration, so that helped to keep me occupied and, on the weekends that Marty wasn't home, I occasionally went out with friends.

Then came the decision to volunteer for Vietnam or not. We decided that it'd be good for our future as far as finances were concerned. A war service housing loan would be available, plus extra payments for a married couple. We'd become engaged just before my nineteenth birthday and our plan was to get married before Marty went away; however, my parents weren't at all happy with that decision. I can still remember my mother saying to me, 'What if he is killed? You will be a widow!' She must've thought I'd end up alone for the rest of my life. It seems so insignificant now, but times were very different then.

In 1969 we bought ourselves a block of land just before Marty left for Vietnam and it was paid for whilst he was overseas. The plan was to build on it once we were married. I don't recall being overly fearful that he wouldn't return. The media coverage of the Vietnam War wasn't as extensive as it would be these days. Marty's letters to me were very general as far as war experiences were concerned; however, he did mention mates, sporting activities and the social side of being in the army base.

I remember the Vietnam War protests held around the country but I don't remember thinking a lot about them. I recall Jim Cairns (a Labor Party politician) being very active against Australia's involvement in the war. All I really cared about was having Marty home, safe and sound. All these years later, I think our involvement was wrong, but I wholeheartedly support the efforts of our Defence Forces, and that goes for whatever conflict they may be involved in.

We both promised to write to each other every night that we were apart. Marty kept his promise. He even wrote on the rare nights when he'd had too much to drink (Bacardi rum was his choice and now the smell makes him feel ill). Whilst in Vietnam, he didn't drink often; in fact, he was a *goffer* drinker – someone who only drinks soft drinks, not alcohol.

I kept writing every day until after he returned to Vietnam from rest and recreation (R&R) in January. I found it really difficult to write every night after that. I missed a couple of weeks, and then started again. When he returned to Vietnam, I was very lonely, even though I had lots of friends and my family around me. We'd spent so much of his R&R together, talking and planning for the future, that I found it difficult to put my thoughts and ideas down on paper. I can't imagine what this must've done to him. Unfortunately, all his letters were destroyed many years ago, but we still have a lot of those he'd received whilst *in country* – a term often used by service personnel to refer to South Vietnam. I'd write to him about what I'd been doing, to whom I'd been talking and where I'd been. Sometimes it'd be very mundane, but I guess it would've been a reminder of life at home. When I read these letters now, they seem so boring! Very much like a one-sided telephone conversation.

This is Marty, left, with our very good friend Kevin Saunders, standing in front of the truck Marty drove whilst in Vietnam. As you can see, he had my name on the front

We were married six months after he came home and life seemed to go back to normal. We rented while our house was built. Thank goodness for the war service loan. Marty went back to all his sports – football, cricket, basketball and golf. Even after our children were born, he was still playing sport two or three times a week as well as working around the house and holding down a job. Looking back, his need to keep active is not much different from life now. It's really difficult for him to slow down. He's always pushing himself to the limit. Now I understand that the effects of PTSD can push a sufferer to keep busy continually as a way of coping and blocking out experiences and memories. Even now, as he reaches his seventies, he's always finding something to do. Rarely does he take time out, just for himself. This can lead to utter physical exhaustion and that in turn causes mental problems. The exhaustion often leads to a breakdown in communication and/or an argument. Sometimes it can take days or even weeks for the communication to be re-established without confrontation or argument. Things will settle down for a good length of time, but then there is another episode.

Our .marriage at St Benedict's Church, Burwood, Victoria, 24 October 1970

Life was okay for a time. Small arguments occurred, but nothing major, until one night in 1976 when he 'lost it'. This particular night he became extremely verbally abusive and he shoved me quite hard. Luckily, I fell on the couch. He stopped and stormed out of the house. I know that it could've been a lot worse, but coming from a family where arguments didn't happen, it was a big shock. I never heard my parents argue. Sure, there were disagreements but there weren't angry words said in front of my sisters or me. When Marty and I did argue, I can remember thinking that he'd leave me, that maybe I wasn't good enough for him. My biggest fear at the time was separation. Things were sorted out and often discussed, sometimes in depth; other times just skirted around. Every now and then, though, he wouldn't be able to hold back from a shouting match. I contributed as well, and often it happened whilst the children were around. On occasions, I'd withdraw into myself for several days until we could have a discussion without the angry words. Even now, we can really disagree about something, major or minor. One of us will say, 'Okay, if that's the way you want it, that's the way it will be.' Often, we both need a break, and then we can appreciate the other's point of view.

We moved from the suburbs to a rural location and made a life for our family. We started with an empty 40-acre paddock, built a house, fenced paddocks, built sheds and stables. Marty worked extremely hard on the farm whilst at the same time holding down a job as a test driver for the Defence Force (as a civilian). The job was quite stressful at times, as was trying to make ends meet financially. Things would get rough: there would be an argument, little or no talking for weeks on end, but no physical violence. Our financial situation was always difficult, as we were developing our property, educating our children and making some hefty mortgage payments. Disagreements with his work colleagues flowed over into our relationship at times, and sometimes the kids were too noisy or too energetic in the house and that would upset him. When he was silent, it was a relief from the angst, but the lack of conversation and closeness was also very difficult to handle. I think the kids learned to keep out of his way at these times. Our children weren't difficult, just normal, active, fun-loving kids who mostly did what was asked of them. There was never any question of his love for the children. He's always been extremely proud of their achievements.

Early in our marriage, Marty's symptoms were quite unknown to me – neither of us had any experience with PTSD. All I knew was that from time to time it was very difficult to live with him. His moods would be up and down from one day to the next. He could be so loving in one moment, then ice-cold in the next. What never changed was his work ethic. He always had a project or three to work on and this could lead to physical exhaustion.

Prior to becoming aware of PTSD, I'd try to get Marty to talk to me about what was troubling him – sometimes he could verbalise his feelings, other times he couldn't. I mostly just went along with what he wanted so that our life could be more peaceful, but as I grew in my self-confidence, I began to realise that this was not always the best strategy, especially where our children were concerned.

I was struggling with my relationship with Marty and I remember thinking that if I didn't do something, then our marriage was doomed. I spoke to the wife of another veteran one day and she opened my mind to the issues relating to PTSD. Her husband was also a Vietnam veteran. At first, I didn't think that PTSD was the issue – it was just his personality and upbringing. I didn't want to end what we had, so I sought help from the VVCS (now known as Open Arms – Veterans & Families Counselling).

Our names were placed on the list to undertake a lifestyle course through VVCS, but when someone from their office rang to confirm our attendance I wasn't home. Marty answered the phone and promptly told them we weren't interested. I was quite upset when I found out so I put our names back on the list, only to have the same thing happen again! Not to be deterred, I rang VVCS and was lucky enough to get on a course within a short time frame, so eventually we participated.

This course was of enormous benefit to me. Marty didn't really participate until the second last day when he saw the video *You're Not in the Forces Now*. Then, and only then, did he think that maybe he had some issues. If you ask him why he went, he'll tell you that he thought it'd be a good break away from work and the farm and that he would have a rest for the week!

He did benefit from it. He called a family meeting and told our children and their partners about some of the issues. He'd taken quite a lot out of the role-play about saying no. A lot of veterans have difficulty saying no, even when it means that they're unhappy about a situation. The role-play showed how to say no without conflict, without anger and without upsetting someone.

Marty explained that he no longer wanted to get up early to feed the horses and that someone else needed to take over this task. I wasn't sure how this would go down, but there was no argument from anyone so he no longer had to get up early. This may seem such a little issue, but to him it was very important. It was resolved without any argument, pressure or nastiness.

Couples counselling was organised with an excellent counsellor who had rooms not too far from home. I clearly remember Marty saying after the first session, 'That went well. We won't have to go again.' Wrong! He hardly said a word and I did most of the talking. Months later, it was the other way around. Marty was talking more and I gave a comment when necessary.

Since then we've both sought individual counselling. I feel that it has made an enormous difference to our relationship. I found a counsellor through VVCS who was extremely helpful and gave me a lot of reassurance about my own abilities to cope with a husband suffering from PTSD. I'd been struggling with having in-depth conversations with Marty and he'd often dismiss the topic without delving into the issues I was raising. My counsellor helped me with strategies to get around these times. I've found that if we both offer a clear explanation, then we can usually reach a good resolution that we're both happy with. This could be something as small as deciding what to have for a meal or something that's a big financial purchase. I wouldn't call it compromise, but maybe respecting the other's point of view.

He enrolled in the PTSD course at Heidelberg, which was live-in for four weeks, with the partners participating once a week. What a life-changing experience. After not participating fully in the lifestyle course, Marty decided that because he'd been given another opportunity, he'd try to get the most out of the program. At the end of the four weeks, he didn't want to come home. He felt very comfortable with the other men in the group and both of us had established close friendships with the partners as well.

Today, we have an easy relationship with everyone in the group. We get together for lunch several times a year and keep in touch regularly via email or phone. Over the winter months, when some of us like to travel to warmer parts of the country, we don't always see each other, but when we get together again, it's as if we'd seen each other yesterday. It's an amazing group of people who are always willing to help, encourage and support each other. I don't think that I have any friends who'd really understand what this group is about. Our connection is unique. We've stayed together for thirteen years and the bond is enormous. Sadly, we've lost two of our wonderful ladies who were part of our original group. Christine and Glenda are still very much in our thoughts, and now Carol and Lisa have become a big part of us!

Marty's shirt and tie – my hat, 2014.
Together always

Since participating in several PTSD and lifestyle

courses offered by the VVCS, I now have the strategies to cope, not only for myself, but also for Marty, for the rest of the family, and for friends as well. Generally, the strategies work, but sometimes there is a situation where nothing but time helps; nevertheless, staying calm and not being forceful is one good strategy. It is, however, often hard to keep the anger out of a situation. Comments that don't antagonise, but instead are positive, make a lot of difference, and enable us to move forward.

Things that have happened in the past can't be changed but you can learn from them. I don't think that you ever stop learning about your life partner. There is always something that will surprise you. It isn't always easy. Just when you think things are running smoothly, up comes another issue. Sometimes it's a minor hiccup; other times it's a major hurdle. If you want to continue with a happy relationship, then there needs to be give and take on both sides.

Closeness, when no words are necessary, is sometimes the best way to resolve issues. I've always tried to make sure that I don't go to bed angry. Every time that I've told Marty I love him, he's always replied, 'Love you more!' After fifty-two years together those words are repeated with just as much meaning as when we first met.

We enjoy being together, travelling in our caravan, seeing this amazing country of ours, but we also enjoy our family and friends at home. It still isn't easy street, but it's so much better than what it was. I can't imagine being with anyone else. Sharing so many good times with him is just fantastic.

Us, 2016

MY CHALLENGE WITH THE ABYSS

Nikko Nicholas

I've been called a lot of things in my life; however, for this read I'm better known as Nikko. As I write this story, I've reached the milestone age of seventy-four years young. You might think it's a strange thing to say, then, that at the age of fifty-eight I started to wake up to myself. Firstly, let's put this down to being a slow learner, and secondly, this was about the time I hit the wall and was diagnosed with PTSD. Before this, I was bulletproof, a leader in my field, triumphant, and too big for my boots. I took no prisoners and could unwittingly leave in my wake a path of ignorance and pain, without acknowledging the damage I'd done during my early adult life.

In my story, I talk about shifting blame and ignoring warning signs, especially from those trying to support me. If only I'd listened to my mother's advice when I first returned from Vietnam, when she wanted me to contact the DVA.

If this story can help anyone out there (and that can be in any form of working life) to see the early stages of PTSD and seek help, then I'd say this no-holds barred read has all been worthwhile.

PART 1: CHILDHOOD

I think the seeds of PTSD were planted in my early childhood – some individuals can be more susceptible to problems later in life by experiencing trauma in their growing years and adolescence. In my case, because of some terrifying experiences during these years, I was always going to be a high-risk candidate to join the ranks of PTSD in my later years.

My father was of the very strict Victorian era. His motto was, 'Do what I say, not what I do.' He also had a cruel demeanour about him. Countless times I can remember getting belted around the head by this brute with plenty of verbal abuse for good measure. On one occasion he chased me around the house cracking a stockwhip around my ears, laughing his head off as he thought he was some kind of entertainer in front of his so-called friends. I was ten years old at the time.

One of his worst offences was for me to witness him punch my mother in the stomach and to see her fall to her knees. He did this terrible act when my mother told him she was pregnant with my youngest sister. I was a mere 2 metres away. Maybe he had a sense of guilt for this cowardly act, as he never laid his hardened hands on my two younger sisters, so at the very least I give him some credit for that.

When I was four, the family lost our little brother to meningitis before the age of two. He had been such a livewire, full of mischief and fun, while I was more on the timid side. I knew in my father's eyes I couldn't make up for this lost son. Soon after this the beltings started. He would look at me with vicious disdain and my fear would grow. Was this because it was me who should have been the one to go?

At this time we lived in a remote rural area. I had a pet dingo – naturally I called him Dingy. We were inseparable. He was my protector. If I could sense my father was coming after me, I'd charge inside Dingy's kennel and he'd stand outside with his teeth bared, saliva dripping from his mouth, and face this monster of a man. Each time, my father would back down and walk away. I thought one day he would shoot Dingy, but as fate would have it, he was run over by a car, and I watched him die beside the road. My protector was gone and I felt helplessly alone.

Around this time, I was in the early stages of primary school. I was a hopeless student. My father made things worse by expecting me to be the best in the class, but he never sat down to help me except to demand that I spell words like elephant or hippopotamus. In a trembling voice, I'd say, 'E ... L ... E ... F', and then he'd whack me around the head for my incompetence! As a result, my confidence and self-esteem were crushed and I remained a hopeless student through all of my school years.

I was now close to sixteen. I was put to work around the house after school, and most of the weekends were spent digging garden beds and chopping all of the firewood while my friends were having fun, fishing and mucking around at the footy oval. This felt like punishment, or as one of my friends said, 'You're nothing but a slave'. All this hard work and wood chopping made me strong and wiry, which would soon pay dividends!

I was almost six feet tall and playing football for the local countryside. I wasn't playing too badly on one particular day, and as I burst out of the centre and kicked a long ball, I missed the big sticks and kicked a point. There, yelling on the sidelines within the crowd, was my father, 'You play like a girl, Sissy'. I sunk into myself and felt ashamed, but then I saw my poor mother next to him, looking very embarrassed as she pleaded with him to stop. She then quickly left, for she feared him too.

So, did I learn to despise this brute? Absolutely.

Leaving home

It was a September evening, the air was growing chilly; we would be in for a heavy frost in the morning. It was 7 pm when my father arrived home. He turned to look at me and immediately started with the abuse. He accused me of not doing all of the tasks he had given me. I said I'd done everything he wanted, then bang, around the head again as he said, 'Don't answer me back boy'. He hit me again with a sickening blow to the head. My mother begged him to stop, but no, this cruel beast belted me again.

This time it was different. I was ducking his wild swings, and when I was hit I refused to fall down. I stood upright and looked down on his stocky frame, and said, 'I told you I did everything you asked for, get out of my way, I'm leaving this house now'. He stepped aside. My mother was distraught, and as I walked out of the house at 7.30 pm with only an old jumper on my back, he said, 'Never are you to return back to this house'. I heard him utter the words, 'Good luck and good riddance.'

I ran for miles, sometimes hiding in the grass beside the road when I saw a car coming with its lights on, just in case it was him. I had been hiding and running for over two hours, full of adrenalin and fearing the worst if found, for I didn't want to go back to that hell-hole again. It was now around 10 pm. When I saw headlights, I thought it was safe to come out of hiding. I thumbed for a lift. The car stopped. I got in. As fortune would have it, this kind gentleman was going all the way into the city.

'Where are you going?' he asked.

'To my grandmother's,' I replied.

It was a strange thing that he didn't ask me where I was from, or what I was doing out there late at night, but I think, somehow, he knew I had been roughed up and was trying to escape from something that was untoward. I sometimes still think about this Good Samaritan. He even dropped me off at my grandmother's front door. It was now midnight and I was safe inside with a loving and caring gran.

PART 2: DEALING WITH NEWFOUND FREEDOM

I hadn't completed fourth form, yet as each day went by I could feel myself growing more confident. I was also mapping out some employment opportunities; there wasn't a moment to lose.

I contacted my headmaster at school and asked for a reference. He had learnt all about my home life. He wished me well and followed up with a reference so glowing I could have applied for the position of CEO with BHP.

I started working at the railways on the station platforms. That was the beginning of my independence and from that point on for the very first time I had the *power of positive thinking* within me. I started to believe then that there was nothing I couldn't achieve.

Furthering my education was high on my priority list. Knowing how difficult it was for me to concentrate in a classroom, I decided to do various correspondence courses, with my first being a Sales & Marketing Diploma. This dummy was now scoring top marks. All of the freezing-up had gone away and I could now learn and was seeing things as clear as crystal.

Life was improving month-by-month as I continued to progress through the junior ranks. At eighteen, I had my first car and I started dating girls. My only problem was I knew I was becoming a little cocky. In two years I'd grown up fast and free of all negativity, though I was becoming more of a smart aleck! So, I changed direction and decided to travel around this great country of ours. The first adventure began after a few beers in a pub (maybe more than a few). I ended up at Essendon airport and disappeared without a trace to Tasmania.

I didn't give a thought about contacting anyone back home for two weeks and I didn't know I was on the missing persons file. Was I in trouble when I returned? Oh yes, especially with my grandmother who called me irresponsible. Oh boy, did I learn how to start sucking up!

I'd really enjoyed my few weeks lost in Tasmania, so much so I went back with my car for several months, trying my hand at a variety of jobs. Amongst other things I even became a surf lifesaver. Then it was time for me to leave the Apple Isle, as there was a pretty girl who had ideas about putting the shackles on me, so I eagerly escaped and started my travels northward into New South Wales and Queensland. I worked in abattoirs, I cut sugar cane, and dug with a shovel, knowing that it wasn't all that bad getting your hands dirty while meeting a variety of like-minded people sharing the same adventure. I really had a great time.

Almost twenty, I was told my mother wasn't well and had become a heavy drinker. I decided to go back home to see her. Living with my father was hard enough for her, and me being out of the picture didn't help.

I arrived at the old house and you'd have thought I was a king walking inside. This stocky man now stood there with a grin from ear to ear. He tried to tell me that he was so proud of me and the compliments kept on gushing. However, I remembered his last words when I walked out at sixteen! But for now, I would tolerate his company and give him little credit for what he had to say to me, as my only thoughts at this time were for Mum. She needed a lot of support so I tried to see her a lot more regularly. Constantly, she would say, 'I've got to get away from your father, as I can't stand the stress and his domineering ways.' I knew she was unhappy living with such a controlling man. Thankfully, her health and drinking problem slowly improved over time, but she never gave up on wanting to get away from him. Several years later when my sisters left home, my mother called me to help her pack and leave. I happily obliged with aiding her escape.

The age of conscription

Back in the big smoke, after my great working holiday along the east coast of Australia, it was now time to put my career back on track. Vietnam was starting to place a wedge within the country. Our then Prime Minister, Harold Holt, was quoting, 'All the way with LBJ', the then American President, Lyndon Baines Johnson. I had a career and objected to the idea. Luck was on my side; my number didn't come up. I pulled my head in and moved on.

My early twenties were exciting, with great jobs in sales and marketing, new cars and lots of female friends. I was a high-flyer. This once timid, shy fellow continued to be over-confident. I was expecting everything to go my way and it mostly did. I was so cocky and full of myself that I was close to obnoxious. Amazingly though, I kept all of my friends so maybe there was a likeable side to me too.

Vietnam was in the news more. We heard all about the Yellow Peril, that if the communists took over Vietnam they would sweep through Asia and beyond. We saw more conscientious objectors and I could feel for them, after all, I worried about it too. On the other side though I was fairly patriotic; I loathed the thought of communists winning in Asia, and the speculation of our freedom at risk. In those days you mainly made up your mind with what was fed to you by the media, close friends, and, to a lesser degree, the pollies. However, we know when the North took over South Vietnam the so-called invasion into Asia didn't eventuate.

PART 3: THE ACCIDENT THAT CHANGED MY LIFE

I remember back on a sunny spring Sunday afternoon I was showing off my new car to a pretty girl. We were driving on a narrow country road, when all of a sudden I was overtaken by some hoons driving a hot rod. They splattered my car with stones, incensing me. I took off after them at great speed, my female companion egging me on.

I sensed danger, as I was pushing my vehicle to the limit. Then bang, the front tyre blew. We went through a farm fence and were heading straight for a big gnarly tree. I was having trouble steering and on the soft soil the brakes were having little effect. Miraculously, I missed the huge tree, but in the process, I took out some smaller trees and the car's undercarriage was badly damaged. My brand-new car was a write-off. Thankfully, we both got out of the accident without a scratch. I wondered if my luck was going to run out.

I looked again at my new car, and realised I didn't have a car anymore – it was on hire purchase and the insurance company wouldn't be pleased with me at all! I dusted myself off, arranged with someone to take my friend back to her home, and headed back to my unit to do some soul searching.

That night I watched the news. The Yellow Peril was pushing ever further south, coming to get us all! In a moment of heroic patriotism, I said to myself, 'I should help to stop all of that and give something back for my fellow Australians.' Filled with bravado, I volunteered to join the army.

Everyone told me I was mad and throwing my career away. Notwithstanding, a few days later I went into the army barracks to join up as a regular soldier. The rest was a blur, with a medical check-up, signing on the dotted line, and, before I knew it, I was on a small blue bus with fourteen other dingbats heading to Kapooka to commence boot camp. Everyone was talking mighty tough talk such as, 'We volunteers are not going to be harassed by the army brass; we'll show them a thing or two if they do'. All of this tough talk carried on, until finally we drove through the barrack gates.

Everyone sauntered off the bus. Some had hair down to their shoulders; others had cigarettes hanging out of their mouths. I was the last to disembark. As I looked around, I saw a striking figure of a man well over six feet tall, with bright red hair protruding from underneath his slouch hat. He had bright blue piercing eyes that could cut through you like a knife. His uniform was starched like a wooden statue, and on his sleeve he displayed three stripes. As we slumped around like a pack of rubble, this imposing figure's face clinched, with his square jaw exposing the top layer of his teeth, snarling. Then came this deep, volcanic-like rumble from within this mountain of a man and he boomed out, 'Speeeeeeeewww'. That word was all it took to put fear into the lot of us. He bellowed, 'Attention!' We all jumped around like lost rabbits and somehow found ourselves in a line formation.

This sergeant couldn't look angrier. With his fists clenched, he yelled out 'Left turn, quick march. Left, right, left, right', and we marched to our barracks. Recruits hanging out of their windows chanted, 'You'll be sorry.'

At that moment, I knew I'd gone from the top of the heap to the lowest common denominator in a flash! Next thing, we hit the barber's chair. Locks of long hair hit the deck and I noticed I had a receding hairline.

Day one. It was 5.30, loud trumpet speakers blaring, and we had to run down to the parade ground with our sheets from our beds. One guy was slowly making his way down without his bedding; it was here we quickly learnt if one mucked up we were all punished. We were all ordered to do twenty-five push-ups and then stand to attention. For good measure we were ordered to repeat the dose. Needless to say, we made sure the once lazy recruit was the first on the parade ground the following morning. This was the system we had to learn quickly. Basic training went on like this for another ten weeks. I didn't do too badly, much to my own surprise, and I was no longer a recruit, but given the rank of private. *Golly.*

I was as fit as a Mallee bull; moreover, I was about to go into infantry training and would come out the other side as an iron man. Army training was tough and intense; again, it was all about teamwork and systems that you learnt in your sleep. As a country boy I was a good shot with a .22 rifle and could shoot a rabbit between the eyes at over 60 metres away. This helped me as a marksman in the infantry, and soon I was ready to go to Canungra in Queensland to complete my final jungle training before I headed off to South Vietnam.

The jungle training camp pushed your belief in what the human body could do. Some things stay etched in your head, like the first day we observed the jungle obstacle course, which included several low-level barbed wire courses to crawl under, various high walls to climb over and rivers to cross, with explosions going off all over the place. Completely spent, I thought I was pretty smart to get through on my first attempt in four minutes, until we were all told that to pass and get out of Canungra you needed to complete the course within one minute and forty-five seconds. *Is this some sort of joke?* I thought. I just couldn't see how this was plausible especially as some had taken over six minutes! So, each morning our day started with a 5 to 7 kilometre run before breakfast, then jungle training, or the dreaded obstacle course, and/or a 28-kilometre forced march with full pack and drill.

The weeks of training were starting to fly by. Everyone was under the one minute forty-five seconds limit. What looked to be near impossible just proved to me what the human body can do when it's pushed hard and the bar is raised. I didn't realise it at the time, but it was this training and methodology that was preparing us to feel confident in our new-found ability. We felt bulletproof. As for fear, this wasn't on the agenda. From here on in, we were part of a well-oiled machine.

PTSD at this point was nowhere to be seen on the horizon. You acknowledged all of the smoke and explosions during training as a game, but nothing really prepared you for the effects of the real thing.

PART 4: VIETNAM'S UNCHARTED WATERS

One day in October 1968, I walked up the stairs to board a Qantas plane on my way to South Vietnam. I was attached to the Army Reinforcement wing, where on arrival I was to replace personnel for the First Royal Australian Regiment (1RAR). After several hours in the air we were flying into the then Saigon.

A turbulent mixture of feelings ran through me. As I saw the landing strip I was feeling excited, but then I also wondered just how secure everything was down there. I looked around me and saw that no one was smiling. What I was seeing, however, was an odd, serious look, and I thought they were thinking the same as me: 'Keep my head on my shoulders for the next twelve months. She'll be right. Be positive and get on with it'.

We touched down. It was hot and humid, but without haste I was shown the doorway to an RAAF Caribou aircraft. I got in with my gear; my shirt was soaking wet with sweat. Down further in the bowels of the plane I could see some mates who had come over on the same trip. It was good to see some familiar faces. We waved and smiled, then the plane fired up with a roar and we took off for a rough ride on our way to our Australian base in Nui Dat. After thirty minutes, we landed and I could see the jungle and the Vietnamese people working in the fields. Again, a great mixture of emotions and feelings, something I hadn't really experienced before.

I was taken over to my new quarters, where I found myself sharing a tent with someone I knew from basic training. We were issued with SLRs with live rounds in the magazines. This SLR was to be kept as clean as a whistle and we could strip, clean, oil, and put those weapons back together quicker than we could blink.

That first night we were sent outside of the secured wire to do a patrol. Talk about being thrown to the wolves. This helped explain the nervous ta-tas!

We were patrolling in an area where there were many banana tree plantations, and I was experiencing a real sense of heightened alert. In our earlier training we were taught to be alert, but this *heightened alert* was something new, and I quickly started to wear it, deal with it and live with it! It was quite dark and we settled down for the night.

Quite naturally, I got little sleep that night; however, I did doze off just before dawn. As the first rays of light filtered through the canopy it appeared foggy; however, as my eyes focused, I was underneath a mass of spider webs, with huge black and yellow spiders with abdomens as big as bananas. Guess what? I have a phobia of spiders. I can pick up a snake and crack its back but these monsters terrified me. Welcome to Vietnam!

I was involved in many fire-fights during my tour; however, there were three occasions where I thought I'd end up going home in a sealed box.

Incident one

Battalion 1RAR was nearing the end of its tour, with only six weeks to go for most of them. All of these guys were getting edgy, as the choppers were still flying us all out to the jungle for weeks at a time to flush out the Viet Cong who were building up in our region.

It didn't take long to experience my first contact. We were dropped off in a clearing as the machine gunner at the door of the chopper sprayed the surrounding canopy of the jungle with a blast of bullets indiscriminately cutting through anything in its path. While this was all going on we jumped out and ducked down to get clear of the twirling blades, then watched as our transport lifted off with haste and quickly disappeared.

There were three sections in this platoon. My section was at the front. I was carrying my M60 machine gun with two forward scouts in front of me cutting a thin path with their machetes.

The objective was to find the enemy's bunkers or tracks that they used to transport their supplies. The Viet Cong were masters of camouflage and it was possible to walk through their camp of bunkers without detecting them. It was in their best interest not to be discovered, as it was their strategy to build a network of tunnel bunkers in wait for a major offensive. The catch-22 was that it was our role to find and disrupt them. This redefined the idea of hide and seek.

On the first day, our forward section didn't encounter any contact and it was with some relief that we were moved back to the third section on day two. This was known as 'Tail-end Charlie'. Three days went by, bashing through the dense foliage and twisted vines, when we came across a narrow track. Almost immediately, there was a loud shout up ahead, 'Contact', and then came the intense noise of gunfire from all directions. Instinctively, we all hit the dirt and positioned ourselves into a right flank. We were in the second section, and the third section took the left flank position. Everything went like clockwork. All the training drills had paid off. The fire-fight was over within a few minutes. We had no casualties and our forward section had a count of three dead Viet Cong. We knew there were at least five in the enemy group, so the plan was to travel down this track and set up an overnight ambush with Claymore mines. These are mines that point forward in an arc. As we walked down the narrow track we walked past the dead North Vietnamese soldiers lying on the ground. One had his head blown open with his brains spilling out of his skull. This ugly death hit me like a sledgehammer and it took several days before I could start to remove this image from my mind.

That night, we took turns of standing guard; eyes wide open, peering into the darkness, expecting a contact to happen at any moment. Eventually light slowly penetrated through the canopy, heralding the start of another day.

All of this kept us on the highest alert; I compare this feeling to fishing. When fishing, concentration and anticipation fill every moment, as you just never know if a fish will strike. When one does strike and you're not altogether ready at that exact moment of time, it's game over.

For the next ten days we moved around the area to find one abandoned camp that had several tunnels running underground. This was destroyed with hand grenades and heavy artillery fire. We found no further evidence of Viet Cong in this area. They had vanished deeper into the jungle! We were told that this exercise was over and the next day the choppers arrived to take us back to our base in Nui Dat.

It was such a relief to be back behind the wire, even though unwanted thoughts intruded, so we would have a few beers and then a few more.

It was the build-up of the wet season and I was breaking out with monsoon blisters. I also had prickly heat with hives all over my body that spasmodically attacked nerves and that could bring one down to their knees. Being out in the bush without a shower all this time didn't help.

1RAR had two more exercises before going home. This time we had some wounded casualties and I saw more enemy deaths, but I was becoming more conditioned to all of this and subliminally I was also becoming more hardened to the daily life and conditions that confronted me. In total, I had been with 1RAR for six weeks and it was time for them to go back to Australia. Boy, did I wish I was going home with them, but

I had to say my goodbyes and welcome 9RAR who had now arrived to commence their tour.

9RAR had a tough time of it. Too many were wounded or killed. I lost several of my mates, including some I trained with back in Australia.

We knew that as soon as we went outside the wire we would be in the thick of it.

Incident two

One day I was up front with my two forward scouts when at the point of a narrow track we ran into a guy dressed in black. He was carrying a rocket launcher. It happened so fast. The forward scouts yelled 'Contact!' then hit the deck and commenced firing. At the same time, the guy with the rocket launcher raised his rocket, pointing it at me. All of this happened only 20 metres away. Our gunfire hit him but with only a flesh wound he still managed to fire his rocket launcher. A loud explosion followed. He missed me but hit a large tree nearby. The force of the explosion threw me to the ground, and I couldn't hear a thing for a few minutes. Eventually, I started to hear gunfire from our section. We almost stripped the canopy and vegetation with machine gun fire. Then we searched for his body, but once again this wounded, slippery little soldier had managed to vanish into the thick of the jungle.

I dusted myself off and saw blood running down my arm. A piece of wood shrapnel had lodged in my right arm. I pulled it out without any problem. The medic gave it a quick clean up, and applied a bandage. Later, I wondered, *Am I fast starting to run out of cat lives?*

Incident three

It was a stinking hot, sunny day.

Our forward scout had stumbled right into the middle of an enemy bunker system. He was suspicious about something and signalled to halt. Seconds later, a wall of gunfire rang out and he fell to the ground dead.

We found ourselves in a nest of enemy bunkers. While the battle was on we called in the air force to bomb the bunker system. We pulled back about 500 metres and the ground started to shake. I thought, *If one of these bombs goes astray, I hope it's over quickly.* After the bombing was over, we moved back in and collected our mate's body. The bunkers were badly damaged, but again not one dead enemy could be found.

The next day we expected more contacts because we discovered a significant area where the enemy had congregated. The fish were biting! We were fired on, but the jungle was so dense that it was hard to see how many there were. The enemy only fired when we tried to move into a flank position, or forward; it was clear that they wanted to hold us down for as long as possible. When the front section saw a flash of gunfire about 25 metres away in the dense bush they began to fire with their M60 machine gun in that direction; however, the AK47 gunfire from the other side then became more intense and they kept firing at us relentlessly. To make our pinned-down situation even worse, the front machine gunner ran out of ammunition.

I was about 15 metres behind him, with two full belts of machine gun ammunition over my shoulder. I yelled that I would bring my ammo over. It was the slowest 15 metres I've ever travelled. I was down as low as I could be, crawling with my heavy backpack placed in front of my head for some protection, although I knew an AK47 round could go through my pack and skull without a problem. As I crawled towards the gunners, a sound took me back to my childhood – the crack of a stockwhip going close by my head. Only this time it was the cracking sound of an AK47 round passing close to my ears, going faster than the speed of sound. I kept going forward and just hoped I could get the ammo belt to the gunner before I was hit. I had some support from some in our section who managed to crawl into a flank position. They fired with their SLR rifles and drew some fire, giving me the chance to deliver my belts to our front machine gunner.

By now they had a good point from where to fire. Soon it was all over. We got them – the whole *three* of them. These guys had sacrificed themselves so that the rest of their troops could retreat to fight again another day.

This was the day I thought I was a real goner. Finally, my number was going to be up, but it was also a time to reflect on those brave enemy soldiers who gave their lives to their cause with no exceptions. This was indeed a formidable competitor.

Vietnam was a lot of hard work, but it made me realise just how much harder it must have been for the First and Second World War diggers, never knowing if they would ever return home. At least we knew that when our twelve months were up we would be going home.

That was worth hanging onto at the time. When I say Vietnam was a lot of hard work, add to the mix jungles with snakes, bird-eating spiders, and a cocktail of wild animals.

Incident four

This is a classic to add to the pile of traumas for PTSD.

One night in the jungle I was on rotation guard duty, peering into the darkness, when I heard something softly and slowly moving through the scrub towards me. I sensed that it was large and I blurted out, 'Halt'. I raised my rifle, and it charged towards me. I threw myself on the ground, felt it jumping over me, then it continued to belt its way further into the darkness behind me. I suspected I'd come across a tiger. It was very big and I was glad I missed the dinner invitation. As for the rest of the night, I couldn't stop shaking, imagining being clawed to pieces and trying to fight off fangs tearing into my flesh.

The wet season was a lot of fun, too. When it rains in Vietnam it falls down in torrents. I'll always remember the lightning and thunder as the most intense I've experienced. The ground would be awash with water pouring its way into the creek beds, and when the lightning hit it sent out massive amounts of small lightning bolts that ran along the wet ground in all directions. It was quite scary the first time. For those who didn't like leeches, it was really too bad. Those little beasties got inside our clothing when crossing flowing, muddy creeks, then would grow into big, ugly, grey beasties sucking up plenty of blood. We found the best way to get them off was to light a match underneath them.

It was always good to get back behind the wire, to clean up with a shower, a container that you poured cold water into and stood under. Generally, I kept to myself in camp, as it wasn't a good place to be when some of the men were having a few too many beers and were itching for a fight. Some of the fights were brutal, and I think some of the guys who were not coping well found distraction in a good punch up.

Vietnam was isolated. When I was there, man walked on the moon, but I knew nothing about it until someone told me in a letter months later. We all eagerly awaited letters from home. One chap we noticed never received any mail so a few of us got together and wrote a letter to an Aussie magazine called *PIX*. We wrote, 'I'm a lonely digger in Vietnam and would like a friendly penfriend to write to me. Signed, John.' A few weeks later we arrived back into camp to find a big mailbag filled with 'Dear John' letters. He was, as we all were, overwhelmed by the huge response. So we all pitched in to write back to all of the kind ladies, telling them John had so many penfriends now and thanking them all for their kind thoughts. To my surprise, one of the girls I replied to wrote back to me and sent a parcel of goodies, including a couple of large cans of Foster's Beer. This girl we'll call Mary, who asked if I'd be her penfriend. I agreed. Mary was a thoughtful girl and regularly sent me little parcels with a newsy letter. I asked her to do some research on a motorcar I was interested in. Without fail, all the technical information soon arrived in the mail. For her kindness, I promised to catch up with her when I got back.

Recreation leave

A highlight of Vietnam was Rest and Recuperation (R&R). About every three months we would go to a beach called Vung Tau. We enjoyed a few drinks, dunk hot chips in tomato sauce, were chased by all the young girls wanting drinks, and got ripped off by all the street shops selling junk. These breaks from the dread of battle were a welcome distraction. The best one of all was going to Hong Kong. Halfway through the tour you could go home, or go to a place like Hong Kong. I didn't like the idea of going home and then having to come back again, so I chose Hong Kong because it was a haven for duty-free shopping.

After a short flight, I checked into my hotel. The bellboy took me to my room. I shut the door and went to the fridge to crack open a beer, when there was a knock on the door. When I opened it the bellboy shoved a young Chinese girl into my room. She couldn't speak a word of English and looked nervous. I didn't want to play this game, so I let her out of my room. Less than ten minutes passed, and there was another knock on the door. Again, the bellboy shoved a girl into my room. She was also Chinese, but could speak some English, had a nice figure and wasn't too bad to look at. But again, I said I wasn't interested. I was looking forward to doing other things, so I let her out of the room too.

I was about to take a glorious bath. I thought, *Each time I turn these girls down, the talent keeps getting better.* There was a knock on the door again. This time, a tall, slim, well-dressed Eurasian girl asked me, 'May I come in for a chat with you?'

Her English was good, and I thought, *Why not? She may be able to point me to some of the good hot spots in town.* I let her in.

The first thing she said to me was, 'Do you find me sexy and attractive?'

I could see what she was leading to and said, 'You're coming on a bit strong, aren't you?'

'Well, do you want me or not? You'd better make up your mind as I have another job to go to today,' she said.

Nope, I thought. *This one's far too bossy.* I let her out and said to her, 'Tell your bellboy boss I'm not interested in paying. Just forget it'.

I needed to run more hot water into my bath. Naked, I was about to get into the tub when there was another annoying knock on the door. I wrapped a towel around myself and charged to the door to give this guy a blast, but there standing in front of me was a beautiful woman, tall and elegant, older than me, about thirty.

She said to me, 'You're Australian right? I love Australia. I've been there. Let's have a talk.'

'I'm about to have my bath.'

'That's okay, I can talk to you while you're having your bath.'

I was intrigued and thought they'd sent me the jackpot, so I let her in. I explained to her that I hadn't paid for this service, so if that's what this was, I wasn't about to start now.

'What other things can you suggest we do?' I asked in a schoolteacher tone of voice. To my surprise she said, 'I'm really okay about that, and I just love your red hair. Would you like me to show you special places in Hong Kong?' Boy, did she say all of the right things.

For the next three days she took me in her Mercedes motorcar to sightsee all over the place. I saw things most tourists would never get to see. I was taken to incredible restaurants, and I even got to meet her parents. The whole thing was bizarre. What was the catch? She said, 'I'm very fond of you. It just feels so right. I want to get to know you a lot more.' Then she said she wanted me to come back and take her to Australia!

I thought, *This is too good to be true. It's time to exit, quick smart.*

I should've known the nice meeting with her parents was a clue. I was quite concerned that this wouldn't be the last of her. Before the bomb dropped, I'd stupidly given her my contact details in Vietnam.

I had one day left in Hong Kong. So I went out to buy stereo equipment. I was assured it'd be delivered to my hotel room within two hours, so I left the store and caught a taxi back to the ferry. I had several small boxes on my lap, including a new watch. I pulled out my wallet and paid the taxi driver, but in the rush to get out some of my parcels fell on the floor. I put my wallet on the rear window ledge of the taxi to gather them up. I ran to catch my ferry back to Kowloon. Of course, the bellboy was looking for his tip when I got back to my room. I reached for my wallet in my pocket. I tapped my other pockets; no wallet was on my person. I started to feel really sick. In the rush at the ferry terminal I'd left it in the taxi on the back-window shelf. The wallet contained over 2,600 US dollars – a lot of money back then!

There are thousands of taxis in Hong Kong and they're all the same make and colour. While feeling sick to my stomach, I knew I had to go back and make some attempt to find my money, as hopeless as it seemed. With my last few dollars I caught the ferry back to the terminal hoping I'd get lucky, despite one in a million odds.

I arrived an hour later. There was a policeman standing on guard duty and I went over to report my lost wallet. I figured he'd fall over laughing, but it was worse than that – he shrugged his shoulders and looked away. He couldn't speak a word of English. I decided to stand at the taxi rank until it got dark. I didn't have to wait very long. Within five minutes a taxi passed by with what looked like a wallet on the back shelf. The problem was it drove one hundred metres further down the road to another ferry terminal.

I ran that one hundred metres faster than the Jamaican Bolt. Getting out of this taxi was a six-foot-six, huge American man. I dove into the back seat. He yelled, 'Whoa there, man.'

It didn't matter to me that I was climbing all over him. I grabbed the wallet, and yes, it was mine, and it was still full of money. Inside I was jumping for joy. I shouted out, 'My wallet has been floating around in the back of this taxi for hours with all of this money in it, and I've got it back. Whoopee!' The American laughed, while the poor taxi driver cursed. He went bright red. Am I lucky or what? It certainly gave a new meaning to a million-to-one-chance.

What did I learn on that day? Number one: I stuffed up. Number two: do something about it and never give up!

I went back to my hotel to celebrate with a few beers and my new stereo. I had a great time in Hong Kong. I promised myself that I'd go back there again one day.

Soon enough it was back to reality and I was on the plane and heading back to Nui Dat. Although I missed home, I was glad I didn't go to

Australia for R&R, as it was hard enough readjusting from Hong Kong.

After a few weeks back on base I received a visit from the Military Police (MP). They had intercepted two letters from my Hong Kong lady. They wanted to know if I'd told her anything about our operations in Vietnam. I told them I'd given her my mailing address before I found out that she wanted me as a ferry ride back to Australia. They advised me not to write back. I was more than happy to comply, but I was intrigued as to why they had intercepted my letters; however, they gave me no information, except to say I was lucky I didn't meet an unfortunate fate. For the life of me I couldn't work out what all the fuss was about! I hadn't seen anything untoward about her, but also had no intention of getting involved. This little interlude was closed.

A challenging incident

There was one other incident in Vietnam where I had a brush with the brass. One evening back inside the wire at Nui Dat, I was playing some music on the stereo system I'd bought in Hong Kong. In my platoon was an officer, who shall remain nameless. He walked into my tent and I could tell he'd had a few too many drinks. He yelled, 'Turn off this music.' It wasn't loud but I obliged. He looked at me with his hands on his hips and said, 'Well!' I gathered he wanted me to salute him. I was sitting down. To amuse him, as I got up, I said in a relaxed and cheery voice, 'Yes, sir, three bags full, sir', and gave him a salute. Was there any humour about this officer? No, not in the least! He slurred, 'You're on a charge for insubordination Nikko', and waddled off.

I thought, *He'll think better of it tomorrow when he sleeps it off.* Wrong!

In the morning, the company commander came into my tent, upset that I had been charged. 'This is not like you Nikko. You'll be taken up to the colonel this morning to be dealt with for your insubordination.' It was no joking matter. If I were found guilty of the charge I'd be handed over to the MPs, who would lock me up and throw away the key. I felt the charge was trivial, but this officer had it in for me. I didn't know why and now he was trying to put me away.

I was marched into the colonel's courtroom, with all the brass looking me up and down, while the officer who charged me waited outside ready to celebrate my demise. The proceedings started with the colonel asking me, 'It's stated here that while you saluted my officer you said, "Yes sir," and "three bags full". Do you plead guilty to this insubordination as charged?'

'I do plead guilty for saying these words, sir, however, I plead not guilty for saying these words in an insubordinate manner,' I replied to the colonel.

'Then I take it you're guilty,' answered the colonel.

I answered, 'Only guilty of these words, sir. These words were not said with any aggression. If anything, they were said with some humour and absolutely no intent of insubordination; therefore, I'm pleading not guilty.' The colonel kept up the heat for a little longer, but I stuck to my guns.

The colonel then asked my commander, a major, 'What can you tell me about this soldier?'

The major thankfully gave me a glowing report: 'Nikko is an exceptional soldier, he's in everything in the field when the action is on, and I see this incident as most out of character.'

The brass all huddled together and then the colonel addressed me. 'We can't let you off scot-free, Nikko, however, I find you not guilty as charged, but will give you an admonishment.' Then he said to my major, 'I want this soldier promoted.' Everyone smiled and I felt vindicated. I marched out to see my smiling assassin. Walking out, free to go, I saw his face start to twitch. He seemed bewildered that I wasn't handcuffed!

He walked across to me and asked, 'So how did you go, Nikko?' I replied, 'Well they did give me an admonishment.' The look on his face was priceless. He knew he'd been rightly outsmarted. While the whole thing was petty, being gazumped by his senior ranks would've been embarrassing for him.

I had a month to complete my tour. I knew he'd make it as hard as he could for me; I had to watch my step, give him no excuse for any further reports.

With no major incidents in the last few weeks, my time was finally up. Thirteen months and I was still in one piece. All I needed to do was get on that aircraft carrier and sail back to Adelaide.

On the final day of my tour, we were about to mount the troop carrier trucks when my assassin-officer handed our record books back to everyone. It was very fortunate for this guy that we were leaving. I was enraged with what he'd written in my record book. He'd unexpectedly put the knife in, with negative and blasphemous comments. I wanted to knock his block off. I went to my major to see if this wrong could be righted, but all he said was, 'Don't worry about it'. That was something I'd hear a lot in the future: 'Don't worry about it,' or, 'Get on with it'.

The trucks rolled out of Nui Dat. Instead of being happy I was seething with anger. The dirt roads were lined with Vietnamese civilians waving goodbye. In anger I threw my arms up and a beautiful watch I had bought in Hong Kong flew off my wrist into the arms of an elderly, grey-haired civilian. The little old man put his hands together in a praying gesture. I thought that was bloody stupid of me, but at least I got a thank you of sorts from this poor man. It has taken me awhile, but I can laugh about it now.

My time in Vietnam had some ups and many downs. This type of war zone was one hell of an experience. The effect on me in the ensuing months and years would be immense, but while I was leaving the real battle, ahead was a cocktail of denial, anxiety, built-up anger, frustration with day-to-day issues, a lack of understanding, and, last but not least, little patience. When I returned to civilian life, I wouldn't accept or understand any of this.

I wish I could've found my way out of this maze a lot sooner, rather than so late in life.

PART 5: GOING HOME TO THE AFTERMATH

I was on HMAS *Sydney* sailing back home with hundreds of other soldiers. There wasn't much to do on the ship and it was quite boring. It was also a time to think about those left behind, and the scary moments, such as the smiling assassin. Most things were challenging my ability to feel good about life when I should've been jumping for joy. After several days, I noticed some friendly chaps playing cards, so I joined in. I played cards for most of the trip; it was an excellent antidote that helped to distract my wandering mind during the day. Trying to get any shut-eye at night in the hammock was a challenge. When crossing the Great Australian Bight, the seas were relatively calm; however, the swell coming up from the south was massive. We were travelling east and that really had our hammocks swinging around, making everyone uncomfortable.

It was with some relief that we finally arrived at the port of Adelaide. I remember this well, as it was on a warm, sunny November day back in 1969.

The Department of Defence paid us for the time we spent in Vietnam in cash. Everyone looked for a way to safeguard the money. As many of us had to travel long distances interstate to get to our families, I thought this was inconsiderate.

We were told that the 9th Battalion would march through the main streets of Adelaide; I thought it'd be nice to come home to a public welcome. I was very wrong.

The band started playing as we marched in unison, proudly swinging our arms. When we came into view of the public, they started yelling and screaming at us. 'Murderers!' 'Demons!' 'Shame on you, you low bastards!' Eggs and tomatoes were thrown at us. I was shattered. Why couldn't the Department of Defence have warned us of the impending protest? This was bad. If I was angry before I arrived, I was now livid. I'd felt good about my service, believing I was doing my part to protect the Australian people from the Yellow Peril. Thanks to those ill-informed protesters my contribution during the last thirteen months in Vietnam now felt like a worthless ordeal.

After the parade, and for our protection on the streets of Adelaide, we changed into civilian clothes. We also had to find our own way back to our respective homes. Mine was in Victoria. I was with a mate who wanted to come back with me so we agreed to share a cabin on a train leaving in a few hours. We carried all our money on our person. Being on the top bunk, I placed all my cash under my pillow and my mate did the same thing in his lower bunk. When we woke the next morning my mate's money was gone! The door was locked all night, with the train conductor the only person who had key access.

I arranged for the railway police to board the train, but they showed little interest in the train conductor. Instead they went through all of my things with a fine-tooth comb and made me out to be the suspect. I was also upset that the army/government gave us all of this cash and just sent us on our way. After about thirty minutes of looking around, the railway police left without even asking for a forwarding address or contact number. My mate didn't have a dollar to his name, and I was the only one who could support him. I felt a great sense of shame about my fellow Australians and knew there'd be people who'd be aware of our vulnerability while carrying large sums of cash. We were easy targets.

After a few days, we arrived back in my small country town. To my surprise the local memorial hall welcomed me home. There were a lot of people there and that evening I was presented with my Returned

Services League of Australia (RSL) badge. To receive it felt good and helped to take the edge off some of the earlier discomfort when we were bombarded on our arrival in Adelaide.

It was good to see my mother and siblings again, even my father appeared pleased to see me. Within a few days, however, things began to turn sour. My father's old habits started to surface again, but this time they were directed at my mother. One memorable incident started with my father complaining about his dinner.

'What's this rubbish you're feeding me?' my father demanded.

I interjected with, 'What are you going on about? This is great food.'

'Mind your bloody business while you're in my house,' he said.

That's when I saw red. 'This is my mother's home too and get this into your thick head: if you speak to her like that again, this time it will be my pleasure to give you a back hander.'

Mum tried to come between us, and fortunately for Dad he took himself outside for a walk. Then Mum asked me, 'What's wrong? You've changed so much.' I replied with, 'There's nothing wrong with me; I don't have to tolerate him talking to you like that anymore.'

A few weeks went by. I could see my father was trying to be a little more civil. Often Mum would try to talk to me, saying, 'You've changed. What's wrong?' I'd keep saying, 'What are you talking about, Mum? There's nothing wrong with me!'

My leave with the army had come to an end. It was time for me to go back to the barracks where I had no idea of my new role. Firstly, though, I had a car to purchase. It was a Mazda coupé rotary motor. I had all the information needed for this vehicle thanks to my penfriend, Mary, who wrote to me in Vietnam. It was good to have a set of wheels again, so I contacted Mary and asked if I could come over to her folks' place to see her. I wanted to thank her for her kindness and I asked her out for a coffee.

'I really don't want you to go to any fuss,' I said, and then we both agreed that I'd come over the next evening.

I arrived at her place the next day. The sun had almost set so my headlights were on. As I drove in, I couldn't help but notice the driveway was adorned with tall, magnificent rose bushes on both sides. These people were proud gardeners, so I was careful not to touch the flowers with my car door when I got out of the car. Before I got to the door, out came my penfriend with a big smile, saying, 'Welcome, Nikko'.

'It's great to finally catch up with you,' I replied. I was asked if I'd like to come in and meet her folks. If I'd known what was in front of me, I would've left there and then.

Her parents were all smiles and very friendly. We went into the lounge room where there were many antiques. It was quite an old home with everything in its place. It was a nice place, but for me everything started to turn into a complete disaster! I was asked to sit down in this old chair but its legs gave way beneath me, and the chair and I collapsed onto the floor. I tried to minimise my impact by rolling to one side on the floor, but in doing so I knocked over a hallstand with a tall antique vase containing long-stemmed roses. The vase was smashed to smithereens all over the floorboards. In a few seconds I'd made their home look like a war zone.

'Don't worry about it,' they all said while smiling.

I was offered another seat. I gingerly sat down then the family cat walked into the room and immediately jumped up onto my lap. I quite liked cats, and this cat started purring, which helped get some small talk back on track. As we chatted away, I offered to pay for the damage to their furniture, but they refused to accept, saying it was an accident. That didn't make me feel better. All I could do was apologise over and over.

Thankfully, Mary said, 'Let's go for that coffee.'

I thought, *Good, let me out of here.*

Outside, I opened the car door for Mary, got in and started my new motorcar. As I was about to drive out I looked up and saw her folks waving at us. I backed the car out of the driveway, mindful of not going too close to the roses, when I felt the back wheel roll over something.

'What was that?' I asked. I got out to see that I'd run over the family cat. It was a nightmare! They all came running to see their poor dying cat. I was shattered. Once again, they tried to reassure me that it was an accident. I must have said sorry ten times over. I felt horrible. They took the dead cat away and started to wave goodbye again. In my haste to get out of the place, I missed part of their driveway and took out a row of their prize roses! I was now looking for a big sinkhole to jump into and disappear. I felt so sorry for Mary. I drove for only a few minutes then stopped the car. I took her hand, thanked her for everything she did for me in Vietnam and then said, 'I think I should take you back home now. The way things are going, I'd be happy to see you home safe and sound'.

I dropped her home. I got out of the car, opened the door, and sadly said goodbye. I drove off into the darkness feeling very anxious. Needless to say, we didn't see each other again! Wasn't she lucky?

Several weeks rolled by. Army life wasn't too bad. Instead of pointing a gun, I was dealing with administration. Around this time I met Blondie. The first time we met was at an army function. Blondie was in the Army Reserves, part-time. She invited me to a party and I accepted.

When I arrived at the party the place was full of females. I noticed one of them was trying to get my attention by waving and smiling at me. She was gorgeous, with long blonde hair. It took me a moment to realise it was Blondie. She'd turned into a knockout, with her war paint and charming smile.

Blondie had it all. She was attentive and said sweet things like, 'You make me laugh a lot with your sense of humour'. The relationship quickly blossomed. Soon after, I took her home to meet my folks. Blondie was charming and at ease with everyone, and the family appeared to be accepting of this confident young friend of mine, with the exception of my grandmother, who I could see was giving her a once over.

Later we went to the local hotel where a band was playing. Everyone was dancing and having a few drinks when Blondie said she was going to the powder room. Over half an hour went by. Another hour went by when finally she came out with some other females who looked concerned. I was told that she'd be all right and Blondie said, 'I've just had a bad turn, that's all'. Another female looked at me and shook her head. I was receiving mixed messages. Blondie looked a little pale but convinced me she was okay. The next day, I was taken aside by someone I trusted deeply.

'Nikko, you only met Blondie a few weeks ago. Take it easy, won't you?' I was alarmed about these comments and didn't want to accept any of it, as I was so keen on Blondie. At the time I couldn't help feeling some uneasiness and confusion about this incident.

Three months later, Blondie had me wrapped around her little finger. We talked about getting engaged. I was in a blind rush, with no thought of feeling for the brake pedal.

In a glow, I went and saw her family and asked if we could get engaged. At the time her family celebrated this news with great gusto, while my folks tried their best to slow down my momentum. Mum continued to say, 'You've changed, and not for the better. Take your time. If she loves you, she'll wait a little longer.'

But Blondie made me feel wanted and I was carried away with her good looks and charm. I ignored my mother's words that, 'Beauty is only skin deep'. I dived headlong into the abyss and we became engaged.

We set a date to get married, but I started to see cracks forming in Blondie. I noticed that she was a whiz at getting her own way. I saw how manipulative she was with her family, and I felt like I was receiving subliminal commands. Instead of asking, 'What do you think about this?' as she used to do, I was told, 'This is the way we'll do things; it's for the best'. Volatility was starting to grow and I was questioning her demeanour and sincerity in our relationship. I went into panic mode. I was turning in the opposite direction, trying to find the brake pedal. One day I blurted out, 'I don't want to get married.'

She raised her eyebrow and said, in a strong mesmerising voice, 'Oh, yes, you'll marry me!' It was kind of hypnotic, and I couldn't find a way to say anything more.

Several days went by. One day I'd be saying to myself, 'I'm still in the army and this is no way to get married.' Mixed thoughts about Vietnam kept flooding my mind, and I thought I was too young to get married. I was starting to doubt Blondie's motives and I began to wonder why my friends tried to tell me to slow down my involvement with her back when we first started dating!

The following day, she smiled at me and said, 'We'll have a great successful life together.' That was music to my ears. I loved the positive sweet-talking that she used to sweep away my negative doubts. Without realising it I'd capitulated and had become a prisoner to her charm!

Confused and half-rattled, I bounced along until the day arrived when I was standing at the church altar. I saw a stunning, beautiful young woman dressed to kill in a pure white wedding gown slowly walking towards me. I was a goner – there'd be no escaping now. I was married to this beautiful woman who I came home to every night.

Within a few short weeks, things were not working out too well. I was calling her selfish, self-centred and manipulative. Blondie said, 'If you truly love me you wouldn't get so angry. If you truly love me you wouldn't say these things about me.'

That's when I said, 'Yes, right, you think it's my fault. Well, take a good look at yourself; maybe it's all your fault!'

I know there are two sides to every story, but my condition wasn't going to be diagnosed for a long time and it was going to be everyone else's fault for decades to come. The next six months were some of the darkest days of my life. Blondie would go missing from time-to-time and I was becoming paranoid that she was up to no good. We would be shouting at each other regularly, and soon I could see fear in her eyes.

This made me worse, and one day I stupidly grabbed her and shook her, saying, 'What on earth are you frightened of?' I'd really done it.

She ran out of the house and I thought, *Well, that's that!* I reached for the bottle and started to drown my sorrows. I felt so depressed that I kept drinking until I was in a stupor. That night is a blocked-out blur, and I'm thankful that I cannot remember this, but I'm told I was walking around outside, swearing at everything that moved. Finally, I collapsed and was taken to hospital. I was there for three days. I'd almost passed away. At the time, I felt so ashamed that I wished I had.

I was taken to the Repatriation Hospital where I was assessed by doctors and psychiatrists and advised to stay there for a while. Blondie decided to see me, which became another disaster.

I told the doctors I needed to change my direction in life, that I wanted an early discharge from the army, and that my young life was as good as over if I kept going this way. I was diagnosed with a Situational Reaction, was considered unstable, and was thankfully granted a medical discharge.

As for Blondie, I thought it was all over and I'm left with strong feelings of worthlessness.

PART 6: CIVILIAN LIFE

Now an everyday civilian, I was looking forward to resurrecting my career. Then something completely out of the blue happened. Blondie came back to me and was alarmingly romantic and affectionate towards me! Once again, I was in a spin and I failed once more to hear the alarm bells. However, there were other hurdles in the way. As a result of recent issues, I'd fallen out of favour with her parents. I don't blame them for that; however, they gave Blondie an ultimatum to leave me, or they'd disown her forever. Blondie ignored her parents' threat, making me feel worthwhile for a change. I couldn't quite understand why Blondie wanted to come back so soon into what I thought was still a very fragile relationship.

One of my main strengths was in sales and marketing, and I soon had a position as a sales representative for a pharmaceutical company. I grew quickly in this industry, winning sales competitions with a prize of a trip for two to New Zealand. This pleased Blondie and our arguments were less frequent. I was promoted and we moved interstate to open up the new branch of the business. Blondie then announced she was pregnant. Being new to the area, Blondie didn't have any close friends or relatives she could talk to, and she felt isolated during her pregnancy. Eventually, the time came when we took off to the hospital and soon we were proud, happy parents of our beautiful son. It was an amazing thing to see the birth of our son whom I loved so much from that moment on. I was very protective of him. All of my thoughts and time were for my son. On the other hand, I didn't give Blondie anywhere near the attention I should have. I was more interested in entertaining my beautiful son and didn't see what was coming.

I noticed Blondie quietly started to become interested in other men. In the end I have to take most of the blame for this. Instead of challenging this problem, I bottled up all my knowledge about it, and so the arguments started up again.

My behaviour was becoming worse. I was now grabbing and pushing her as I went into a new level of undisciplined control. Understandably, she was becoming increasingly more distant. I felt that I wasn't wanted as a partner any more.

I found it hard to talk to her about what was on her mind. Did she want to leave me for someone else? I bottled it all up. Instead of finding solutions, I blamed her for the whole mess. The end soon came when I went interstate for a conference. While I was away, Blondie dropped our eighteen-month-old son at a neighbour's place and went out with a good mate of mine.

The next morning, all panic broke loose and she acquired a one-way ticket back to her parents, who accepted her back with open arms.

She flew out in the afternoon and I arrived back that evening. I returned home to a stripped house, but far worse for me was that she'd taken my son away from me. This was a dark day. I was completely heart-broken. I felt so cheated on, and I was enraged. My anxiety was immense, as was my sense of loss. I had no ability to think logically and I kept going around in cloudy circles as all this unfolded. I just wanted to see my son again.

Without thinking sensibly, I placed the house on the market, accepted the first offer, and headed interstate to see my son. Blondie won her way with the settlement and played hardball with my rights to see my son. She was in another relationship and wanted my son to call him 'Daddy', and so a long, protracted court case went through the Family Court as I attempted to gain access. It was a bitter fought case, but in the end, I had a win and felt relieved to be granted regular access.

All was fairly stable until a few years later Blondie met another fellow in the northern half of Australia. She left her existing relationship in Victoria and took off yet again with my son. We were thousands of miles apart and my son had another daddy to answer to, and I was stressed out with more court cases. It became grubby, with her barrister trying to convince the court that I wasn't fit for access, and that I was a nut case affected by Agent Orange. Blondie looked confident in court, while I was shaking inside at the thought of not seeing my son. I was relieved though that the judge ruled in my favour and threw their argument out of court. He then ordered access to be available during the school holidays, and when I was in their state.

The next few years were difficult. I tried hard to see him regularly, but I was constantly presented with negative excuses from Blondie. Somehow she had managed to change my son's surname to that of her current partner.

Years have passed by and I'm happy to see my son growing with a strong independence. Despite the upheaval in his life, he's managed to cope well.

I began going out with plenty of nice females. There was no thought of falling for any of them. Then one evening I met the sexiest woman alive at the time. I should've done my homework about this one. We'll call her Kitten. I fell out of the frying pan into the fire. Kitten, full of brimstone and fire, had a history of pursuing her prey, me included!

We lasted several years. It was a hot and bothered relationship, with many aggressive and heated fights, until one day Kitten pulled out a knife and stabbed me. I took myself to hospital to get stitched up.

I found out that Kitten had done this before. Maybe I bring out the worst in the opposite sex. I felt we were both near the end of our demise, and at the time I blamed her – it couldn't possibly be my fault! In truth, we were both to blame. I ended the relationship, but we remained friends. Following this, I convinced myself that I wasn't intended to have a meaningful relationship and I wallowed in self-pity.

I often caught up with my mother who would quietly suggest that I should contact DVA. She suggested exploring with them why I'd changed so much since coming back from Vietnam. I said, 'It's not all that bad. I have a great job. I keep getting promoted. It's not necessarily my fault about broken relationships. I obviously haven't picked the right ones, and I don't think there is really anything wrong with me, Mum.'

I was forty years young and was director of a large company. Interestingly, I could get the best out of the people I worked with and could motivate and give good direction to staff. It was all going very well in the workplace. I wondered why I couldn't make my relationships work out as well as they did at work. My mother thought she had the answer. 'Nikko,' she'd say, 'you're an angel by day and a devil by night.' I resisted contacting DVA. I wanted nothing to do with the Defence Force; it brought back so many bad memories.

As a consequence, there were many difficult and blinkered years ahead. I wasn't interested in another committed relationship, but then I met a pretty redhead with a fiery temper. While I enjoyed Red's company and was fascinated by her personality, she also had a dark side. Out of nowhere, she would cut me down with an ambush of insults and rants. It fast became a cocktail of oil and water and I never quite knew what was around the corner. It was a big shock when Red declared she was pregnant!

I told Red I'd help and support her. During the pregnancy, I managed to control most of my anxiety and tried to stay calm; however, every now and then Red would let fly with so much negativity that I'd let the team down and would end up shouting and yelling back. Red didn't back down. One day I found myself walking out the door, slamming it behind me.

I saw it through though, and after nine months Red gave birth to a healthy and handsome son. I felt overjoyed about the birth of another son. Helped by the nurses, I gently bathed Handsome, wrapped him up and presented him to Red.

Once again, I had another strong purpose to protect and nurture this little bundle of joy.

Red and I tried for several years but her negativity and my outbursts occasionally led to me throwing her clothes out the door and telling her to go.

Red moved out with Handsome and I vowed to give him all of my time and support. It was agreed that I should see him regularly. I looked forward to seeing him mid-week and on the weekends.

I still feel guilty that both of my boys were subjected to the arguments and abuse, yet I blamed others for making me angry. Any separation has its effect on young children and, as much as you wish, you can't take all their pain away.

I was about to hit the wall. Instead of seeking help, I kept a stiff upper lip while slowly spiralling. At this stage of my life I was convinced more than ever that I wasn't meant to have a meaningful and happy relationship, so I worked myself to the bone to keep myself occupied and became a general manager for an international company to head up a new Australia-wide business. The business grew quickly to have a string of interstate offices.

I questioned myself. *How come I can run a multimillion-dollar company and motivate the people I'm working with, yet I cannot find a partner to share my life with?* Frustrated at these thoughts, I phoned my mother and asked her the same question.

Her response was, 'I've been telling you for years, you've changed – you're still the angel by day and the devil by night.'

I thought, *Maybe one day I might go and see the doc and have a chat.*

PART 7: WHAT'S THIS DEPRESSION THING

I was forty-eight. Fate was about to take my hand and convince me that I had one final chance to find my soul mate. It was a warm Saturday night and I was a guest at a city hotel. Across the room, I saw this gorgeous blonde, and I thought she looked classy. I walked over and started to chat to her. Instantly, we had a great rapport. We talked about what we did for a living and it turned out that she had my business card on her desk after a referral from a customer. We both thought that was uncanny and started to laugh. Another bloke came over and I was introduced to him as her friend! I walked away thinking to myself, *I can't see what on earth she finds interesting about him.* I looked around for another friendly face.

For days I kept thinking of her, and then out of the blue I got a phone call and this voice said, 'Remember me? I said I had your card on my desk and was wondering if you could provide me with some of your product knowledge'.

Without answering, I asked, 'Are you still with that chap?'

'No,' she said.

'Good. How about you give me your home phone number?' I said.

That was over twenty-four years ago and she still is my darling superwoman. You might ask, just how did this one happen to go the distance?

First, I must be blessed to have My Darling, who won't accept me if I rant and rave. But My Darling saw the good side of me, and I thank her constantly for hanging in there through our trials and tribulations. I know that I'm a pain to live with. My Darling would argue that we must always talk our differences through, never at a time of a heated discussion, but at a time when all is quiet and the dust has settled.

Despite all of her patience and understanding, I still cause some worry by continuing to rock the boat, but at least in this relationship I'm now trying harder to learn from my mistakes. I celebrated my fiftieth birthday with her and I can't bear the thought of being without her. I think about My Darling's feelings more than I did in any other relationship. There are still hiccups, but at last I'm seeing the benefits of working hard at this relationship.

The downside of wanting to keep the relationship on track was that cracks began to form at work. At the time I didn't understand, or didn't want to understand, that having a condition such as PTSD meant I could only do one thing successfully at a time. In other words, if work had all of my positive energy, I had little left in the tank for home life, or vice versa. I'm not saying everyone would react in this way; this was how it was in my case. Work and business were becoming more of a drag. I had no feeling of winning.

At the office, I'd drink several cups of coffee with the door shut, instead of my normal open-door policy. When things went wrong, I'd demand results instead of achieving them through good motivation. It was becoming harder to get out of bed in the morning, and I didn't want to socialise as much. Instead of working smarter, I was working harder for half the results. At this point, I finally went to my doctor for a check-up. I told him about how I wasn't getting as much out of work as I used to, that I didn't have the same level of attention to detail, and I was giving my staff a hard time. He said I was depressed, and had been for some time.

That was a bolt out of the blue; I thought there was nothing wrong with me! He tried to convince me to take anti-depressants, arguing it would help to put me back on track again. Still in shock, I declined to take his advice but agreed that if I couldn't turn myself around within six months I may take up his recommendation. The power of positive thinking was something I used to believe in, but over time it had fallen through the cracks so I challenged myself to resurrect this power once more. I was trying harder to be more aware of my moods and so I concentrated more on my surroundings. By the end of the day, to relax, I'd have a few drinks, then a few more. Quite often My Darling would have to wake me up out of a deep sleep on the lounge room couch and pack me off to bed. But then the nightmares would start, with the jumping and the kicking of blankets onto the bedroom floor.

I avoided going back to the doctor as I was trying pretty hard and was using relaxation techniques to whitewash the depression issue. To add to the depression and anxiety, my international parent company situated overseas went into liquidation. The Australian arm of the business was doing well and was profitable; however, the banks moved in to sell it off to recoup their debt. The banks took everything, and My Darling and I were out of pocket with money owing to us. We decided to change direction and formed our own sales and marketing company. Starting everything from scratch placed a lot of pressure on me and I started to fray around the edges. Despite everything, we landed some big contracts that regularly took me overseas. Sometimes I'd arrive home with the flu and would be tired and grumpy. This would try out any superwoman's patience.

I was almost fifty-four. I had a bad day at work one day, and I said to My Darling, 'Let's go up to our boat for the weekend'. I was feeling more anxious than normal. I wanted to have a few drinks and try my luck at fishing. My Darling was concerned about me and wanted to know what was wrong. She stood close to me and without thinking I pushed her out of the way. Thankfully, she fell backwards onto the couch, without hurting herself. I should've said sorry, but I became very angry, and this frightened My Darling.

My Darling wasn't happy and reminded me that we'd been on shaky ground before this. She talked about taking another break for a while. I felt like I'd been given twenty lashes, and I realised I had to sort this out quickly. When my mother became aware of the incident she demanded that I contact DVA.

The next day I felt like a lost soul, more nervous than ever, and I had a sense of fear about the future. I picked up the phone and called DVA. I gave my service number and name to the DVA representative, and, to my astonishment, he said, 'You poor fellow, you're going to need our help'.

'What do you mean?' I asked. 'I've only called you because of my mother's insistence.'

'Good,' he said. 'Give me your current address and I'll post you a White Card within a few days.'

Within a few days, I opened up my DVA letter, revealing a White Card that enabled me medical cover for all the things that were wrong with me.

I often wonder how I was granted my initial disability DVA card without an interview or assessment. I can only think that I must have made a real mess of myself before I was medically discharged. A few years later, the RSL suggested that I apply for a full Gold Card disability pension. I was then asked to see some medical professionals and I was granted my Gold Card without any objection from DVA.

Feeling depressed that I had a disability pension, there was no denying that I was about to face up to some more demons. Yet again, My Darling got right behind me and suggested we go to the VVCS. Amongst other things, the service provides counselling for partners and offers relationship improvement ideas for couples. My heart and my soul weren't in it. I found it very hard to open up completely, so we had limited success, even though My Darling put in more effort than me and got quite a lot of good ideas from them.

Two more years passed and during this time the nightmares became more frequent and my mood swings became wilder. It was a period of extreme highs and lows. I felt like I was on a roller coaster. One day I'd be the life of the party, the next a horrible grouch. I felt like everyone was crossing my path. I was accused of being a workaholic; however, the truth was that while it appeared that I was putting in many hours behind my desk, I was floundering, running out of steam.

Despite all of this, our business managed some very healthy contracts and we started discussing retiring. We worked out that we had enough to retire on. I was fifty-seven. I thought it was a blessing that I was able to leave the workforce completely behind me. In the meantime, My Darling wanted to keep working for a few more years part-time before she fully retired as well. We then commenced travelling, which we both enjoyed. We haven't had a boring day since we retired.

All of the workplace pressure was off my back, but I was becoming more of a 'Cranky Hank'. Another demon would arrive and then I'd get myself worked up over trivial things. I wondered why I couldn't just get on with life. I looked for another fork in the road to wash away my negativity.

It'd been several years since I'd spoken to the doctor about depression. My six-month timeframe had well and truly expired. Back I went and was offered anti-depressants immediately. I reluctantly capitulated. At this point, I want to stress that everyone is different and most of the time these drugs can be very beneficial for most people. I'm the odd one out. When it comes to this type of medication, I really struggled with them. I was listless, and at times my moods became more intense.

I persevered for another year, trying several of these drugs, until one awful day in 2005. I came home with the weight of the world on my shoulders and hit the wall! My head was spinning. I was feeling very intense. I was angry at everything, and couldn't explain why. My Darling handed me a toasted sandwich for lunch, then she said something to me that I couldn't hear or understand, and in a rage I threw the toasted sandwich across the room and onto the wall. This frightened My Darling and she bolted out of the house fearing I had completely lost it. I was a complete wreck and couldn't control my thought processes at all.

It was decided that I should go up to the houseboat on my own for a week to cool down and get myself back in order (if I could). After a week of being by myself, I didn't feel any better about things and decided that the anti-depressants were not helping me. I started to wean myself off them. I returned home to see the doctor again and told him that I was giving up the medication. He highly recommended that I see a psychologist at the Defence Repatriation Hospital.

I agreed this time. After spending several days with the psychologist, he diagnosed me with PTSD and recommended that I do a four-week live-in course that offered a group treatment program.

I went home and talked things over with My Darling and told her that I was thinking of doing a PTSD course. I could see she was relieved. She said, 'If you do this, I'll again be behind you all of the way.'

PART 8: SENDING MY DEMONS INTO EXILE

On day one we had an introduction and explanation about the four-week PTSD Program. I was introduced to seven other men and their partners.

Although we didn't know it then, we would go on to form a strong bond and understanding that stands firm to this day. Our group of guys come from all different walks of life and social backgrounds, yet we've all become very special to one another, as it was always all-for-one and one-for-all.

Why was our group so successful and why did we get so much out of our course? It was unique because every man and his partner decided to give it their all. This meant there were no weak links in the group, only full-on commitment by everyone.

On day two of the course all of this commitment developed. Tony, the facilitator, was talking about anger management. *What does he know about my behaviour and feelings?* I thought.

He started to write on the whiteboard. 'Have you felt this?' 'Do you think about this and that?' 'When you feel hurt do you react this way?' I felt he was somehow exploring my soul and knew my immediate thought processes. I had to agree with him. That was me he was talking about. As I looked around the room I could see all of the other guys' jaws dropping to the ground with eyes staring in astonishment as their souls too were being invaded by the words on Tony's whiteboard!

We had four more weeks to go and already I had a strange sense of fear, a feeling that I was lost in space. Was it because I was about to be challenged within these walls for the good, the bad, and all of the ugly, too?

Our group had meals together, with dinnertime being the most talkative period. Initially some of us talked with much bravado, while some would just shake their heads, saying things such as, 'I said to my wife I don't know why you wanted me to come to this PTSD thing as there's nothing wrong with me, but when Tony started writing on that whiteboard about symptoms, behaviour and feelings, all I could see was that he was talking about me!'

By the end of the first week no one had any bravado left. Some of us were having trouble facing up to things and we wondered if we could continue. In truth, we were all confronting our issues of denial. That's when we started the teamwork thing. Our group would rally around these guys and talk to each other about their feelings. None of us tough nuts could get involved and do this in the past, but knowing we were all in the same boat meant we all started to talk.

This is quite foreign for a bunch of blokes to do, but strangely, it was somewhat therapeutic. Instead of going to war to help your fellow man, offering support felt more worthwhile. We talked and listened to each other dealing with our demons. This gave us confidence to speak freely and we agreed that all questions we raised within our group had 'merit', and there was no such thing as a 'silly question'. As we continued to talk and to open up I wondered if I was becoming vulnerable, and that maybe these thoughts were some of my demons screaming at my subconscious. These doubts and demons, however, soon faded as our group quickly began to believe in each other.

During the course there were many topics to digest. Some of the things I found helpful were:

- Trauma memory network
- Common problems associated with PTSD
- PTSD and its impact on family and relationships (one topic that was hard to swallow but had to be faced)
- Education to obtain skills, on things such as:
  » substance use
  » communication skills
  » anxiety and anger management.

Each of us had a one-on-one counsellor who would help us deal with some of the difficult issues that we confronted during the course. Believe me, it would happen frequently! Again, I was totally honest with my counsellor in talking about my feelings, hoping for some magical cure. I soon realised that wasn't going to happen without a lot of working on strategies on my part.

During the four weeks, the partners were also very active with a Partners' Program that helped them understand and learn skills for living with a person with PTSD. The course offered us twelve highly skilled professionals, including several psychologists, social workers and psychiatrists. In day-to-day meetings with them I never deviated from the truth. There was nowhere to hide from it anyway. I'm pretty sure our entire group wanted this, too.

As each day went by, I hoped and waited for the magic wand that would tell me I was cured of PTSD. Early in the course, however, they hit us with another sledgehammer – they told our partners there was no certain cure for PTSD, but they went on to say the course would help everyone to better manage some of the complications of PTSD.

Then it was the men's turn to be told the same thing. I felt numb for a while, then I realised there was no magic wand after all and that the only person who could control this beast within was me. It was thought provoking and that night all the guys snuck out of our accommodation and headed to the pub for a few beers and a local meal.

The next day we were back to reality; we all knew we had an even bigger mountain to climb. We could sink or swim. We all decided to take the swimming option.

For the next few weeks, together with our partners, we discovered how to recognise the early warning signs of mood swings and anxiety. It was pretty full on and intense, especially with the emotional guilt of past sins. On occasions, some of us would, for the first time, become human again by shedding a tear or two. The demons were going into exile.

Towards the end of the course, we were asked to do a collage to describe our past, present and future life – like a snapshot of our lives. I found this quite confronting. The hardest part was starting. Then I got to thinking of my life as going through windows and so I started to put windows into my collage. It was like I was in a dream. My life was going through all of these windows, including relationships and of course Vietnam, but there was no real purpose that I could see in the past or the present. But there was a silver lining in my collage. It was the last door to walk through, it was the future and there waiting for me was My Darling. I started to well up with tears. It was staring me in the face. Let go of the past, it's the future you now need to grab with both hands, and for certain go forward with My Darling.

At the end of the PTSD course, I'd learnt a lot about myself, but more importantly I'd learnt about my partner's feelings and difficulties, which included an awful feeling of walking on eggshells and having to cover up for my behaviour and mood swings. It must have been suffocating having someone so demanding one day, then quite reasonable the next. I also found that after all of the pain I had inflicted, I have a lot of good qualities too; I just have to put them into practise a lot more. Now I understand that I can still be a Cranky Hank at times, providing I don't bring back the over-demanding demons. I need to keep working on my strengths and accept that I have some weaknesses that need to be kept in check. I've become better at accepting that I can still have a bad day and get angry without feeling worthless for days. It's time to move on; tomorrow will be a better day, that's the plan.

I said in the beginning I really only matured at fifty-eight, when I stopped acting like a child and blaming everyone else for all of the negativity in my life. The PTSD treatment program gave me the skills to put the brakes on the blame game. I now look at things differently, and think to myself, *So what? Move on.*

One of the best things about the course was the involvement of our partners. I liken it to dancing. I'd be dancing to the tune of the samba; My Darling would be dancing to the tune of the Pride of Erin and now, most of the time at least, we can dance together to the tune of the tango. Up until then, these girls were living with someone they couldn't fully understand. They were alone and now they not only have a better understanding of this condition, but they have each other. To this very day they remain as thick as thieves.

With all of the hard work and commitment to the course, many good things eventuated. I accept that I'll never be *fully* cured; however, I do have an arsenal of skills at my fingertips, and my plan is to keep working with them in the belief I can keep all of the demons away. Before the course, if I saw conflict I'd be in there playing Mr Vigilante. Now, I'm smarter and let the law deal with it!

Life today still has its ups and downs but I now accept that nothing and no one is perfect. Amazingly, I'm still the happiest man alive; I'm with My Darling, who stands beside me every day. Now, just how good is that? If I hadn't done something fifteen years ago, I'm sure I'd be a lonely, grumpier old man. I'm also grateful that I have a great and happy relationship with both of my sons. Several years ago I got to tell them how sorry I was. I never hit or slapped any of them, but I know I created a lot of bad memories for them. It was brave and generous of them to forgive me and I thank and love them for it every day.

My mother passed away nine years ago in 2011. I can't thank her enough for trying to get me to see the light and wake up. If only I'd listened to her, then I could've done something a lot sooner instead of carrying around a chip on my shoulder.

If you're out there alone reading this, and you can see any similarities to you, this is what I'd ask you to consider. If you've been threatened, traumatised or have feared for your life, this can lead to PTSD. PTSD is not restricted to the Defence Forces. It can happen to anyone, especially police, ambulance personnel, or an individual exposed to heightened fear. If someone close to you is saying that you've changed and not for the better, I hope you won't ignore it for as long as I did.

Putting this story together has been quite difficult and confronting. I've disclosed a lot of things that I'd suppressed for many years and some of my loved ones and friends reading this for the first time may also feel confronted by it, too. I hope, however, they'll understand that if this story is to have any effect on people and help them see some light at the end of the tunnel, then I had to tell the truth, the whole truth, warts and all. By telling it as it is, readers may see what can cause an individual to live with and suffer with PTSD. In my case, the following are the symptoms and complications that affected me, which I can now share:

- Feeling anxious and nervous

- Feeling jumpy

- Experiencing a sense of high alertness

- A resistance to socialise, particularly if it continues to grow

- A feeling of being weighed down

- Having difficulty with coping, or feeling that you can't go on

- Thinking that you might turn to substance use in the hope of easing negative feelings

- Experiencing a growing temper, including yelling at or over people, and lashing out or starting to become violent with loved ones

- Blaming others, especially if one is made to feel upset and angry

- Blaming your partner, who, in your eyes, can't do anything right

If you relate to some of the above, there are two things you can do:

1. You can deny everything and convince yourself that there is nothing wrong

OR

2. Go and see your doctor as a first step, to check if you may have the symptoms of PTSD. There is absolutely no shame in that. It may even save your life, and at the very least save you and your close ones from going through years of anguish and heartache.

I wish I hadn't ignored it for so long! I wish I'd reached out sooner.
Finally, I hope my mistakes will help others seek help.
Like the old Chinese Proverb: *every great journey starts with one step*.

RIDING THE ROLLERCOASTER

Marney Nicholas

In March of 1994 I was co-hosting an over-thirty-five singles function in the city with the guy I was seeing, when I met this charming, blue-eyed man. Nikko was friendly and very easy to talk to, and we were soon chatting about many things, including our work. As it turned out, an associate had given me this man's business card to contact for a work-related issue. We laughed at what a small world it was.

I had the impression that he enjoyed my company and thought maybe we might spend some time together. Unfortunately, when he found that I was with someone the shutters went down. I thought, *Well, that's the end of that*.

Several weeks went by before I contacted him. The first thing he asked was, 'Are you still seeing that guy?' 'No,' I replied. He then asked for my home phone number.

We seemed to connect and went on our first date to an Italian restaurant. We were so busy talking we hardly ate dinner. I remember when he took me home, we were having a rather deep and meaningful conversation on life, and he asked me if I was a 'wandering generality' or 'a meaningful specific'. What a question – and on the first date! I thought he was an interesting, although intense, person.

Things moved quite fast, with him inviting me to his houseboat for the Anzac Day long weekend. Sensing my hesitation, he also invited my two children who were then twenty-one and nineteen. We all had a great weekend and, to my surprise and delight, he sent me flowers at work the following week to thank me for such a great time.

Within a couple of months, I accompanied him on an interstate trip and met his eldest son. We went on business trips overseas and it was during one of these trips to New Zealand that he proposed. This was most unexpected, as we'd both been married before and it wasn't a priority for me, but it was important to him. I was in love and I accepted. He was warm, caring and affectionate, and would sit for hours talking with me, encouraging me to communicate and express my thoughts and emotions, not bottle them up as I'd often done in the past.

He spoilt me and made me feel so special and important. When I look back at my previous marriage, we were busy raising two children and doing quite a lot of socialising, so much so that we rarely sat and talked in depth about our feelings.

Nikko and I were both working full-time, with him in a very high-powered position, so our weekends were precious to us. Spending as much time as we could with each other, as well as our children, was our priority, especially Nikko's youngest son, who was only seven.

I'd always had a busy social life, and my friends and family were very keen to meet this man that I was constantly talking about. It was quite a juggling act working through all these issues, plus combining two sets of children of varying ages into one family. I'd made a career change when my first marriage broke up and I was now attending night school two nights a week. I would race home to his house after classes to see him and have dinner. He'd often have flowers on the table for me, also some of the most beautifully written cards expressing his feelings for me. I tell everyone that he courted me with beautiful meals and piano recitals – he is a great cook and an accomplished pianist.

Within twelve months of meeting, I moved into his home, put my home on the market and we were married. Life was wonderful. We were on the same wavelength. We'd know what the other was thinking, and would frequently finish each other's sentences. So attuned were we that I knew when the phone rang at work that it was him even before I answered it. I'd met my soul mate.

One year after marrying, Nikko's sister and her husband stayed for a few days. Nikko blew up over a small incident. I was shocked. This was the first time I'd seen him show any anger. His sister said, 'He is just like Dad.' He was very upset by this statement, as their father was a bad-tempered man. He was a WWII veteran, a very volatile man who, in hindsight, probably suffered from PTSD.

As the years went by, I started to notice the occasional outbursts of anger. Where was this anger coming from? What was the cause? To me, the anger was in response to the most trivial of things, but they were major to him. He began to blame me for these things and said I'd changed from the girl he'd married. Had I changed? Was I doing things to upset him? I didn't understand what the problem was, and as he couldn't or wouldn't talk about it, I felt quite helpless. I wondered how a man could be so confident to run a multi-million-dollar company with a large staff, but be so insecure in his private life.

When we visited Nikko's mother, she'd question me about his behaviour, because she thought he was such a different person when he returned from Vietnam. As I hadn't known him before he joined the army and went overseas, I had no comparison. This worried her greatly, and over the ensuing years she frequently talked to me about it. She thought he should seek some help, but you can't make anyone do something they don't want to, so the ball was in his court.

For months, everything would run smoothly, and then out of the blue I'd be blamed for whatever had upset him. He'd be loving one day and withdrawn the next. He'd then be full of apologies. Boy, was I confused! I suggested that he should take responsibility for his actions and not blame me for the way he felt.

My fiftieth birthday loomed and he suggested a party. I chose a cocktail party. As my parents had recently gone into aged care, and my brother into residential care, their home was vacant, so we decided to hold my party there. This was fully catered for and was complete with dancing to a string quartet. It was a fantastic evening celebrated with family and friends. Again, I was made to feel number one in his life.

After my parents and brother went into care, my eldest sister and her family began harassing my parents by letter and phone calls about their wills and finances. This caused a huge amount of upset and worry, not only to my parents, but also to the rest of the family.

A few months later, my father unexpectedly passed away. This was devastating, especially to me as I was the youngest and was always his baby. My eldest sister didn't stop fighting to get control of my mother and brother's finances, going so far as taking them to the guardianship tribunal. I don't know how we, as a family, would've got through this terrible ordeal without Nikko, my tower of strength.

Following this trauma, my mother and brother made changes to their wills, and thought they'd made them airtight. Little did we know what else was in store.

Three years later, my mother passed away and we had to endure a challenge to her will, which dragged on for a couple of years. Once again, Nikko's advice and support was invaluable to my family and me. He was my knight in shining armour, with his logical thinking and strength of character. Unfortunately, we came through all of this quite scarred and haven't had any contact with our eldest sister since.

Sadly, after this, Nikko's mood swings were becoming more obvious, but I endeavoured to keep our busy life as normal as possible. I started doing everything I could to cover things up so people wouldn't notice, often making up stories as an excuse for how he was behaving. I would say, 'We double booked an engagement,' or, 'Nikko has made other plans,' or, 'I was unwell'. The list went on.

I didn't know from one day to the next what mood he would be in. I felt like we were riding a rollercoaster, with such highs and lows!

A few years later, with increasing outbursts, I suggested counselling. Initially, he wasn't interested, but after some time he reluctantly agreed. I felt counselling was important for our survival as a couple; I was desperate. I phoned the VVCS for help.

In the first session, the counsellor started with family history. As she delved into his childhood, he became defensive. The session wasn't all that successful and he didn't want to go back. To his credit, he persevered and got some ideas on how to improve things at home; nevertheless, we were struggling big time! He made rules that all seemed to be on his side and I felt that I didn't have a say. Some of these were: do not make any spur of the moment decisions; do not make any plans without consulting him first; if it isn't on the calendar and we haven't agreed to it, then we can't do it; and, specifically for me, do not change my mind after making a decision.

A few years later, we tried counselling again, but I felt intimidated by his attitude and didn't feel comfortable opening up and expressing my feelings, as he was again blaming me for making him angry. We also found that there was little or no continuity in some of the counselling, as the counsellors seemed to work on a twelve-month contract. This was very frustrating.

Nikko's doctor prescribed him anti-depressants a few different times during these years, but they seemed to have an adverse effect on him. This was worrying to us both, as his anxieties and hyper-vigilance were already high. He worried about me when I went out and needed to know where I was and if I was all right. If I came home later than expected and I hadn't let him know, anxiety would kick in, causing an upset. Afterwards, he was sorry and very loving; he thought I was making a fuss over nothing. At times it was like living with two different men, never knowing what to expect from one day to the next, and sometimes one minute to the next. I was walking on eggshells, not wanting to cause any problems that might make him angry or upset. I felt that I had to be alert at all times as to what mood he was in and how he was feeling. Sometimes, when things were going smoothly, I'd relax, but it seemed that was when a problem would arise and he would get angry and explode.

By this stage, he'd been retired from the workforce for a couple of years, and apart from managing our investments and doing some volunteer work, he had a lot of time to brood over things. In looking back, early retirement was difficult, but it was a catch-22 situation – when someone isn't coping with work, what is the better option?

These angry outbursts seemed to be happening more often and in 2005 he had a major episode. He'd been depressed for a few months and went to see a psychiatrist at Heidelberg Repatriation Hospital who'd taken him on a tour of Ward 17. This brought back some very disturbing memories, having been a patient there on his return from Vietnam. When he came into our home after this visit he was anxious and just exploded. He then took himself into the Repatriation Hospital for treatment. Sadly, we spent our tenth wedding anniversary apart because he didn't want me to come in to see him while he was at the Repat. He was very depressed and saw me as the problem. He was often irrational, giving me ultimatums and then going back on them. I couldn't understand the problem and I didn't know where I stood in our relationship. All of these ups and downs in our marriage were taking a toll on both of us, although we still deeply loved one another. I knew he had to work through his issues and it was going to be a difficult time. He has great inner strength and I hoped he would use this to get through the rough patch, and things would be better.

During his hospital stay he was encouraged to enrol in the PTSD course. He came home and talked this over with me and I encouraged him to go ahead. This was an intense four-week live-in course, with weekend leave for the veterans. Partners were invited to attend one day a week. I thought this course would be our miracle cure. I just wanted my lovely man back again.

This was a very difficult four weeks for him, being a very private person, and I know he struggled with opening up and talking about himself and his feelings. This was obvious to me, as when he came home for the weekends he was very tense.

He often asked me if everything was all right with us, but he didn't want me to talk about our problems with my family or friends. If I did so, he would feel betrayed. The only person I could talk with was his mother. As I'd come from a family who shared their problems, I found it very difficult not to be able to talk to my middle sister to whom I was close.

People suspected at times that things weren't good, especially with his mood swings, and he was sometimes brusque with family and friends. His outbursts were often followed by withdrawals and a downward spiral into depression that could last for days or sometimes weeks, only speaking to me when he had to.

When he was like this he refused to have friends in the home or to go out and socialise. I felt very isolated and lonely. For years, I put on a brave face, even though I actually felt that my world was falling apart. My daughter suspected that things weren't right. She didn't like the way Nikko spoke to me and she didn't think I should put up with it. It was very confusing, as we also had lots of great times together.

When I started to read more about this condition I was mind-blown by the complexity of the symptoms and the effects on everyone. I remember the first day we met the group of guys and their partners over a coffee prior to going into the lecture room. The facilitators introduced themselves and one of them started writing symptoms of PTSD on the white board. *He's writing about my husband*, I thought.

After the morning tea break, the women went into another room, leaving the men to begin their course. We were told that there was no cure for this condition, only self-help and/or medication to help control things. I knew medication wasn't going to be of much help to us as he'd had bad reactions to them in the past, so it would have to be self-help.

I think initially we all felt a bit shell-shocked until the leaders began explaining things in depth. We were encouraged to open up and talk about our situations. I felt rather uncomfortable about this until we were told that everything that was said in these groups stayed within the room. To be able to be frank and talk about these issues helped enormously. Hearing that these women were all going through similar situations was an eye-opener! I realised that it wasn't just me. Learning that all of these problems were part and parcel of PTSD was enlightening, to say the least.

Our whole group bonded, especially the women, and we all remain good friends to this day, meeting frequently at each other's homes, talking and counselling one another through good and not so good times.

Although I didn't get my miracle cure, I learnt a lot about what causes the outbursts, how to try and defuse situations, and I became better at anticipating what could happen before the volcano erupted. Putting all this knowledge into practice is the hardest part! I found this course excellent and it's one course I'd recommend to anyone suffering from this condition, not only veterans.

The following year, Nikko turned sixty and he decided he'd have a party for this one. On the day of the party he was very anxious for everything to go to plan. It did and he went on to have a great night with many friends and family in attendance.

It seemed from the PTSD course that it'd take a long time to master all of the ways to overcome the turmoil within. Over our twenty-three years together, we've had a couple of splits; the last one in 2009 was the worst. It was over the Christmas/New Year period that his mood swings were out of control. He was very depressed and irrational; if he couldn't control a situation, he'd explode, with much ranting and raving at me. It was as though I was the enemy! I thought this was the end of our marriage and moved out to my daughter's home for six weeks. Despite having told me to go, after a few days he started calling me and telling me to come back home. I refused, as things needed to improve in a big way before I could consider this.

I contacted the counselling service and we both attended individual counselling sessions. He put in a lot of hard work to get back on track, and we had many meetings and coffees together to try to iron out our issues. I turned sixty during this time apart and I was sad that we were not together for it. Fortunately, we did get back together and have celebrated many birthdays and anniversaries together since then, and look forward to many more.

We still have the occasional time when anxiety, anger and hyper-vigilance come to the fore and things need extra attention to remedy the situation. The good thing is that on most occasions we can talk later about the problems without blame.

Overall our life is pretty much on track, and we are busy doing the things we like to do together. I now have much of my lovely man back.

In 2011, we attended the Residential Lifestyle Program at Flowerdale. This is a five-day live-in course with group sessions. We found it very beneficial, as it reinforced the things we'd learnt at the Repatriation Hospital, such as staying positive and being kind to ourselves through yoga, exercise and meditation. A little romance added to the mix doesn't go astray either. We also learnt the importance of mindfulness and caring about each other's feelings and needs on a daily basis. A lot of importance was put on communication and making quality time available for one another, rather than taking each other for granted. These things often take a back seat when life gets busy.

On the final day of the program, we were asked to sit with our partner and talk about the relationship and what we'd learnt. We then set goals, aiming for a smoother future together.

We're very pleased to have had the opportunities to attend the courses that have been available to us and, although our relationship is still a work-in-progress, we are always open to each other's suggestions for improvement. The good news is that with lots of input these strategies do work.

Nikko and Marney Nicholas

A JOURNEY OF HOPE

Pekka Hirvonen

I was born in Finland on 2 December 1945, the second oldest of four boys. Dad was a strict no-nonsense sort of a man. He didn't show much emotion or love towards us kids, although we knew he cared for us. He was born in Eastern Finland in 1918. He learnt very early about survival under very harsh conditions. I think his experiences explain why he was so hard on us, mainly me. He went through the Finnish/Russian war, and he was wounded three times and decorated for bravery three times. He didn't talk much about his early life or the war years.

Mum was a gentle, loving person, born in Central Finland in 1922, the youngest of seven children, four boys and three girls. Her mum died when she was two years old. Her dad couldn't look after her and so an elderly schoolteacher raised her from an early age.

I had a fairly normal childhood – most of the time. We lived in a small village surrounded by water and forest. Summers were full of fishing, swimming and playing in the forest. Winter was different, some days it was so cold we couldn't play outside (temperatures of over -30°F). Skiing was the main sport in winter. We skied ten kilometres to and from school. In winter, we went to school in the dark and returned in the dark, so there wasn't much time to play once homework was completed. My three brothers and I would be stuck inside, and though we fought we always looked after each other, like brothers do. I had a knack for getting into trouble. I was my own worst enemy. A belting from my father followed many episodes of mischief. When you get knocked back to reality, you get up and carry on. 'Why won't you ever learn?' Mum often said. I never did seem to learn my lesson, as there were many of these instances.

I lost my freedom to school. I still remember my first day. Mum dragging me by the hand and me screaming and swearing like a trooper.

She often reminded me about that day and how I embarrassed her. The first two years weren't too bad and I almost started to enjoy school, but then it started getting harder and more time-consuming; too much homework. I started to fib to Dad about doing my homework. Of course, it all backfired and there were more beltings and tears. End result? I failed the year when I was about nine years old and had to repeat it, plus I had to do extra summer school. Every day I had three hours of maths and reading. It was embarrassing and it hurt, as everyone else was having fun. I called that year the lost summer.

There were summer camps organised by the school every year, and I had to attend to keep me on the straight and narrow. Because of my home life and annual trips to Helsinki to have my sight tested, I started to feel unwanted and lonely and spent more time by myself, while my brothers played with their friends. It wasn't all doom and gloom though, as Dad did teach us all about fishing. He also showed us how to prepare soil for gardening and how to plant vegetables. Gardening wasn't much fun at the time, but later in life I appreciated the skills he'd taught me. We had our yearly family camping trips and would load up the rowing boat with waterproof material to make a large tent and other provisions to last two weeks. It was all about bonding and having fun. Fishing, swimming and playing games. Some nights I had to help Dad row the boat when he went trawling for pike trout and other game fish. We always returned with some fish. It was hard work rowing for five hours but at least I was allowed to sleep in in the morning. I could see a tender side to Dad that he didn't show too often and I couldn't get into trouble during holidays. It was heaven for two weeks.

Life went on. When I was seven I had my first cigarette. It knocked me for a six doing the drawback, but I soon started to enjoy it. Sometimes I pinched smokes from Dad, other times older boys gave me some, and other times I picked up butts and rolled them in newspaper. Then I made my own pipe out of pine wood, which was nice and soft to work with but wasn't very nice when lit, so that was the end of the pipe. I was a little worried about the smell of smoke on my breath, so I started chewing on onions. I didn't get caught out until I was about thirteen.

When I was about ten there was a talk about moving to Australia or Canada so the boys didn't have to do National Service at eighteen. We learnt about different countries in geography, so I knew about Canada with its mild summers and cold winters but I had no idea about Australia. Dad decided on Australia. I imagined it was the South Pole: very hot with black people and kangaroos in the main streets. When the decision was made to move, my brain went into overdrive. I thought I should run away or do something. The last year of my schooling in Finland we learnt about the Australian culture and customs. Realising that the culture and customs were like ours in Europe, I started to relax. Then the sad part of moving was saying goodbye to family and friends knowing we might never see them again.

The week we left was a big adventure. We took the overnight ferry to Sweden, then a train ferry through Denmark to Germany. Our ship was an old German troop carrier, SS *Skaubryn Arprin*, converted to a passenger liner. It sank the trip after ours with no lives lost. Poor old Mum was seasick for the whole trip. We kids had the time of our lives. There were games to play, a swimming pool, and the ship to explore. By our standards, we had three good meals a day. In Finland we had porridge three times a day, sometimes twice a week. I saw an Arab for the first time at Port Said, and they scared the crap out of me. Saw the pyramids from a distance, too. Next stop, Colombo, Ceylon (now known as Sri Lanka), where we had to stay for a week due to mechanical problems. We all had blond hair and the locals wanted to touch our hair for good luck. There was cow and human excrement on the streets. We swam in the Gulf of Mannar, our first time in ocean salt water. It was a bit hairy, with strong currents and large waves, but we learnt where to swim from the local kids who befriended us. It was fun while it lasted.

We arrived in Fremantle, Australia, then on to Melbourne. Surprise: no kangaroos or black people. We left Finland in -27.22°C and arrived in Melbourne to 37°C. The only hotter place I'd been was a sauna bath. We caught a train to Albury in the late afternoon, then a bus to Bonegilla Immigration Camp, arriving after dark. Our accommodation was a long hut – three rooms, two beds and a table in each room. A window and a bar heater on the wall. Communal ablutions, with male and female toilets. Separate dining and kitchen rooms and three meals a day. Sunday lunches stick in my mind: roast chicken, lamb or pork with vegetables. It was the first time we ate a roast. Years later, Mum told us about our first Sunday roast lamb. Mum and Dad noticed the meat moving with maggots. We ate it anyway; it was all about survival and we needed the protein.

Bonegilla was on the shores of Lake Hume. There was plenty of fishing, swimming and exploring the countryside in temperatures of 38–40°C.

Then the old nemesis returned: school. Not knowing the language, it was very hard. The first couple of weeks we each had an Aussie kid who read to us and we had to read it back. They didn't teach us how to pronounce the alphabet in English. It was frustrating. What made things worse was my tutor was the headmaster's daughter and not at all nice to me. Maths was even worse. Not knowing how to add up pounds, shillings and pence, I soon lost interest. In Finland there is no corporal punishment in schools, but it didn't take long for punishment to find me in Australia. On a Friday afternoon, the whole school went swimming. The rule was to wait until everyone got there and for the headmaster to read out the safety rules, but I was in the lake already. I got three straps on each hand. Shock, horror, pain and tears. Did I learn anything? Yes. No tears next time.

After two months, Dad went to Melbourne, and we followed soon after. Our next home was Broadmeadows Army Camp. Part of it was an immigration camp. Our house, if you can call it a house, was a half-round corrugated shed like an igloo, hot in summer and cold in winter. We had our meals in the army canteen. The mess made cut lunches every day consisting of vegemite and peanut butter sandwiches. It took a long time to adjust to the taste but we had cold meats and jam as well. I managed to get into trouble again. Wanting to collect soft drink bottles to exchange for cash, I decided to steal bottles from the back of the shop. I was caught, but luckily the police weren't called. The camp had a junior soccer team so I played and it kept me out of trouble for a while. The person who Dad worked for was a farmer and racehorse owner. He had a property in Moira in New South Wales, just over the border from Echuca. This became our next home. They had over 2,000 head of sheep, some cattle and wheat, and it was where the owner spelled his racehorses.

We had expected a large farmhouse but what we saw was a rundown old house of four bedrooms, a kitchen, and a bathroom with half a floor and a bathtub. No lounge room, no electricity, no running water other than water tanks and an outside toilet. Dad, being a carpenter, soon made the place liveable.

School was no big deal this time. It was an early start in the mornings, a 5-kilometre bike ride to the highway, then a half-hour on the bus to school in Echuca.

After a month, the manager decided to give us two milking cows. Of course, I had to learn how to milk them in the morning before school and again at night. At this point, life really started to piss me off. In all my childhood, I'd seen my older brothers getting belted once and the younger ones never, though they got a smack across the ears sometimes. It did get lonely. I had no mates to play with, only my brothers.

School was a drag, but I loved sport. I learnt to play Aussie Rules and baseball and enjoyed swimming and athletics in summer. Smoking was a favourite pastime and was still getting me into trouble. At times, smokes were hard to come by. One day I was walking along the riverbank and I picked up a length of tree root and discovered it was like a honeycomb. It was a rootstock of a Mallee Eucalyptus. Like a good boy scout I always carried matches. Lighting the Mallee root was easy but it was a bit rough. It burned my throat, but when you're desperate you try anything. The dumbest thing I did was on the last days of school holidays. Dad always got a carton of Camel cigarettes each Saturday and they were very strong. As I'd had no smokes for two weeks, I took his last packet and smoked three. I hid the rest under the house. When Dad came home he came rushing out of the house yelling, 'Where are my smokes?' He looked straight at me. I knew I was in deep shit. I tried to plead innocence. He got his smokes back and said nothing. At dinner that night there were only five plates on the table and there was a chair and bucket in the corner. Dad told me to sit down and start smoking. I thought all my Christmases had come at last! Boy, was I wrong. I had to smoke them all, one after another, no breaks. After seven smokes I started to get sick and when I finished the bucket was half full. I gave up smoking for three weeks after that! I was more careful after that. Dad said, 'When you earn your own money, you can smoke.'

I gave up school halfway through form three, due to my lack of English and receiving no help from the teachers. I was fifteen. I knew deep down it was the wrong thing to do but my dislike of schooling was too strong.

After three and a half months of hanging around the farm, doing my chores and hunting, I found work on a small property. They had 500 head of sheep, 100 cattle, 40 pigs, 1000 hectares of wheat and a few horses. There was never a slack moment. I learnt to drive a tractor, other farm machinery and a car. After a couple of weeks, I was ploughing the fields and sowing the seeds for wheat. The most enjoyable part was droving the cattle and sheep in the countryside. At night I herded the animals into a narrow lane with a dog at either end and never lost an animal. Later, when the farmer came to take me home, we had a campfire and a brew. What a life!

To save travelling time, the boss decided to give me a horse and I was rapt. I'd never ridden a horse before. Galloping was no problem but when it came to herding, sudden turns and stops, I was out of my depth. The horse didn't respond to my commands. Suddenly, the horse stopped and I flew over his head. That was the last time I ever rode a horse! I had a five-mile walk home that night. I was bruised, with hurt pride. Then the boss gave me more driving lessons so I could drive his Holden ute to and from work. Herding cattle and sheep was done by bicycle. Taking the cattle 25 miles to the market was hard work along the road and railway tracks, through a small town called Moama, and across the bridge to Echuca. It was no fun and took two days to get there. At least I could drive home. Driving came to an end after three months. One night driving home I decided to race a two-carriage diesel train across the railway crossing. I was flying. I went from third gear to first and destroyed the gearbox. I was lucky; the train missed me by a few inches. Boss wasn't happy.

I worked long hours, seven days a week in summer. In winter I played football on Saturdays and worked on Sundays – there was nothing else to do. The wages weren't much, and Dad took it all. He said there was nothing for me to spend it on and that I was too young to smoke. The boss helped me out with roll-your-own papers and tobacco.

To make things easier, the boss me got me a 500cc Triumph motorbike. Dad wasn't happy about it and said to look after myself, and no speeding. One night, it was pouring rain and the only way I could stay on the bike was to go flat out. I passed Dad doing 60 miles on the way home and when he got home he wasn't too happy. I explained it all and he calmed down a bit. Having the bike made it easier to herd the cattle and sheep. Like everything else, it came to a sudden stop. One wet day herding cattle, there were a couple of runners. While the dogs were keeping the rest of the herd in check I went after the runners. I didn't see the tree stump in the grass and went head over heels. I had cuts and bruises and the bike was totalled. Back to the pushbike.

What I'd learnt so far in my young life was how to be independent, how to look after myself, to respect others and to try to be friendly to one and all.

When Mum got sick and was in hospital for six weeks Dad was the cook. Our meals consisted of stale bread fried in butter, and bread boiled in milk with sugar. Living on the farm, we had plenty of milk, eggs, bread, vegetables and meat so the boys took over the cooking after one week so we didn't starve. Mum came home and everything went back to normal.

To our surprise, Dad announced we were moving back to Victoria, to a place called Wandin Yallock to a large property, a cherry and apple orchard with a few hundred sheep. I wasn't happy about the move. I was enjoying life, my work, and I had a good boss. I'd met nice people through football and work but had to leave all that behind.

We settled down on the farm. Dad worked the farm and my younger brothers went to school, but there were no jobs for me at any of the local farms. For a couple of months I hung around the farm, met a few locals and made friends. I was bored to tears. After a couple of jobs off the farm, Dad's boss eventually gave me a job. I learnt how to prune fruit trees, how to use pesticide machines and I gave his son-in-law a hand shearing the sheep. I enjoyed it but it was backbreaking work. I started playing football and in the second year I won the club runner-up trophy. My playing days came to an end after a couple of years when I tore ligaments on both ankles. I was disappointed but life went on.

There were girls in my life, one I really fancied. I started spending time with her and lost contact with my friends. She was a bit demanding. Out of nowhere, I lost my job and I was devastated. I started to hang around with the wrong sort of people. I went missing for a week and a half and when I did return home, Dad said, 'Pack your things and get out'. I was about nineteen.

I found accommodation with a couple of workers in an old hut that had electricity, running water, wood stove, toilet outside and four rooms. At night I'd sometimes wake up feeling rats running over my body; I was never bitten so I got used to them. I did get some work from time to time. Luckily we had a fridge but it was mainly for beer. I lived on canned muck and biscuits during the week and sometimes had a meal with the family of friends.

Four months into my exile I really hit rock bottom. I started to drink more and when I couldn't afford beer, I went onto cheap plonk. I even tried my own cocktail of methylated spirits, shoe polish and milk. Yuck! It took me two days to recover.

I started to get stomach pains and lost weight. I was 1.75 metres tall and 44.45 kilograms. I lost 15.87 kilograms in thirteen months. Doctors confirmed my fear that I had stomach ulcers. I gave up smoking and drinking for a while. Medication cured the ulcers. It was time to move back home. I had a cool reception from Dad but Mum was happy to see me. I got my old job back on the farm and started to save money for a car. I bought a blue and white 1956 FC Holden sedan. I started to knock around with my old footy mates. We weren't angels and we weren't too bad, but we still did a few stupid things. I was back smoking but not drinking yet.

I was twenty-one, and again there wasn't much work on the farm. After a string of jobs I didn't really enjoy, and without a trade to fall back on, I started to consider my future. A lot of ideas went through my mind about what to do, such as working on a cattle or sheep property, driving trucks, cutting sugar in north Queensland, and joining the armed services. The list went on.

I decided on the army. Dad wasn't happy at all, and he told me the reason – the Vietnam War. I had a long talk with him over a few beers and I told him I was over twenty-one and that the army had free medical and dental services and opportunities to learn a trade. He mellowed, so I enlisted as a carpenter. I passed the medical only to be told that I had to be a fully qualified tradesperson with papers. I joined the railways. I had an active social life and stayed out of trouble. Early in September 1968 I gave the railways two weeks' notice and enlisted in the Royal Australian Air Force (RAAF).

THE ROYAL AUSTRALIAN AIR FORCE RAAF

It was the same deal as the army; I needed tradesperson papers for any building trades. I enlisted as a general hand and hoped for a re-muster to something else later on. I passed the interview and medical; however, I had to be a naturalised Australian citizen and have my birth certificate translated into English. To my amazement, I was naturalised and had my birth certificate translated within two weeks.

On 26 September 1968, I signed on the dotted line and had a final briefing from the recruiting sergeant: no smoking, no drinking on the train and good behaviour.

There were four of us and we had a few hours to kill before boarding the Overland, so we went to the pub. We had a few beers and we had the sense to have something to eat. In mutual agreement, we decided to buy a slab of VB beer. We managed to hide the beer by rearranging clothes in the suitcase. A bag of ice went into a waterproof bag. No sleep that night. After breaking our first two orders, we arrived in Adelaide somewhat sober. A driver met us at the station and drove us to our home for the next three months, RAAF Base Edinburgh.

We had twenty-four recruits in our course. The first week went in a flash. We took the oath, wrote our final signature, and got our hair cut, short back and sides. There was a trip to the tailors to get overalls, boots and measured up for our uniforms. The daily uniform was boots, spit polished every night, overalls and a hat. On the first weekend I had my worst punishment washing pots and pans in the kitchen. During the week, the Warrant Officer Disciplinary (WOD) caught me walking with my hands in my pockets, sleeves rolled up and smoking whilst crossing the parade ground. Week two came and the real work started. Up at 6 am, shave and shower, sometimes a shampoo, room panic (cleaning one's room), and doing a blanket roll, which was part of the training. It took a couple of goes to get it right.

Training was intense but rewarding and somewhat enjoyable. Going to all the lectures, having tests at the end of each week, preparing every night for the next day and then studying, sometimes until midnight. It reminded me of school! At long last, I learnt that it takes theory as well as practice and common sense to have a better future.

After morning parade, there was marching, parade ground drill, gymnastics and sport. We marched everywhere we went. We learnt to work together. It felt good. I learnt to take orders and respect rules and regulations.

After six weeks we were let loose on the weekends. Every Friday afternoon our corporal gave us a brief: look after each other and stay out of trouble. It did work, in a fashion. The drinking age in South Australia was twenty-one and we had four mates who were underage. They could serve their country, but they couldn't drink.

The longer the course went, the more confident I became. I no longer had fear of failure. Study and hard work paid off, but three weeks from the end of course I had an accident. It was a stinking hot day. After drill practice, we had a swim. The pool wasn't large or deep but had a diving board. I did a couple of dives, then, not knowing there was a water pipe on the bottom of the pool, I hit my head. I blacked out for a couple of minutes and was sent off for X-rays and 24 hours of observation in hospital. I had concussion and stitches on the forehead. Luckily, I had no damage to the neck or spinal cord. I did miss out on a couple of exercises, including going into a room filled with tear gas without a gas mask. The other was to dive into water and retrieve an object in overalls and boots and float and swim for ten minutes. The base closed the pool following my accident.

The last two weeks of the course were intense, with rifle practice and marching practice for the marching-out parade. A lot of family and friends attended but none of mine. It went very well. We were told later on that some of the NCOs (Non-commissioned Officers) and junior officers thought we wouldn't make it but we proved them wrong.

Reflecting on the course, I found it most rewarding. I finished up in the top ten of twenty-four and was super fit.

I was posted to the RAAF Photographic and Publishing Unit (RPPU) at RAAF Laverton in December 1968.

The next night I was on the Overland back to Melbourne. We arrived at Spencer Street and then took the train to Laverton and to RPPU. We were allocated our room and after lunch we did our clearances. At the end of the day we were exhausted and slept well that night.

The next morning we met the CO who informed me that I was to be posted to Base Squadron Laverton (BSLAV) down the road because I came from Finland and it was too close to Russia. RPPU had a very high security level and mine wasn't high enough. I mentioned I was a naturalised citizen but no matter, I had to go. With clearances out of RPPU and clearances into BSLAV I was almost ready to go AWOL that night.

Things settled down and I got into a routine for a few months. Monday night was panic night, which involved polishing and dusting furniture, sweeping, mopping and polishing floors and also cleaning the ablution block or hallway once a month. Once this was done, we often went to the boozer and then had to redo our panic the next morning.

My jobs were many: opening up Headquarters (HQ), polishing floors, emptying bins and ashtrays, picking up messages from the Communications Centre (Coms), printing orders and photocopying. Sometimes I helped out in the postal area. On Saturday mornings, I sorted and delivered the mail to the married quarters on the base. What a waste of a morning. Here, there was no time off, as we were employed 24 hours a day, seven days a week. After a while, a civilian was employed to do the post office work. My parents lived in West Footscray, about 12 kilometres from the base. Normally on Fridays we knocked off early and

I hitchhiked home with my weekly washing. Mum had it ready for me to pick up on Sunday nights in time to return to base. I didn't think about it at the time, but I didn't give her any money and I felt guilty later on.

One Friday night walking home in uniform, a bloke came out of nowhere and king hit me for no reason. I got up and retaliated and down he went. Being the gentleman that I am, I went to help him up and on the way up he hit me with an uppercut. Next minute I was on my back and counting stars. I heard a crack in my jaw. Some people in a car saw what happened and they drove me to the RAAF Hospital at Laverton. The Duty Medical Officer that night was the Hospital CO who was a qualified gynaecologist. My luck. He grabbed my jaw, shook it a few times and said, 'I don't think it's broken so report to medical on Monday'. I could hardly talk all weekend and eating was out of the question. Monday morning, the officer took one look at me and said I had a broken jaw. The X-ray confirmed this. They operated and put a two-inch metal plate in my jaw. I was in hospital for ten days.

One day I noticed a new member in the Orderly Room; a young female pen-pusher, Robyn. We became friends and after a while we started going out to functions where she met my mates. I was glad they got on well. As the time went on, things got more serious and we fell in love and started to talk about the future. Best thing that ever happened to me. Whilst all of this was going on, I still managed to get into trouble twice. I was knocked down by a reversing car and ended up back in hospital with concussion. Soon after, having had a few drinks with my mates in Footscray, I was asleep in the back seat of the car when it rolled a couple of times on a bend. The driver had a cut foot. I had a sore body and another concussion. I spent a night in hospital. I wondered how many lives I had left.

Following a few days away with mates over the Christmas break, and on return home, Mum and Dad had news for me from the Orderly Room; I was posted to Vietnam, Phan Rang Air Base on 13 February 1970. Dad wasn't happy about my posting to a war zone. I rang Robyn, who flew back from leave that afternoon. We only had a month and a half before I had to fly out. We talked about what to do in the future and decided to get engaged, though the parents weren't too happy about it. We had a very enjoyable combined engagement and going away party with family and friends. At the end of the night it was sad to say goodbye. There were a few tears. I was the first one in our group to go to Vietnam. The weeks flew by and next thing I knew I was doing outwards clearances. I was surprised that there was no briefing about the war or what to expect. One Friday afternoon I received my documents but no passport. I was told to pick up my passport from Air Movements section when I arrived at Mascot Airport, Sydney.

Robyn and I spent the weekend at Mum and Dad's place. Dad was a bit of a drinker. I was surprised that he was sober that weekend. We talked about the past and he commented on how different I was from twelve months ago and that they were proud of me. We did talk about his war experiences and how they were out-numbered and out-armed and how they used Molotov cocktails against the Russian tanks or rolled a heap of heavy logs to de-track them. It worked at times but the loss of life was great. Dad was wounded three times and although he didn't elaborate on his injuries, he did say it hurt like hell and they didn't have ration packs as they do now. They were very undernourished and they didn't get to the soup kitchen every day. They only had dry biscuits and water and when the soup kitchen did arrive, it was watery porridge, ham and pea soup with little ham, or meat and vegie soup with little meat.

Clothing and footwear for the Finnish soldiers was inadequate. At times they got frostbite in winter. Mum said Dad came home lost and depressed and had no vision for the future. He did improve, but they had no medical help for their problems. Unfortunately, he ended up an alcoholic and it hurt their marriage. He once said you never hear the bullet that has your name on it, meaning be careful and look after yourself.

Not much has been said about the Finnish and Russian War. In 1939, Finland was attacked by Russians and defeated under brutal and harsh conditions. This was called the Winter War. In 1941, Finland allied with the Germans to invade Russia, advancing to its old frontier. Three years later, the Russian offensive regained the disputed territory that led to armistice in which Finland also ceded the Petsamo area, on the Arctic Coast, to Russia. A total of ten percent of Finnish territory was ceded to the Russians.

Saying goodbye to Mum and Dad on the Sunday was really hard. A hug and kiss for Mum and a handshake for Dad. When we walked to the taxi, I heard Dad cry for the first time. That memory will stay with me forever.

It was sad and very hard to say goodbye to Robyn. Next time we would see each other would be on 29 July 1970 for our wedding. I was hoping that everything would go as planned.

At the Air Movements section of Mascot Airport I was asked who I was and where I was going. I showed them my travel orders only to be told they didn't have my passport. A few phone calls later I was informed that my passport would be there on Friday morning and I'd be flying out by civilian flight. I spent all day roaming the airport and at 5 pm a duty driver picked me up and drove me to Bankstown Air Base Stores Depot. I had limited money so I stayed on base. I ate at the Airmen's Mess and had a couple of beers at the Airmen's Club. On Wednesday night I met up with a mate from Laverton. We had a beer and then he asked me if I could lend him some money, which he would return to me tomorrow. I never saw the bloke again – another notch against my fellow man. Friday morning back to the airport. Sydney, even in those days, was a nightmare with peak hour traffic. When I arrived at the airport the passport was there for me. There were another two airmen going to Vietnam as well, one to Vung Tau and the other to Phan Rang with me. We arrived in Singapore late at night. In the hotel we ended up in the penthouse, the only room available. After settling in, the boys decided to hire a taxi to see the sights. By this time I was flat broke.

We arrived at Saigon about mid morning. The traffic noise, with sirens blaring and jets taking off and landing, was unbelievable. I spent my first day in Vietnam at Saigon Airport in all the noise and chaos. I didn't think I'd ever get to Phan Rang. Finally there was a flight going north. After a delay with an engine problem, we took off and arrived at Phan Rang late at night.

A bus picked us up and dropped us off at 2 Squadron (2SQN) domestic area. There the squadron interpreter showed us to our barracks. The other blokes went to bed. Not having eaten for two days, I needed food but the bars were closed. There was a Yankee 21 Club open and, as late as it was, the interpreter and I walked in darkness for twenty minutes to the club. I had a couple of Yankee hot dogs with ketchup and sauerkraut. Never again! We had a couple of cold Yankee beers. The beer came in a plain glass half-filled with ice and topped with warm Budweiser. I had the trots for a few weeks after that night. Then the interpreter decided it was time to go. He left and I stayed. He gave me some Military Payment Certificates (MPCs) and asked if I'd remember the way back. I said, 'Yes. First right, another right and I can't miss it!'

At closing time, after a few not-too-drinkable beers, it was time to leave. The only lights were in the flight line hangars in the distance. I started walking and after twenty minutes I knew I was lost, but I kept walking. Then I heard a car coming behind me. It was the Yankee MPs. One said, 'Aussie, are you lost?' 'Yes,' I said. 'My first night in-country.' They explained that the air base used to be an animal sanctuary and that there were still some wild animals about, and that the dim lights up the hill belonged to a South Korean Army unit who received bonuses for each set of ears, and it didn't matter to whom they belonged. They drove me back to my barracks.

Next morning, while I slept, there was a rocket attack on the base and I slept through the siren. During an attack it was compulsory to go to the bomb shelter. When I woke up, I was under the bed with the mattress on top of me. Our living quarters/domestic area was directly in line with the Base Commander quarters and the Officers' Mess where some of the rockets were aimed. Welcome to the Vietnam War.

Next morning, I reported to the Orderly Room for briefing with the WOD. I collected my SLR and magazine of ammo, gas mask, helmet and flak jacket. I was ready for war.

I was assigned to the Barracks section. Part of the job was to supervise the local labourers. It was a challenge at times. We had four hut girls to each two-storey timber hut. The girls made our beds, did our washing and ironing and swept the floors. I washed my own underwear while having a shower. Our washing was numbered to coincide with the number on our bed. At times we lost some of our civilian clothing. I learnt early that anything of value had to be kept under lock and key. Didn't matter who it was, the locals would lift anything they could. Once I was an escort on the bus to take the local workers to the main gate. They knew there was going to be a search so at the parking lot there was stuff flying out of the windows: cigarettes, watches, money and lighters. Nothing was found on the local workers. Stuff continually went missing.

We noticed that our washing wasn't returned every day so I asked one of the ladies, through the interpreter, what was going on. She said the machine was full. The washing machines were like concrete mixers, same sort of motion. After checking the machines, I found them to be full of some hard substance. After further investigation, I found there were two identical 40-gallon drums side-by-side, one with laundry powder and the other full of sawdust. When the laundry powder ran out the women used sawdust and after a couple of months it got thicker and harder and there wasn't any room for washing. The machines were replaced, the sawdust was disposed of, and the problem was solved.

We had young and old locals working for us. One of them we nicknamed Clary the Claw. We didn't know how old he was but he looked about ninety-nine. All day he sat on his haunches and picked up cigarette butts with steal snippers and said, 'Ugt a lai', meaning number one, or good. At times, I was a driver on base and outside the perimeter. One outside job, which I called meals on wheels, was interesting. I drove a garbage truck and picked up rubbish from the Flight Line, HQ and domestic area, mess hall and bars. I had four labourers to help me. On the way to the tip, three were on the back going through the rubbish from the mess hall, scavenging for stale bread, meat scraps, and fruit and vegies to put in plastic bags to take home. One morning I wasn't feeling too well after a heavy night on the slops. I lost it and tossed their goods off the truck. I was number twelve (not good) after that.

The rockets and mortars kept coming. Sometimes they flew overhead and we knew we were safe. We still had to go to the bomb shelter. It wasn't all doom and gloom though. We had one day off a week, usually a Sunday. 2SQN had a boat shed and beach hut on Phan Rang Beach along the South China Sea. We had a speedboat called *Six Dozen*. We paid the Yanks for it in Aussie beer.

The first time I came under rifle fire was when returning from the beach, after installing a water tank to the shed. We'd been there four weeks. The road from the base to the beach was approximately seven miles of straight road with high hills on one side and shrubbery and swamp on the other side with an oil pipe running along the road. It was late morning and we were travelling along on alert at a good speed. I felt a gush of wind hit my cheek and almost at the same time three shots rang out. Adrenalin set in. My SLR was in the cabin so it wasn't much use and I was hanging on for dear life. If it was a bullet I felt, I was glad he was a bad shot. I was unharmed but shaken.

There were a few more ambushes on Sunday mornings travelling by bus to the beach but luckily no casualties. We had an Airfield Defence Guard (ADG) escort. Quite often we would see black smoke coming from the direction of the pipeline. This would mean no beach that Sunday as the pipeline was blown up.

I learnt early that you couldn't trust the locals; they worked for you during the day and for the Viet Cong during the night trying to blow you up. Experiencing the way the war was going, and hearing things, I had a feeling that our contribution was making no difference.

My routine looked like this: duty until 4 pm, Airmen's Club for a couple of beers, dinner, shower and then writing letters to my loved ones assuring them I was okay. At night there were outdoor movies, or table tennis, billiards or darts and the odd poker game. There was also a library and some board games. Some nights we went to the 21 Club or other Yankee bars.

One night, five of us decided to do a bar crawl. First three bars we went to we had one beer. There was no atmosphere and no one to talk to. The fourth one I'll remember forever. We walked in. I was in the lead. It was dark inside with some red lights flickering on the walls. Next thing I came to a sudden halt. It was like walking into a brick wall. I looked up and standing there was a giant about 7 feet tall – four pick-handles across the shoulders. He grabbed me by the throat and said, 'What are you doing here white trash?' I managed to utter, 'All we want is a beer.' Then he realised we were Aussies and put me down, invited us to join them, and shouted us drinks all night. It was a black fellas' bar. No whites dared put their feet inside the door. They said if we had been white Yanks, we wouldn't have walked out in one piece. That's one thing I couldn't understand; the whites, blacks and Mexicans didn't get along but they were all Americans in the same service.

The squadron was running smoothly and the morale was high, marred only by incoming rockets and mortars and the Viet Cong trying to get in through the perimeter wire. Being a rank of corporal and below, we had to do armed guard patrols at night. One particular night will stay with me forever. I was paired with an elderly corporal who was on his second tour of Vietnam. He decided it was a waste of time as no one was around, so I did the patrol by myself. My adrenaline levels went up a notch. Around 4 am I heard a commotion and a shot from the Airmen's bar balcony where our command post was. Later, rumours confirmed that there were black panthers on base.

A few weeks later two incidents happened in one day. When leaving the base, we had to ensure our rifle was ready, safety off. This particular morning, I was thinking about my return trip home to get married. I forgot to take the safety off. Just as well because nearing Phan Rang I saw this kid throwing something towards our vehicle. Thinking it was a bomb or grenade, I pointed and fired. Thank goodness nothing happened. As it turned out it was a rock he had thrown. He was one lucky kid.

We were showing some new sergeants around Phan Rang Orphanage and market. It was very smelly; it was an eye opener. On our way back, we stopped in an out-of-the-way bar for a drink. Walking in, we were fronted by ten Vietnamese dressed in black pyjamas, the typical dress for the Viet Cong. As far as we could see they weren't armed. I don't know who was more surprised, but they came after us so we left quick smart. Phan Rang was known to be a Viet Cong R&R (Rest and Recreation) Centre. I'd say we had a lucky escape.

A few days later I got a call informing me my flight back home was leaving in two hours. I was rushed, but I made it and had an enjoyable flight back home.

I'd come home a day early so there was nobody to meet me at the airport. I caught the last train out of Sydney to Wollongong, in summer uniform, in the middle of winter; it was bloody freezing. The train had no heating. The conductor was kind enough to lend me his overcoat. I knew to get off at Woonona station and I had the address of Robyn's parents so I started walking. I had no idea where to go but luckily there was a taxi coming, so I flagged him down and gave him the address. It was around 2 am when I knocked on the door. It took a while for the door to open and when Robyn's dad saw me, he said, 'What are you doing here?' It was a very happy reunion when Robyn came out of her room with curlers in her hair. After some cuddles and kisses, I was never more certain than in that moment that I loved this woman and I wanted to marry her. I knew I had changed while in Vietnam. I had lost the ability to show emotions and feeling. I was hoping she still wanted me and, happily, she did.

First thing I asked for was real coffee with real milk, and toast with plenty of real butter. I was glad to be alive and back home. I met Robyn's three brothers, who were nice people. Time flew and it was our wedding day. Then the shit hit the fan. I received a telegram that I had to report back to RAAF Richmond for my return flight to Vietnam that afternoon. There were fuel strikes at the time and flights had to be taken when they were available. I phoned Richmond Air Movements and explained that we were getting married that afternoon, so they gave me five extra days. I remember standing at the altar with my best man and the groomsmen, talking and waiting. Then she was there. After that, everything was a blur. It was the happiest moment of my life. My family came up to Wollongong for the wedding and it was quite emotional meeting up with them and friends from Melbourne. The reception was a blur also. Photos were taken, speeches were made, and we ate, drank and mingled with the guests. Then it was time to change clothes and leave for our honeymoon. We rented a car and spent a few days down the coast.

It was over all too soon. We stayed in Sydney for one night, then had a sad and emotional farewell in the morning.

With six months left of my tour the rockets and mortars kept coming in, luckily not too close to us. Unfortunately, I was drinking more than usual, mainly due to blocking out the noise of incoming and outgoing artillery, aircraft taking off and landing at night and the Yankee Gunship blasting at a valley between Radar Hill and us. We nicknamed that hill Nui Dat.

Then tragedy struck. The day, 3 November 1970, started like any other. Late afternoon an announcement came over the loud speaker that one of our Magpies, A84-231, a Canberra bomber, was missing and had gone off radar. The loss of this young crew was a severe shock to 2SQN. Only the night before we had all-rank drinks at the Airmen's Club and I had a chat and a few drinks with the pilot, Michael Herbert and the navigator, Robert Carver. They were down-to-earth blokes. We expected casualties in war, but to have two of our own go missing, the feelings were of deep sadness and loss, and it will stay with us forever. Over the next week or so, it was obvious how much the loss affected everyone. I think the bond between the members grew stronger. The Canberra bomber was lost in deep jungle and wasn't found until April 2009 after an extensive search. The remains of the two young men were finally located in July 2009.

Letters and parcels from home kept us from going around the bend. I knew when I had mail, as I could smell the perfume on the envelope. Robyn would also send the Monday edition of *The Sun* during the footy season so I could get the results, plus the Melbourne *Truth* just to read some scandalous stories. The first time, I didn't know there were personal messages amongst the pages. I read *The Sun* and a mate grabbed the *Truth* and started reading it. After a while he waved the messages around saying they were better than the stories in the paper. After that I had to check the papers for messages from Robyn. No more embarrassment. It was a nice touch though.

I received fruitcakes from Robyn's mum throughout the year and shared them with my mates. Then Robyn started to send cakes as well. I enjoyed them but the mates preferred her mum's cakes. I didn't mind at all.

We got an invitation to two weddings of two Vietnamese workers. The service of the first one was held in an 800-year-old Cham Temple – or what was left of it. The ceremony was quite interesting. The boss drove to the reception and we followed the wedding party, and would you know it, he lost them. We ended up in the country. After a quick turnaround we found our way back to the base. The second wedding was more enjoyable. The week before we gave them some beer and cans of food. I noticed they had a cute little dog running around the house, not like the skinny runts running around the villages. This one was well looked after. On the day of the wedding, we missed the ceremony due to work commitments but we got to the reception and we were treated as long lost friends. They were Cham people, shy and friendly. We sat down to eat and drink. There was a lot of food: soups, meats, fish, vegies and fruit. Most of the food didn't appeal to me but I tried some soup and the smell put me off. I didn't want to offend them, so I tried some meat wrapped in banana leaf. It wasn't too bad, a bit tough but edible. I didn't see the little dog around so I asked where it was. They said, 'You're eating it!' I managed to keep it down. After that I lost my appetite.

One delicacy we had most mornings at Barracks was French rolls. The carpenter's labourer, a local, would bring six rolls in the morning. Some called them nogi rolls; sometimes they were called hepatitis rolls. We had to pick out the cockroaches, rats tails, flies and other insects before we ate them. Even with the butter we used, they were delicious. As far as I know, no one got sick.

We had a lot of used timber and iron sheets lying around after the old barracks building was knocked down. One of the labourers asked the boss if they could have the timber for their hamlet about 12 miles away. He gave his okay and they loaded up our flat top truck with everything. We had to watch what they loaded. They even took the rusty nails. Next morning, we headed off with an ADG escort and three mates came along for the ride.

The first village after the base was Thap Cham some four miles from the base. Half a mile out of Thap Cham we came to a two-way bridge with a railway track running through the middle. It was an old, rusty steel bridge with wooden planks and some planks were missing or loose. The bridge was about 50 metres long and there was a drop of 70 metres to the river below. The rail line hadn't been used for years. As we crossed the bridge it swayed quite a bit and there was a lot of creaking. Getting to the other end there were five rather grey faces and shaky bodies. We knew we had to return over that same bridge.

On the other side there was a dirt road with lots of potholes and surrounded by jungle that wasn't too dense. The hamlet itself had a school, a few shops and some houses. They were going to extend the community hall with the material we'd brought from the base. They even had an old man straightening the rusty nails. Nothing was wasted.

They fed us and gave us Yankee beer and local beer called Barmi Baa. It tasted like dirty water but had a kick to it. They showed us around. The houses had two to three rooms, an open fire for cooking, and the toilet was in another building with a large deep hole in the middle and very smelly. It was fairly primitive living.

The time flew by. It was getting dark. We were well past our 4 pm curfew. It was a bumpy ride back. On the way, we heard gunfire close by. We didn't know if it was aimed at us or someone else. I put the pedal through the floor. There were cars and bikes coming towards us, but they disappeared into the bush. The adrenalin went sky high. Coming towards the bridge there was no traffic about so without hesitation we crossed it, flat out with a lot of creaking and shaking, but we got across safely. Back inside the base we parked the truck and headed for the bar. I forgot to ring the Base Security Control. The next morning I was summoned to headquarters to explain my action. I wasn't charged, but was reprimanded. No other action was taken. I did mention the shooting and all they said was that the area was out of bounds.

My last trip to the beach on a Sunday nearly ended in tragedy. We decided to have some drinks with some Yanks we had befriended. The only beer they had was the local Barmi Baa. I had three bottles and later on decided to try water skiing for the first time ever. I got up on the skis and then the alcohol hit me – after three beers, I couldn't believe it. The sea was quite calm but in my drunken haze there were 3-metre waves. I fell off the skis and swallowed a lot of sea water. If it wasn't for the quick action of the boat crew, I might have drowned.

The boss noticed some tension in me so I was sent to Vung Tau for R&C (Rest in Country) for three days. Nothing changed. I came back as tense as ever. On return to 2SQN the boss gave me the rest of the week off. In early January several of our group went to Butterworth, Malaysia, for a seven-day R&C. We stayed in the RAAF Hostel in Penang.

The last two weeks of my tour in Phan Rang were quiet except for a couple of mortar attacks that I slept through. Then the day came when we boarded the 'freedom bird' to Saigon. Ours was a Yankee Baby Herc that came from Da Lat with a lot of local civilians being evacuated. They had all their belongings with them: chickens, ducks and pigs in cages. Air con was good – broken windows – noisy, smelly and bloody cold. Spent the night in Saigon and from then it's all a haze. I caught a Qantas charter flight full of army and RAAF personnel and Aussie civilians.

My last memory of Vietnam was the barren landscape and bombed craters. I have no memory of the actual flight home. I remember landing in Sydney late at night and that going through Customs again was a hassle as members were trying to bring in banned items. I had a whole volume of *Sex to Sexty*, a Yankee magazine of sexy cartoons and jokes, nothing dirty. I don't think my Customs officer had that magazine and so he confiscated mine. Finally all the RAAFies who were flying interstate next morning were loaded onto a bus and taken to a hotel in the back streets of Kings Cross. On arrival, we were told to stay in our rooms for our own safety.

We were loaded on the first flight out of Sydney to our destinations. Mine was Melbourne. We were still in uniform and we had our ribbons on. Coming home from war, you expect to be treated with respect, but that wasn't the case when I arrived in Melbourne. Walking along the concourse, I felt like people were avoiding me, and one young, longhaired person spat at me and called me a baby killer. At least I got a happy reception from Robyn – hugs and kisses. I remember getting into a black limo courtesy of the RAAF and arriving at my parents' house. I remember catching up with my brothers soon after. It was really good to be home.

We stayed with Mum and Dad while we were looking for accommodation. As I was posted to Melbourne Telecommunications Unit (MTU) in Frognall, near Camberwell, we found a small one-bedroom flat in Balwyn not far from Frognall. Robyn worked in the city, which took an hour by tram to get to.

I started work in Base Squadron Headquarters Orderly Room collecting messages, cleaning and making coffee for the officers. I was then shifted to Barracks and put in charge of five civilians in their late forties, some of whom were a handful. They didn't like taking orders from a leading aircraftman (LAC). I had, however, passed my corporal exams and was soon promoted to the dizzy heights of corporal. Things were a bit more cordial from then on.

After a few months we moved into third-floor high-rise married quarters in Prahran. Nothing flash. I knew a lot of people at Frognall and with that came an active social life. Sunday football matches against the cadets; hit and giggle cricket match at a local park; and drinks and barbeque at someone's house. Most of us lived in the flats. We also had good sporting competitions on base with volleyball and basketball at lunchtime all year round. It was quite competitive.

One of my mates was a bar member at the Airmen's Club and it wasn't long before I got phone calls at 10 am to help him with the Bar Recce. By lunchtime we'd had a few beers. From then on my drinking was out of control. Some nights I didn't know how I'd driven home or where I'd parked my car. One morning, walking to the car, I noticed a scratch on both sides of it. I asked a mate what'd happened and he said I'd driven on the footpath between gateposts and a fence. On the way to work he showed me where it'd happened.

My first Anzac Day was a disappointment. I was up early, put the 'bag of fruit' on together with my two medals, and headed to Box Hill RSL for the dawn service, only to be ignored by the older diggers. It was a kick in the guts and took a long time to heal. I learnt to live with it; I was a hardened veteran and nothing could hurt me.

Then our first anniversary came and I was out drinking with the boys after work and forgot all about it. I felt very ashamed afterwards and it still haunts me at times. My time at MTU came to an end and I was posted to No 1 Stores Depot (1SD) Tottenham. We remained at the married quarters in Prahran. Being posted away from my mates, I thought I'd be drinking less but that lasted only a few weeks. As the time went on I got to know my work mates and one bloke I served with in Vietnam. He was a Corporal General Hand, same as me, and we had ten civilians to look after between the two of us. It worked out well. Our Corporal Storeman lived in flats in Richmond and had no car so I picked him up every morning and dropped him home at night. We soon got into a routine, stopping on the way to work at an early opener for a couple of beers and a flask of brandy near Victoria Market. The brandy was gone by smoko.

By now I had settled into a happy married life and it got even happier when Robyn announced that she was pregnant. I was over the moon. Happy as I was, I couldn't show my feelings or emotions, but I didn't think anything of it at the time. With news like that, I should have settled down, but no, life went on as before. In 1974, I was posted to No.

75 Squadron, Butterworth, Malaysia with Mirages for two years. I hoped this posting would assist us financially. After settling our affairs, selling the car and putting our meagre furniture into storage, we said goodbye to friends and were on our way.

Being pregnant, Robyn couldn't have the inoculations and at the airport we had some friends seeing us off. After checking in for our flight to Sydney, I decided to have a joke with Robyn saying she couldn't come, as she hadn't had her inoculations. I felt like a dickhead when she broke down crying. I should have realised how vulnerable she was, with the trauma of going overseas and leaving her family, especially her mum.

We travelled by bus to Penang to our married quarters. During our drive I made another king-sized stuff up. As we passed a kampong (Malaysian village) I told Robyn our married quarters were like that; house on stilts. More tears. What a piece of shit I was.

Bus, ferry trip and another bus and we arrived at our married quarters to be greeted by our next-door neighbours with house keys and documents announcing me as the new neighbourhood warden. The reason for having area wardens was that there was still a slight chance of a communist uprising and it was up to the wardens to inform the public of the plans to be put in place if something were to happen.

Getting to work involved a bus to the ferry terminal on Penang Island, then a ferry to Butterworth and a bus to the air base. The trip normally took over an hour. My main job was to tow the Mirages from the flight line to the maintenance hangar. I also serviced aircraft hydraulic jacks, cleaned and repainted the flight machinery, was a unit driver and supervised local Muslim labourers.

With six sports clubs, sport was a big thing. Volleyball was popular and the team I played with reached the grand final every competition and we ended up second. It was the same with softball. We also played ten pin bowling, which was most enjoyable, had darts competitions, social tennis with mates and wives, and golf on Sundays when we had time. I had a very active sporting life.

Our social life was also active. We had dinner dances, dinners out with friends, and card nights once a week where we learnt to play canasta. They were fun nights. Then I started to get upset and angry with my wife for making the wrong decisions and losing the game. It upset everyone, but I thought nothing of it.

Then the happy day came. Robyn went into 3 RAAF Hospital in Butterworth and, being two weeks overdue, she was induced. After a long and difficult labour, she had an epidural and then our baby girl arrived. We were very proud parents. Jacqui kept us on our toes right from the start but she was the apple of my eye. With a family comes responsibility and at times I didn't show it, because of my involvement in sport and thinking about my next drink.

My posting to Butterworth didn't go without incident. There were three of us playing rugby, volleyball and softball for the same club. Most nights after a game or practice, we had a few beers at the local bar called The Cartwheel, which wasn't far from where we lived. After losing our second volleyball grand final, we had a few commiseration beers. As the night went on, we noticed that every time we bought a beer, the price went up. We didn't like being ripped off, so we fronted the head barman and of course he denied it and he ended up wearing a couple of pints of beer all over him. Out of nowhere all the locals turned up and, with a bit of pushing and shoving, we got kicked out. Luckily, someone had phoned the RAAF Police and they were waiting for us outside. They saved us from being badly beaten up.

When Robyn's parents came over for a visit we showed them the local attractions: the snake temple, Reclining Buddha and monkey gardens. We hired a car and went for a drive in the country, but when we came upon a group of armed men coming out of the jungle I had a bit of a heart flutter thinking they were communist guerrillas, then I noticed their uniforms. They were men on patrol from the Malaysian Army. Months before there had been an incident up north in which some guerrillas had robbed, but hadn't hurt, some tourists. Thankfully, the rest of our trip went without incident.

Being an area warden, I was supposed to meet all the new families who arrived in my area. It was the security section's responsibility to send me details of the new families. I didn't get one memo but I did meet some of the families socially. Security section was supposed to brief all the wardens once a month about the alert levels. Not once did we have a briefing. The lack of concern for everybody's safety worried me at times, but it was out of my hands.

We lost three Mirages within a couple of weeks. In the one incident, two were lost when one was ready for take-off while another was landing, and it landed on the stationary Mirage killing its pilot instantly. Then it skidded onto the grass and exploded. A few weeks later a Mirage on its landing circuit lost its power and crashed into a cemetery. The pilot ejected safely only to end up with back problems. I knew him from

Vietnam – a lucky young man. I was in the recovery team and it was a mess.

After the events of those two weeks, memories of Vietnam began returning. No escape from the flashbacks and nightmares. But I managed to live with them.

At times work was challenging, in particular towing the aircraft. I was told, 'You damage it; you pay for it!' It was nerve-racking at times. I only had centimetres between another Mirage and the hangar door. Even if I say so myself, I got very good at it and didn't have any crashes.

While spray-painting the flight line equipment, I was asked if I'd like to re-muster to a Surface Finisher. I jumped at the chance and made an appointment with the Flight Sergeant (FSgt) Surface Finisher. When I arrived, he had returned to Australia. I was disappointed and somewhat relieved because of my self-doubt and fear of failure. I didn't go any further with the re-muster.

Time flew and my time in Malaysia came to an end. My new posting was to the RAAF Academy, Point Cook, Victoria in November 1976. I was very pleased. After final clearances and goodbyes, we were on our way home. It was a good feeling. At first we stayed with Robyn's parents, then we moved into a three-bedroom house in Laverton, which was only twenty minutes by car to work.

RAAF Academy was a school for pilots and navigators and the course lasted for four years. I got friendly with a group of lads from one course and still keep in touch with them. I worked at the Academy hangar, which had everything you needed in a workshop: carpentry, paint, fibreglass, welding and metalwork sections. We had a staff of six in the hangar: one FSgt, one Sgt General Fitter, one LAC Airframe Fitter, one corporal general hand (Cpl GH) and two leading aircraftmen general hands (LAC GHs). The trouble was we all liked a beer. We all got along well together and as long as the work was done, we were left alone. We had a couple of beers every day at Werribee South beach or a counter lunch at the Werribee Hotel. FSgt and Sgt weren't involved but they knew what we were up to. When the administration heard about our trips I was given a friendly reminder about NCO responsibilities. The reminder was noted but ignored.

Over the years, Robyn had expressed her concern about my drinking and the change in my attitude towards people and life in general. I assured her there was nothing to worry about. As it happened in the services, people get posted, so in the next two months my hangar mates got posted out one by one.

My life slowed down a bit at this time and then I got a bellyful of good news. Robyn announced she was expecting our second child. A little brother for Jacqui, I hoped. Life couldn't get any better. With the new FSgt came changes to the hangar. No more drinking at South Werribee, though we still had the occasional counter lunch and we had staff drinks on Friday afternoons as long as the work was done. Sport was a big part of Academy life. We put a team into the base badminton competition and did quite well. I was picked for the RAAF Victorian Inter-service team to play against army and navy teams. Navy won, we came second. I also played volleyball. At least with all the sport we played, I kept fit and enjoyed it. I was an all-round sportsman, but master of none. Then the big day came in March 1978 when Robyn went to hospital and came home with a baby brother for Jacqui and I was over the moon. It was a long celebration. Robyn's parents came down to babysit Jacqui while I was at work. It worked out well, now we were a complete family. We named him Warwick.

In the following year, a few of my mates from Vietnam were posted into Point Cook. Not a good idea; more drinking and late nights. I found it was easier to communicate with them than other people. My life was controlled by an alcoholic fog. I wasn't remembering things, then, at times from nowhere, I had tears in my eyes and started to cry watching movies on television and with real life happenings. Of course, Robyn was worried and she mentioned the VVCS and suggested I go and see them. After some discussion, I said I didn't have a problem, everyone else did, end of discussion.

Robyn's dad had been sick and in and out of hospital for a while. We knew it was only a matter of time, but when the time came at the end of 1982, we were not prepared. It was a sad and emotional time for us. Robyn went to the funeral and I stayed home with the kids.

Then my two veteran mates were posted out and I slowed down, but was still in a haze.

In 1984 I was posted to Base Squadron Barracks at Point Cook and was promoted to Sergeant. With my track record, I was surprised but elated. My work involved supervising sixteen troops in jobs such as weeding, trimming and mowing. The promotion required doing an Orderly Sergeant roster three to four times a year. The jobs included raising the flag at sunrise and lowering it at sunset, patrolling the hangar area along the waterfront, and handling any disturbances at the Airmen's Club before getting the orderly officer or Service Police involved. No drinking was allowed but rules were meant to be broken.

At this time, my dad was seriously ill with inoperable lung cancer. Seeing him suffer and waste away to nothing was sad. Then Robyn phoned me to say he had passed away. Instead of going home to be with Robyn and the kids, I got on the grog and drowned my sorrows. What a creep! No matter what sort of relationship you have with your father, you feel sad and miss them when they are gone.

Once the kids started school, Robyn decided to join the RAAF Reserve (21 Squadron) doing one hundred days a year. She was able to align working hours with school hours. It suited us fine and she enjoyed the work.

Things started to change in the services, including amalgamating and getting rid of some musterings, and bases were closing down. You either had to re-muster or resign. At this time, for me, a new problem arose in the form of horseracing. Both Robyn and I had a bank card to be used in emergencies only. My betting got out of control. During the week, I'd go to the bank for a cash advance of $20 to put on a horse, hoping for a win to help with the finances, but no luck. When the card bill was due in I tried to get home before Robyn to check the letterbox so I could pay the bill without her seeing the withdrawals. Like all my great ideas, it backfired. When Robyn found out, shit hit the fan, big time: tears, my card was destroyed and I wasn't given another. Once more I felt like crap and a feeling of helplessness came over me; a feeling I hadn't had for a while. My betting soon ended. My aim was to stay in the RAAF until compulsory retirement at age fifty-five or I could take a Defence Force Retirement and Death Benefits (DFRDB) pension after twenty years of service. I still had eighteen months of service left until my twenty years was up. Having no trade, and hardly any money in the bank, we wondered how we were going to survive in civvy street. Jacqui and Woz were in school and we needed somewhere to live. We talked it over. Even with my drinking increasing, crying sessions and fits of anger directed towards the family, I was convinced I was okay and everyone else had changed. At the end of 1988, I decided it was time to hang up the boots before I did something stupid and lost privileges. My discharge papers went in. At work they tried to talk me out of it, and even talked about another promotion, but I knew that wouldn't happen as they were getting rid of the GH mustering. I still managed to get into trouble with drinking.

Unknown to me Robyn had been penny-pinching here and there to save money for a house deposit. She'd started working full-time at this stage, while I was pissing it against the wall. I'd realised by then that without her, I wouldn't be here, and she'd saved our marriage by staying with me.

After a few weeks we found a house and, after signing documents and organising bank loans, we were ready to move into our home. I left the RAAF with mixed feelings, more happy than sad. On leaving, I got a retired member's card that gave me access to most bases and Sergeants' Messes in Australia. Very handy.

BACK TO CIVVY STREET

Life slowed down a bit, with no more late nights drinking at the mess or card games. I did have a drink at the mess on Fridays at lunchtime with the mates. The first few weeks I was lost, with no idea of what to do. I checked the papers daily for jobs but found nothing suitable. Then I started a gardening business but with the cost of tools, equipment and fuel, there wasn't much left each fortnight. Just enough for my beer. Luckily, Robyn was working and we had my DFRDB pension and, thanks to Robyn's management skills, we survived.

With increasing nightmares, crying and losing my temper over the smallest things, Robyn tried to convince me to get help at the VVCS. I was adamant that I was okay. She gave up but left a phone number for VVCS on my bedside table.

I go to the Werribee RSL for the dawn service and diggers' breakfast every year, then to the city for the march with the 2SQN WWII veterans. In the early days, it meant a loss of memory for two days at Anzac Day time. There was one Anzac Day that stands out from the rest. I managed to get my mate to come along to the march, even though he wasn't a veteran. He said it was a bit emotional with thousands of people cheering and clapping. I always get emotional and teary.

After the march we went to the Sergeants' Mess in Dorcas Street, South Melbourne. Between drinking and playing two-up and crown and anchor, the time flew. We both had a good win. The mess closed at 6 pm. We had money in our pockets so off to town we went. First stop was an adult only movie-cum-live show theatre. We bought a six-pack of VB, paid our entry fee of $5 and went inside. It was quite dark and hazy inside. We sat down and cracked a tinny and I had a smoke. Then two bouncers materialised from nowhere and escorted us out. No smoking or drinking allowed. We continued looking for places to drink but eventually ran out of options so we found a taxi and arrived home at 4 am. That was my mate's first and last Anzac March with me. We did meet at the mess afterwards but no pub crawls.

It wasn't long before I had a new job as a handyman. It was a public service job at Defence International Training Centre (DITC) at Laverton looking after twelve units, each with four bedrooms, a lounge and a bathroom. Very appealing. It was only for eight weeks until they made it a permanent position. When the time came I applied for the position and went through the interview, which was a bit nerve-racking. Eventually the boss asked me if I wanted the job. Oh boy, was I pleased. I shook his hand and said thank you. My job was safe for now.

I started to notice that things weren't the same at home. Every time I walked into a room the family seemed to tense up like they were afraid of me. My relationship with Jacqui, who was no longer a little girl, was becoming strained, but I had no problem with Woz. As well, at about this time, my younger brother died of cancer. These things started to worry me a bit but I didn't know how to handle them at the time. There were times when I knew I couldn't live like this. I realised I needed to think of my family instead of myself. In trying to find a solution, I thought about moving out and living in the forest in Gippsland somewhere as some veterans had done. I didn't mention this to Robyn.

I found the phone number for VVCS on my bedside table and made the call, hoping that they could help if I did indeed have a problem. When I had a session with the VVCS counsellor, somehow I couldn't communicate with him. I stopped going, even though I knew I might have a problem.

My drinking habits hadn't changed. If anything, I was drinking more. The social life at DITC was great, but it wasn't one that I needed. There were barbeques once a month on Fridays.

Work was going well, although the job was still temporary, and dark clouds had appeared in the distance; the public service was closing down positions across the board. My job classification was GSO2 and I was in danger of losing it. Robyn drafted a letter stating I was a Vietnam vet, a retired member of the RAAF with twenty years of service, and that it was supposed to be government policy to look after veterans.

After a bit more correspondence, I finally got the job permanently. The threat of getting rid of the public servants was still there, so our CO fought for our positions, stating that we were a vital part of DITC. They left us alone after that. In 1995, I was awarded with Department of Defence Australian Day Medallion in appreciation for my outstanding performance at DITC.

Things at home were improving: happy family, happy life. Health-wise, I wasn't in great shape. My way of dealing with any ailment was to ignore it and hope it would go away. At work things started to change, but not for the better. The CO made an announcement that we would be getting Vietnamese students in the near future. My first reaction was, *Bloody Viet Cong*. Workmates said I went pale and started to shake. I knew the war had been over for years but I wasn't ready yet to forgive. I wasn't happy about it, but that's life. Time came for the CO to get posted elsewhere. It wasn't long before they tried to get rid of our jobs. This time they succeeded. The new CO gave up without a fight. I'd been in a depressed mood for a while and with the Vietnamese coming and my job going, I went on my last staff development exercise for four days at a Yarra Valley resort. No BYO alcohol. Stuff them! I took a dozen cans and two bottles of red. I wasn't there for the lectures just for some time off work. One lecture was about workplace safety and atmosphere in the workplace. I voiced my feelings about workplace morale and support for the staff, stating that there was none. I was cut off. I was fuming. Then came a talk, with slides, by an army captain about his experiences in East Timor. I'd had enough. I walked out, got my last bottle of red, found a nice tree, watched the stars and drank the red. I saw a rope dangling from a branch and a tree stump nearby so I jumped on the stump, got the rope, made a loop and put it around my neck. I jumped off but the rope broke. It wasn't my time. I hoped not to do it again.

On return to work they gave me six months' notice and a good redundancy package. The redundancy package and my super paid the mortgage on our house and outstanding bills. It was a good feeling to start retirement debt-free. Robyn was working at the university and had a good job and seemed to enjoy it, so I became the chief cook and bottle washer. I didn't mind the housework and shopping as it kept me occupied. The pay was lousy, no holidays or weekends, but I recommend it.

Unfortunately, my drinking once again got out of hand. I cracked the first tinny about 9 am and during the day I drank while doing my chores.

Before long I was drinking one slab a day. At the time it was light beer, 2.7% alcohol. Most nights I also had a bottle of red.

Jac and Woz were both grown up and working and happy with their lives. Robyn was still working so in May 2004 we decided to take three months off and travel around Australia. Robyn took long service leave. Jacqui got engaged. Happy times. We left on our trip quite excited. We left the kids in charge of the house – no wild parties. We shared the driving: two hours on, two hours off.

After our trip, Robyn returned to work and me to my old habits. It wasn't long before I hit rock bottom. Going to the march on the train on Vietnam Veterans' Day, I noticed six young hoons creating a disturbance. Having had a few beers already and feeling good, I tried to calm the situation. Next minute they turned on me, six against one; not good odds. After a bit of pushing and shoving, I got off the train at the next stop to prevent things escalating and returned home feeling sorry for myself. I had a few more beers and then decided to go to the RSL to await the mates' return from the march. By 7 pm and several more beers, none of them had turned up. Feeling down and out I phoned my son and he took me home. Left alone, I had a few more beers then I decided to ring my daughter to have a chat. I had a feeling she thought something was wrong. (She was in early stages of pregnancy.) Robyn was out with work friends for dinner. After that my mind went blank. I felt so alone, no mates, no family, so I decided I'd had enough. I jumped on a chair outside and attempted once more to take my life. The clothesline slipped and I landed on my ass, somewhat shaken up. I had another beer and after a while Jacqui arrived. She asked if I was okay and I said nothing. She helped me inside and I went to bed. Next morning it was like nothing had happened.

After that it didn't take me long to realise I had a problem. I went to my GP for help and he referred me to a psychiatrist. At that stage I admitted to two attempts on my life. I then made an appointment to see an alcohol counsellor. I said I wasn't an alcoholic but was alcohol dependent. She only laughed. After a few sessions, I was admitted to Ward 17 at Heidelberg Repatriation Hospital for two weeks. I went in voluntarily and after two weeks of counselling and medication, I walked out alcohol-free. After a few sessions with the psychiatrist I was diagnosed with PTSD. It was explained to me that anyone who has been through a life-threatening or traumatic experience could get PTSD. It was nothing to be ashamed of and that I could get help by taking medication and attending the PTSD course. I attended the course with seven other veterans. The group was made up of six from the army, one from the navy and me from the RAAF. We came from different walks of life; some were CEOs and some were labourers like me, but it didn't make any difference. We all had our own demons to get rid of, and we all got along well together. The course, in 2005, went for four weeks. We lived-in during the week and went home on the weekends.

Our accommodation was outstanding and not far from the hospital. It was a block of flats owned by the hospital. We each had our own room with a shower and toilet and a communal dining room for evening meals that I collected from the hospital kitchen each night. At the start of the course I was as nervous as a new kid on the block. Some of the old doubts returned: lack of self-confidence, poor spelling skills and communication. Trying to fit in and be noticed by the group, I started to make some smart-arse comments during the lectures to ease my anxiety only to be told to 'give someone else a go'. Back to reality. We were asked to do a collage, which to me was double Dutch. I had no idea what to do and I was too stubborn and proud to ask for help. Prior to the course, I'd had some blood tests done for diabetes and for cholesterol, both of which came back positive. So more bloody medication! Even though I'd given up drinking, my concentration and thinking was getting all screwed up. Plus, adding to my problems, I was diagnosed with severe sleep apnoea. I gave up smoking as well, from forty a day to nothing. Going cold turkey was hard. Completing the course was, therefore, not easy. Only with the help and support from my loving family and the mates on the course did I manage to finish it. We did cover a lot of subjects during the course and I did absorb some of it, which came in handy later on.

All eight of us formed a lasting friendship with each other and we have barbeques regularly at someone's house. At these meetings, with wives in one room and the husbands in another, we try to help one another with any problems. We had a follow-up program one night a month for twelve months. This had its benefits; so far my no alcohol and no smoking approach is going well and our life is somewhat back to normal.

We had more sad news when my second youngest brother was diagnosed with a brain tumour and nothing could be done for him, but we still lived in hope. He said he wasn't in any pain and that was a blessing. Meanwhile, I started my anger management course once a week for eight weeks at Heidelberg Repat. Being on strong medication, I wasn't allowed to drive, so Robyn drove me everywhere. It was an informative course and with the help of medication, I lost a lot of my anger. On the last day I received the news that my brother had passed away. Another sad time.

Our monthly barbeques were going well and all of us were still on the same planet. We heard about a seven-day live-in lifestyle program so we decided to attend. Unfortunately, the concept of the program was somewhat lost on me. My lack of concentration and little interest in the course didn't help. Even though we were all Vietnam vets, somehow I didn't connect well with the others. Might have been my fault. I don't know.

Life goes on and you face it as best as you can. I bought myself a boat, a five metre half cabin cruiser and it comes in handy when I feel down in the dumps and I can go fishing for a week and think things over. It does relax me. Another tragedy hit us when Robyn's mum passed away. I think she knew her time was up so she flew down to spend her last Christmas with her daughter. She was ninety-two.

As the years went by, I started to slow down and the memory got hazier.

We did a trip to Vietnam with a few mates I served with in 2SQN and it was a bit nerve-racking to start with. Our bus broke down on the way to the hotel in the back streets of Hanoi. It was dark, hot and the smell of incense brought back memories and feelings I hadn't had for some time. We stayed for two days and saw the sights. The war museum was interesting and very anti-American, referencing how they destroyed the country and how badly they treated the Vietnamese. Nothing was mentioned about how the Viet Cong treated their own people to get information. They called it the American War. We went through the 'Hanoi Hilton', Hoa Lo Prison for prisoners of war, and saw the inhumane way in which they treated the prisoners. It was sickening.

The people were friendly with many in military and police uniforms, which made me feel quite uneasy. The highlight of our trip was going to Phan Rang and seeing the air base and an orphanage built by the Australians (now a government school). We laid a wreath at the War Memorial there. The air base was a no-go area but we were able to view it from the top of the hill at the Charm Temple. It was still operational and we saw the Russian Migs on the tarmac. We noticed the Russian influence in Phan Rang and surrounds. Saigon, like Hanoi, is a vast metropolis with millions of people and no road rules to speak of. The locals still call their city Saigon. We visited the old Presidential Palace and it was like a fortress. We did a cruise on the Mekong River, which was very dirty. I'll never complain about our Yarra again!

The trip itself was a bit of a disappointment to me. The first time I really relaxed during the trip was on the flight home. Back home to golf and the occasional fishing trip. Life was good.

Then my mum decided she'd had enough. She was ninety and had dementia. It was sad to see her go.

The memory hasn't improved – must be old age. I fell off the wagon. I had a couple of sly drinks behind Robyn's back; red wine only. She found an empty bottle in the cupboard and confronted me with it. Boy, it made me feel like a real piece of shit. What was I thinking? You can't hide something like that. I'd drunk red wine before but this time I drank it for enjoyment, instead of getting drunk. Still no beer or smokes, which I'm happy about.

Then I turned seventy and everything turned to shit. I got sick. I thought it was flu but after a few weeks it got worse and I had difficulty in breathing and developed a bad cough. I almost passed out after some coughing fits. I had lots of tests done; X-rays, lung function tests, and they even drained my lungs under general anaesthetic. The diagnosis was some sort of lung infection and the appropriate antibiotic was prescribed. No fishing or golf for a while. It got that bad I ended up in hospital for a week with more tests done. Same result. They had no idea. To top it all off, I developed bursitis in the hip and it was painful. There were some days I couldn't get out of bed and was almost in tears. It was cured by medication and exercise. After more trips to hospital with my lung problem, different medication and inhalers, I started to improve after hanging on for twelve months. Even with the way my mind and thinking had been, I managed to keep my thoughts rational and started to put my life in some sort of order.

Then the unthinkable happened; every parent's nightmare. Coming home from golf one afternoon, I noticed two police cars in front of our house. Thinking nothing of it, I walked inside. Jac walked in and my first thought was something had happened to her husband or to our grandchildren. She told us to sit down and then announced that Warwick had been killed in a car accident on the way to work. We didn't want to believe it but the police came inside and confirmed it. Just a little after

6 am on the sixth of October, Warwick was driving up a hill; a car and truck were coming up on the other side of the road. The car overtook the truck on the crest of the hill and hit our son's car head-on, killing him instantly. At least he didn't suffer.

I must have gone into shock because I wasn't much comfort to Robyn and Jac. I remember having difficulty with breathing and going to hospital in an ambulance. After a few hours of observation and some medication, I was able to think more rationally and absorb what'd happened. Then I was able to show some emotion and comfort the girls. Viewing his body was the hardest thing a parent could do. Seeing him lying there, looking so peaceful, I wanted to shake him and say, 'Wake up, son'. When we left, we knew it was the last time we would see him, but he'll always be in our hearts and we have many memories.

Our hearts went out to our son's partner and children. All we can do is be there and support them when they need us. She has her family living in Adelaide to support her as well. The funeral was huge. To see how many hearts our son touched filled me with pride and happiness, as did having complete strangers come to us with tears in their eyes saying what a gentleman he was.

On the flight home, I became anxious and had breathing problems. I ended up in hospital again. With the loving support of my family and friends, I got through the darkest time of my life and we're very supportive of each other. As time goes on, you learn to live with your loss. I think of him first thing in the morning, during the day and last thing at night, and even dream about him at times. I'll never forget him.

Over the months, my breathing settled down to a manageable level and is checked annually.

I decided to cut down on my medication, so I went to see my psychiatrist who recommended I gradually decrease my tablets. After six weeks, I was feeling good in myself, but I didn't notice any change in my ability to think or any improvement in my memory. Then I started to feel irritable, angry and emotional over nothing. I had more nightmares and began thinking, *What's the use? Life is full of disappointment.* I knew then that I was in trouble again so I returned to my psych and he suggested I increase the medication again and monitor it. To my delight it worked fine. From two and a half tablets to one, I might've been over-medicated for a while.

Life is looking a bit brighter but the sadness remains. I've found myself thinking more and more about our son's accident, if you can call it that.

With my health improved, I started playing golf once again and I do a bit of fishing. We did another relaxing and enjoyable cruise around the Pacific Islands. So far this year has gone by without any hassles.

So in closing, your life is what you make of it. Some of us obey and follow the rules to the letter, some of us bend the rules and use them to our own advantage, and there are those who have no regard for rules and the law. I think I've fitted into all three categories at some time in my life. It depends on how you deal with the ups and downs of your life. People can tell you that you have a problem but it is up to you, and only you, to do anything about it. The PTSD Program and my loving family helped me. My advice: don't leave it too late to seek help.

OUR JOURNEY ON MY OWN

Robyn Hirvonen

Pekka and I met in 1969 at Royal Australian Air Force (RAAF) Base Laverton, having come from quite diverse backgrounds. I came from quite a religious family and joined the RAAF in 1969 as a rather immature twenty-year-old, having left school at sixteen. Pekka's family immigrated to Australia from Finland in 1958 when he was twelve. He had difficulty learning the English language and was often taunted at school, so he wagged regularly. He left school and worked in many and varied jobs, including farming and the railways. At twenty-three, he joined the RAAF as a general hand. I worked as secretary to the Commanding Officer.

We met in the Orderly Room and dated for about three months. He was very handsome and had a lovely accent, but he came across as very shy. We started dating and soon became very close. My family was concerned that I was dating a foreigner! Following a posting to Phan Rang, Vietnam in February 1970, we decided to get engaged. Once my parents met Pekka, they soon warmed to him. We married at my home in Woonona, New South Wales on his R&R (Rest and Recuperation) leave in July 1970, and his family travelled up from Melbourne. I was able to stay in the Women's Royal Australian Air Force (WRAAF) as a married member, as new rules allowing WRAAFs to remain in service following marriage had recently been introduced. When he was away we wrote letters nearly every day and we numbered them on the back of the envelope, so that if many letters arrived at the one time, we were able to read them in sequence.

This is a poem I wrote in one of my letters:

My husband to be; so far away from me
I long for your touch, and I miss you so much;
My love for you will grow; but never will you know
How much you mean to me; my husband to be.

On Pekka's return in February 1971, I resigned from the RAAF and we started our married life together, virtually as strangers; the person who returned from Vietnam was quite different from the carefree, loving man who had left. Pekka told me that he'd lost the ability to show love and affection and I felt this deeply. For the first two years, we both had sleepless nights from his nightmares and night sweats. He never spoke of what his nightmares were about or of the bad experiences he had, only about the light-hearted pranks and escapades he and his mates got up to.

Having moved into RAAF married quarters in Prahran, I was a long way away from family and friends and felt very lonely, but I had a very good job managing an Australia-wide account for an insurance broker, so I put a lot of time and energy into that.

We had some friends from Pekka's work and enjoyed regular card nights on pay night at each other's houses. Pekka regularly stayed back at the base drinking with his friends and would often come home in the early hours of the morning, sometimes forgetting where he'd parked his car. I felt very much alone at this time and I worried that he didn't love me anymore. I also worried that he'd have an accident in the car when drinking. I didn't drink or smoke and I often felt like an outsider at social functions.

Three significant things happened in 1974: I got my driver's licence, which gave me a boost in confidence; we were posted to Malaysia; and I fell pregnant. We lived on Penang Island and Pekka caught the ferry every day over to Butterworth for work. He really enjoyed his time in Penang and was involved in many sporting activities. I had difficulty coping with the heat, so I often stayed home alone. It was then that I developed a love of reading. We also had a good group of friends and played canasta at each other's houses.

Pekka was 'over the moon' when our beautiful little girl arrived, though he'd been pretty sure we'd have a boy. Three years later, on return to Australia, our gorgeous little boy arrived. Pekka was involved with the golf club, so as the children grew up, I took them to all their sporting events on a Saturday. I also taught the kids to drive. Each year, we went on camping trips with friends, which the kids enjoyed immensely. One passion Pekka passed on to his son was his keenness for fishing and they've enjoyed a couple of fishing trips together.

I didn't work in the early years after having the kids, and finances were a struggle, which caused a lot of stress for me. But Pekka never went without his beer and smokes. Once the kids went to school, I started working part-time and eventually full-time, which made an incredible difference to our financial situation. Pekka was always very much in charge at home and if I tried to talk to him about his behaviour, he'd shut me down by saying, 'Don't nag me, I can't stand women who nag'. I had very little confidence during these years.

He went to a few squadron reunions with his No 2 Squadron friends, as well as the Welcome Home Parade in Sydney in 1988. He found a lot of solace from meeting up with these mates. They'd drink very heavily. He always went on the Anzac Day marches and would come home in the early hours of the morning completely inebriated. On one occasion, he'd had recent surgery and wasn't able to attend the Anzac march. As we watched it on TV, he began to cry; yet another indicator that he needed help. During this period, I focused my energy on the kids to ensure that they had the best I could afford to give them.

After completing twenty years in the RAAF, Pekka retired. As I'd worked full-time at Victoria University for a few years, we'd saved for a deposit on our home, which we purchased on his retirement from the RAAF. He worked for himself as a gardener, but wasn't able to earn much, so we were back to one wage, which became a struggle as the children grew older. He then got a job working as a civilian in the RAAF International Training Centre as a maintenance person, a job he enjoyed immensely until such time as the Vietnamese students came to the centre. His attitude changed and he wasn't coping with day-to-day contact with these people. The kids said the atmosphere in our home was like walking on eggshells, as any excessive noise they made would cause their father to be annoyed with them. The nightmares returned and I knew that something was very wrong. I tried to talk to him, but as far as he was concerned he didn't have a problem. I telephoned the VVCS and told them, 'My husband needs help'. They told me that he had to ask for help himself and they couldn't help until he contacted them, which was very frustrating. I left the phone number of VVCS on his bedside table. A year or so later, he decided to make the call, which was followed up by having counselling with a VVCS counsellor. He didn't have much faith in the counsellor and said, 'How could he know what I'm going through when he hasn't been to Vietnam?'

At work his bosses noticed his behaviour and he was cautioned on a number of occasions. Eventually, in 2002, he was made redundant. Following this, unbeknown to me, he began drinking heavily during the day.

We had a good relationship as long as I didn't confront him on his drinking or behaviour. Once again, he didn't want to be nagged. The kids loved their father dearly, but they always knew there was a limit to how much he would tolerate. I think the reason our marriage survived was that, even though there were difficult times, we always showed respect to each other and never swore or fought, but there were times when we didn't speak for a week or so!

Eventually the GP referred him to a psychiatrist, to whom Pekka revealed that on two occasions he'd attempted to take his life. I was shocked beyond belief and very upset. He was prescribed anti-depressants and referred to Heidelberg Repatriation Hospital, where, in Ward 17, he underwent a month of detox from alcohol. Next he participated in the PTSD Program at Heidelberg that involved a live-in period of four weeks, then weekly sessions with the PTSD team. A counsellor phoned to see if I'd be able to attend the wives' part of the program. She asked me how I was coping and I burst into tears, as no one had asked me how *I* was coping – it was always about Pekka. I felt a sense of relief. My boss at the time was very understanding and allowed me to attend a weekly session for the wives at Heidelberg. I also commenced counselling with VVCS and it helped me enormously.

It was very hard to leave him at the hospital for detox, but once we started the PTSD Program, I felt quite comfortable that he was finally receiving the help he needed. On the first day wives and husbands attended a session together in which the psychiatrists outlined the symptoms of PTSD, telling us there was no cure, but that the guys would be given strategies to cope with their symptoms.

The class of 2005 was formed. The wives' group met weekly and we soon became very frank in our discussions of our experiences living with our vets. There was a great sense of relief that I wasn't the only one dealing with life with a vet and a great camaraderie was formed with both the men's and women's groups. The psychologists who were helping our husbands also came to speak to the women's group and we told them our stories. They gleaned a lot more information from us than from our men. Following the Heidelberg part of the program, we then met weekly at Kew with a VVCS counsellor. The men and women met separately. There was a great trust built up within the group and we knew that we couldn't lose touch, so decided that we'd continue to meet monthly at each other's houses on a Sunday for a meal and get-together, which also included a time in which the girls and guys would separate to discuss how we were progressing.

Sadly, we lost one of our girls to cancer, but Chris will be with us always in our hearts. There were many occasions in the girls' group when there would be tears. The support from the other women was wonderful. Even though the boys touched on their various issues, they'd often use the sessions to catch up on the latest jokes; they didn't seem to use the social group to get the same support that the women were able to give to each other. We could talk very frankly about what we'd been through over the years and how we were coping at that time.

A few years ago, Pekka decided that life was too short to miss out on the things he enjoyed and he started drinking red wine again; secretly at first, but soon discovered! I was very concerned so I contacted the Repat Hospital. As he'd abstained for a few years, the counsellor said he could perhaps go ahead, as long as it didn't get out of control. At this stage he's been able to keep it at a reasonable level, although I still worry when he's been drinking and driving.

Our group still meets a number of times a year and, even though there are still a lot of ongoing issues, we know that we're only a phone call away from someone who will listen and understand. We recently went away for a girls' weekend and enjoyed it so much we decided to do it again. The support from these girls is unbelievable.

One important thing I learned from the PTSD Women's Program was to take care of myself so that I'm well enough to care for and support my husband. There have been occasions when I haven't coped and became anxious, and I found the VVCS counselling sessions were very helpful. On occasions I've taken anti-depressants.

A few years after he'd completed the program, we holidayed in Vietnam with a group of friends from Pekka's old squadron. Pekka felt very apprehensive about the trip. When our bus broke down near Hanoi, Pekka became very agitated, but eventually a local Vietnamese man came along and shook all the boys' hands, showed them his photo in a North Viet Cong uniform and said, 'No hard feelings', in broken English. We all found it hard to hold in the emotions.

My husband continues to take anti-depressant medication, along with other medications for various conditions. He doesn't have the arrogance he used to have and will try to listen and participate in a discussion, if I have some concerns to air. Following the program we've settled down to a quiet lifestyle and we try to get away on holidays each year. We have two absolutely wonderful and supportive children and four equally wonderful grandchildren. We also have a little puppy, Molly, whom we both adore!

It's been about two years since I first wrote my story and, in that time, we lost another one of our girls to cancer. Glenda was such a kind and gentle soul and she is sorely missed by each and every one of us.

Then the most unimaginable thing happened. We lost our son, Warwick (Woz to most), in a tragic car accident in October 2016. He was only thirty-eight and left behind a lovely partner and two beautiful kids, aged five and six. The accident was the result of a driver who may have been afflicted by alcohol and drugs and was escaping police custody. This has been such a devastating blow to us and something we'll never come to terms with, but we are a close family and have stuck together through our grief as best as we can, with the help of our beautiful daughter, Jacqui. I'm having grief counselling through VVCS. The support I got from Pekka during this time was enormous and I couldn't have got through it without him. Also the support from 'the Class of 2005' and our friends has been wonderful. We miss Woz every day and find it hard to get through life without him, but we must.

There are so many women still out there, living with their vet husbands and enduring a difficult life. These guys might be sitting quietly, but you can be sure there are many thoughts spinning around in their heads. I try to pass on the information that we received to women I meet, but most won't follow through with the advice. If, however, you're reading this and you have a husband experiencing post-conflict difficulties, please contact either your GP or VVCS yourself. They can and will help you.

Robyn and Pekka Hirvonen

FOR WHAT IT'S WORTH

Terry Wolff

Spring has sprung and the Wolff can no longer hide in his den. The best way to tell my story is from the very beginning until the time my marble came out of the barrel and I went into the army, then to Vietnam and finally, the direction my life has taken since then.

I was born in Camberwell on 22 February 1949, third in line, after my older sister and brother. Our family consisted of Mum, Dad and seven children, four girls and three boys. After my mother's death, I discovered she'd had a daughter prior to marrying my father. This and other issues may have caused tension between my parents, which had quite a detrimental effect on us as children.

On the surface ours seemed a normal, happy and good Catholic family. My father held a senior position with the Olympic Tyre and Rubber Company, where he worked for forty-five years. He could be a very affable, affectionate, loving dad, but was inclined to severe mood swings that changed his personality and affected my mother. His mood swings usually occurred when he'd been drinking, so we children would try to keep out of his way at these times. Strangely we never weathered the storm together. I distinctly remember my two brothers and I sitting in our bedroom, not saying anything to each other, waiting for the situation to improve. In a relationship like this, there always existed in the back of my mind a question as to when the next confrontation might occur. As I moved into my teens, I began to stand up to my father, which sometimes caused physical confrontation.

I mention these negative aspects of my life and the effect on me in relation to how I coped with stress during my two years in the army, especially in Vietnam. While I'm on the negatives, I was a victim of bullying around my mid-teens when I started a new school. This lasted for a couple of years and didn't do much for my confidence, academic pursuits and general self-esteem.

Enough of the negatives for the moment. As a kid life was full of excitement. Roaming the neighbourhood with friends and spending a lot of time at the local creek where there was plenty of open space, bush and blackberries; building forts with rocks; digging underground huts; making tunnels through blackberries; constructing shanghais, bows and arrows; then graduating to slug guns. Talk about training for the army! When everything was running smoothly at home, life could be very pleasant. Dad had a good sense of humour and could be great company. Memories flood back of holidays at Rye and Dromana over a period of years. When I think of my mother, I feel a great sense of love and gratitude and always felt close to her.

When I left school, I started work with the ES&A (English, Scottish and Australian) Bank at Blackburn. I was there for about five months then went onto the relieving staff. I enjoyed my time in the bank but felt, at the time, it wasn't the career for me. Work wasn't hard to obtain and I worked for a while in a factory, then as a storeman. The following year, I decided to go back to school to complete my matriculation at the local high school. During this year, I was called up for National Service. As it turned out, I only passed a couple of subjects, pure and applied mathematics and calculus – should've been a mathematician! Anyway, I worked in a factory until the Big Day.

The first of September '69 found me at Swan Barracks with a few hundred other lottery winners. At this stage NCOs (Non-commissioned Officers) were quite jovial and pleasant as we boarded buses for Puckapunyal. The situation changed when we arrived at Pucka. Sergeants and various NCOs shouted out harsh commands. A march in fast time to the barbers – like an assembly line. Even guys who had smart, short haircuts prior were shorn. Issue of uniforms and other associated paraphernalia. Then we were sent to our companies and platoons. I was 3 Platoon, A Company. The guys in my hut were a good bunch from different walks of life, all thrown together, many of us sharing the same birth dates.

Basic training was a hard slog. As recruits we were treated as sub-human until the day we finished and were promoted to the great rank of private. They needed to teach us basic army skills and to obey orders without question. The training was very effective, with a strong emphasis on teamwork and developing a real sense of camaraderie.

After basic training, I was posted to infantry training at Singleton. Infantry wasn't one of my choices. I guess more 'grunts' (infantrymen) were required at that particular time.

Corp training was fairly demanding, but we were treated a lot better by officers and NCOs. The role of an infantryman was definitely drummed into us.

After completing Corp training, the next stop was Ingleburn where we filled in time, waiting to be sent to Vietnam as reinforcements. We spent three weeks at the Jungle Training Centre, Canungra and flew to Vietnam on 12 August 1970.

I served in Vietnam from 12 August 1970 to 12 August 1971. Most of this time was spent in D&E (Defence and Employment) Platoon attached to Headquarters Company, 1ATF (1st Australian Task Force), Nui Dat. Although not attached to a battalion, D&E was a very active infantry platoon that operated around Nui Dat and throughout various areas of Phuoc Tuy Province. In the previous year, D&E had a tally of thirty enemy killed in action. One of the first things I remember seeing at D&E was a large tally board with small figures representing the number of Viet Cong (VC) killed.

I arrived at D&E with six other reinforcements to replace members of the platoon who'd been injured when an armoured personnel carrier (APC) on Operation Massey Harris had reversed over a 30-pound land mine. They'd been on an operation to destroy and eradicate enemy agricultural plots, bunker systems, tunnels and building structures, and any enemy personnel they made contact with.

On arriving at D&E, I initially noted that it was potentially quite an effective killing machine, but at the same time I knew that I was also replacing casualties on our side. I came to the realisation, while being airlifted by chopper out to Massey Harris, that this wasn't a game and involved people being killed and injured. As a result of this revelation, I can honestly say I genuinely feared for my life.

OPERATION TO MASSEY HARRIS ON 10 SEPTEMBER 1970

While patrolling, D&E located a 1000-pound unexploded aerial bomb from which the Viet Cong had been extracting explosives. It was decided that the remainder of the bomb be destroyed with plastic explosive. While we were taking shelter in thick jungle about 300 metres away, another huge bunker system and garden were discovered. After clearing the bunker system and establishing a secure harbour position, some members of D&E were sent back to the bomb to blow it up. While this was happening, contact was made with enemy on the perimeter of our harbour position. After shots had been fired with no result, my section of the platoon was sent out to sweep the area to locate and capture or kill the enemy. All this was occurring while waiting for the bomb to detonate. The enemy was not located but on returning to our position, there was an almighty explosion, much greater than anticipated, where the earth shook and bomb shrapnel flew all around us. The combination of these events proved very traumatic for me and the other members of the platoon. The experience set the trend for the remainder of the operation.

A Platoon Commander's Perspective

D&E Platoon was involved in (Op) MASSEY HARRIS. The units on the Op were tasked with finding and destroying enemy vegetable crops and camps in an area to the East of the Task Force's Area of Operations.

Apparently these crops had been established sporadically throughout the area, mainly under the cover of the vegetation canopy and every other endeavour had been taken to camouflage them. I understood that the gardens were managed from enemy located in the May Tao Mountains and provided food for the enemy in the area. Most of the gardens that we'd found had a small camp of some kind, located either on its edge or close by. Camps normally consisted of a small hut/humpy and one or two bunkers. The people [we expected to encounter] were local guerrillas, sometimes with family. Their normal reaction was to avoid conflict. The locations of these gardens were previously established by SAS and air photographs. We located the others during our searching for those already identified. The destruction of the gardens was carried [out] by exploding a combination of 44-gallon drums of defoliant, diesel and petrol over the area. When [detonated], this combination created a fireball, which covered the area, destroyed the crop and contaminated the area.

Whilst clearing the surrounding area with clearing patrols, a bomb was discovered standing on its tail, leaning against a tree. The top [had been] cut off and it appeared from its state that someone was trying either to take the explosive from it or it was being set up as a booby trap. I decided that it should be destroyed. Receiving permission to proceed, I then tasked Cpl Jack McIntyre to destroy it.

Cpl McIntyre's group were still out at their task when a single shot rang out. This was followed by a considerable amount of firing by members of the platoon engaging in the immediate area. Apparently an enemy soldier had been watching us from behind a tree, some 30 metres out from the perimeter.

Just prior to the contact I heard Cpl McIntyre call out, 'Fire on', from the area of the bomb, an indication that he'd set the explosives to destroy the bomb and had lit the fuse.

As the contact gained momentum, it appeared as though we were being engaged by a number of enemy because of the heavy weapon fire ... coming from the area. This was reason for concern because of our location in relation to the May Tao Mountains, distance from other friendly forces, our size, and [signs of enemy presence] in previous days. It was obvious from freshness of various tracks that we'd crossed that there were enemy in the area, at least platoon size, with the potential to be a reasonable threat.

Shortly after the commencement of the conflict, the bomb set for demolition exploded. There was a horrendous noise accompanied by considerable amount[s] of shrapnel and debris. The explosion and subsequent fallout seemed to have a sobering effect on all of us because everyone seemed to stop firing and it caused a significant lull in proceedings. After a short break, some intermittent fire resumed with a considerable amount of noise from the scrub beyond the contact, which seemed to indicate that the enemy were withdrawing. The enemy's disengagement was influenced by the uncertainty of the explosion and the sound of the APCs and tanks starting up and moving in our direction. Their situation could've also been compounded by the impact of naval fire support being ranged into their area from the north from a destroyer off the coast to our south shortly after the commencement of the contact.

At some time after all this chaos, a section was sent to clear the area where the enemy were believed to have been.

Further investigation of the area established that the enemy had probably withdrawn along tracks [formed] by cutting brush up to head height, and fresh boot prints and scuff marks [were found]. The combination of this contact and enemy 'sign' increased our concern about the enemy and made us extremely apprehensive [of] their intentions.[1]

MAY TAO OPERATION
28 JANUARY – 30 JANUARY 1971

The May Taos were regarded as a VC and NVA (North Vietnamese Army) stronghold. The enemy felt safe here. It was an area honeycombed with bunker systems of various sizes. The Australians never tackled the May Tao hills in force. We were taken to the area by choppers, but because the jungle was so heavily forested the helicopters couldn't land. While a small squad of Special Air Service (SAS) troops covered the area below, we had to be winched down individually with all our gear. This was a risky business as the stationary chopper, plus those being winched down, were sitting targets from enemy fire. We hadn't been patrolling on the ground for long when we came across an extensive bunker system and discovered a large cache of weapons and explosives. One of the greatest fears was of stepping on a mine or triggering a booby trap. This operation only lasted a short time because it was discovered through intelligence that there was a large NVA force in the area. I found this whole operation to be very stressful.

OPERATION OVERLORD 18 MAY – 16 JUNE 1971

Operation Overlord required D&E Platoon to man and defend Courtney Hill, which was 250 metres high and commanded an all-round view of the surrounding area. Our job required us to do daily foot patrols around the base of Courtney Hill. As well as this we did reconnaissance patrols with a section of armoured personnel carriers from 3 Cav (3rd Cavalry Regiment).

On 10 June 1971, while patrolling at the base of Courtney Hill, 2 Section came across a mound containing a body. I, with another member of the section, was asked to unearth the body for identification and then re-bury it. This was a very painful and stressful experience. The corpse was partly decomposed. It made matters worse knowing we had to continue the job of identifying the body and then re-bury it. I'll never forget the impact the smell of that body had on my senses. It's something that my sense of smell hangs on to, even now.

On 11 June our section, with other members of D&E and a section of 3 Cav, came across footprints of about eight to ten people, moving along a track by a creek. We followed this track for about two kilometres before we returned to Courtney.

The following day, 12 June, some members of D&E with 3 Cav, returned to the track that was discovered the day before. Peter Tebb, a member of D&E and the machine gunner in 2 Section, had volunteered to go out and asked if I'd be his Number 2. I genuinely said that I didn't much feel like it, as I'd gone out the day before. Driscoll, another D&E member, volunteered to be his Number 2.

The patrol had been out for about two hours when we heard an explosion followed by a much louder one, then gunfire. Courtney Hill, which included the remaining half of D&E, went into high alert, expecting the worst. Within what seemed like a long time, we found out through radio messages that the patrol had been ambushed and one of the APCs had been hit by a rocket that'd detonated claymore mines and an ammunition box on top of the APC. We knew that there were casualties and later found out that five of our platoon had been killed, plus two from 3 Cav.

Those of us who remained at Courtney were shattered. We felt helpless to do anything. Our feelings were mixed – great sadness and a rising anger that made us want to even the score and seek revenge. I felt something I've only become aware of recently: survivor guilt. In a way I wished I'd been there.

To lose five comrades was a great shock and I still feel angry when I think of this terrible loss – for what?

Every time we went outside the wire at Nui Dat base, someone was potentially trying to kill us. It's not a very pleasant thought.

DISCHARGE

I was discharged from the army on 1 September 1971 and I expected to slip back into 'normal' civilian life. I became very restless and decided to head off. I travelled up the eastern coast of Australia, working for the Water Board in Sydney for a while, then a factory in Brisbane and finally finished up in Mareeba, North Queensland, on a tobacco farm.

This type of lifestyle continued for quite a few years, coming back to Melbourne for a time, and then deciding to take off again. I worked in Cairns for about six months and then headed down to Alice Springs, picking up work there for a few months.

In the winter of 1974, I was back in Melbourne working for the Fuel and Grain Merchant in Blackburn, bagging briquettes at the railway siding and delivering the 'black diamonds' to the local area. This also included delivering grain, hay and chaff to various places including dairies in the area, which were still using horse and cart.

Early in 1975 a mate and I caught the train to WA. I stayed there for a couple of months then bought an old Holden and drove back across the Nullarbor to Melbourne. The Nullarbor road was still dirt at that stage. For the remainder of that year, I worked again for the Fuel and Grain Merchant and in 1976 returned to the west, where I worked on an Aboriginal mission as a baker and bus driver for two years.

After leaving the mission, I worked in Perth for about eighteen months then headed north with a friend up to the Kimberleys, across to Darwin, over to North Queensland and down the eastern coast to Sydney. Then it was back to Melbourne.

I worked in Melbourne for a swimming pool company, The Pool Doctor, mainly installing outdoor spas, which were the big thing at the time.

At the end of 1980, I decided to head back to the west with the idea of finding work in the Kimberleys. On the way I stopped off at Wandalgu, the mission I'd previously worked on, to say hello. They needed a bus driver and baker for '81 and asked if I'd volunteer my services. After thinking about it for a couple of days, I decided to stay. This was also when I met the lovely Glenda, who was working there as well.

At the end of 1981, Glenda and I returned to Melbourne. She resumed work with a previous employer and I worked for a friend who was a house re-stumper. Not the most pleasant form of employment but with a couple of good mates we worked for Ron, the boss.

Unfortunately we were involved in an industrial accident in August when a house collapsed, killing two guys, one a very good friend and the other, a brother-in-law of Ron, who was out from England on a working holiday. This very unfortunate incident had an adverse effect on me and left me in a fairly bad state for a few months.

Due to my state of mind and indecisiveness, my relationship with Glenda was affected. She decided to head back to the west to volunteer her services on the mission at the start of 1983. About a month later, having come to my senses, I joined her.

After catching up with Glenda again, I moved to Geraldton and picked up work as a shed hand on a shearing team. The contractor I worked for talked me into doing a wool classing course at Geraldton TAFE College with the view of running one of his teams after I'd got my classer's stencil. While I attended TAFE in Geraldton, I worked as a shed hand in my free time and stayed in touch with Glenda, who was about 170 kilometres away.

At the end of 1983, Glenda came into Geraldton and we moved in together. This was the start of a great partnership that still exists today.

Glenda picked up different work in Geraldton and I continued on in the wool industry, classing for a shearing team. Our run was mainly in station country throughout the Murchison and part of the Gascoyne areas. This meant being away from Geraldton and Glenda, sometimes for up to two or three weeks. It was a different lifestyle altogether and reminded me somewhat of my army days.

During 1985 Glenda became pregnant. At first it was a shock but after a long time I decided to take responsibility for our situation and made a commitment to her, and our impending offspring, to play the role of partner and father. I'm so glad I did.

Glenda decided she'd like to go back to Melbourne, closer to family. It was going to be for a year, but after the birth of our beautiful daughter, Meagan, signs of our next child, Chris, appeared. Our lives changed fairly dramatically and we decided to stay in Melbourne.

Within less than five years we had four children: Meagan, Chris, James and Emily. We decided after Meagan was born to make the full commitment and were married in June 1986.

We bought a house in the Upper Yarra Valley after a couple of years and have lived there ever since.

I mainly drove trucks work-wise, and then ran the shed for an organic food company for the last twelve years of my working career.

In 2004 I started to suffer from fairly severe anxiety attacks that led me to being very re-active and paranoid in situations that, in the past, I could handle or cope with. In 2005 I had a very bad panic attack one Saturday morning in Yarra Junction. I went to my GP whose initial opinion was that I was suffering from depression. He prescribed anti-depressant medication and referred me to a psychiatrist in Lilydale. The psychiatrist altered my medication and in turn referred me to a psychologist.

In talking to the psychologist, my experience in the army and especially Vietnam started to come to the fore. After a few sessions with her and doing some tests, she suggested I may have PTSD. I had a few more sessions with the psychiatrist in which Vietnam was also mentioned.

My psychologist suggested that it might be a good idea to apply to do the PTSD course in Ward 18 at Heidelberg Repatriation Hospital. I was eligible to do the course and this is where I met other vets who had similar problems to mine.

We all came from different backgrounds and had been exposed to different life experiences. I feel that the only common thread that linked us was that we'd all had fairly difficult childhoods in one way or another. It was a remarkable and valuable experience to do the course with such interesting guys and so was the fact that we got on so well and still do to this day.

Our partners are also a very close-knit group and with their efficient organisational skills have probably been more responsible than the men for keeping the group together.

The PTSD course was invaluable in helping us identify and understand why we sometimes felt the way we did and gave us strategies to use in coping with our stressors.

In April 2006, after a session, my psychiatrist said to Glenda and me that he felt I wouldn't have a great problem getting a TPI (Totally and Permanently Incapacitated) pension. I received the TPI within a couple of months after that appointment.

Since the PTSD course over ten years have passed. With the help and support of our group of 'crazies', and being able to personally rationalise and understand more clearly the problems we face, life has improved greatly.

GLENDA'S STORY – SADLY INTERRUPTED

Glenda Wolff

When I first met Terry, he was eight years out of the Army and it was nine years since he was conscripted. Mutual friends in Perth introduced us in January 1981.

I was working in a remote part of Western Australia and he was travelling through to Broome. He had ties to where I was working and, a few days after we met, he called in on his way north and ended up staying and working on the property for a year. We hit it off from our first meeting and the rest, as they say, is history.

I knew that Terry had been in the army and I think I knew that he'd been to Vietnam, but it's not something I remember being concerned about, so obviously not a subject we talked about.

Terry had spent eight years travelling the length and breadth of Australia and had many funny and interesting stories to tell of people he'd met and the jobs he'd done. He seemed footloose and exciting to me, not unsettling and confusing.

Our relationship was on reasonably solid ground and we lived and worked in Geraldton for a few years. Terry had completed a TAFE course in sheep management and became a wool classer. He joined one or two shearing teams and travelled and worked throughout the Murchison area. I worked in and around Geraldton. Life was good in our cute little duplex in Beachlands.

When we started our family, I wanted to return home to my family and, luckily, we both came from Melbourne. We always had a loose idea that we'd return to settle in the west, but a rather quick succession of four babies changed our minds!

Our first two children, Meagan and Christopher, were born in Williamstown and our second two, James and Emily, were born in the Yarra Valley, where we settled and have lived for the last thirty years.

Terry worked locally initially and both of us were kept busy raising our children. We were involved in our community and then school. Those were happy and busy years and we all thrived in one of the most beautiful areas in outer Melbourne. As we both came from large families, we spent a lot of time visiting 'down the line' and had many pleasant barbies and sleepovers at home.

I was a busy mum, a part-time worker and a driver of children in our people carrier, so I'm not sure when I started to take notice of Terry's mood swings and slow disconnection.

On reflection it could've been on his fiftieth birthday when we had a big all day and night party at home for family, old friends and new friends; after which, and for the following few years, we entertained at home a bit less. Quite often I took the kids to Melbourne alone, as I knew Terry needed his own space, but I'd no idea why.

Terry was a truly loving husband, supportive and kind. His devotion to his children was so clear. He was a very hands-on dad and they all adored each other. But underlying all that something was wrong.

When Terry was fifty-five he had a breakdown and sought help from our local doctor who was also a friend. Peter recognised something in Terry that I'd completely missed. He knew Terry was a Vietnam veteran and proceeded to diagnose his symptoms. Terry was then referred to a psychiatrist in Ringwood.

Vietnam! I thought. *What's that got to do with the now?* He'd slowly withdrawn from me and I hadn't particularly noticed it. I thought we were just bogged down with normal family responsibilities and commitments. I thought that our marriage was strong and as we loved each other we would survive this. The children were getting older and more independent of us, so we'd have plenty of 'our time' together when fun and happiness would again surface.

Terry still seemed able to function with people. He was always the life of the party and liked by all. We'd holiday, usually camping with family and friends as much as possible. I felt I was the only one who truly knew the dark times Terry was going through and that's a lonely place to be in. Terry's bouts of moodiness and listlessness were occasional but progressed over a couple of years to something a lot more troubling

– depression. Not something I had a lot of knowledge about, but soon became an expert on.

The psychiatrist Terry was seeing over this period of time didn't seem to be helping things (in my opinion) until one day when I was invited to accompany Terry to a session. Terry had written out a statement outlining events that took place during his time in Vietnam and I was shocked.

It was the day I understood Terry's torment and realised the pressure that must have been building for years and had no release, trapped inside his mind. Feelings of helplessness, flashbacks, guilt, vulnerability, fatigue and loneliness.

Terry told us of his Vietnam War experiences. Stories I'd never heard before. I was crying my eyes out by the end of that session. The hard-faced psychiatrist was equally moved and started the ball rolling to give us access to more intense help than a session every few weeks.

Di Cronin from Heidelberg Repatriation Hospital contacted me at work in mid-2004 and invited Terry and I to participate in a PTSD group therapy course. It was a live-in situation for the blokes and a one-day-a-week commitment from the partners.

That phone call changed both our lives. I was versed in depression but I'd never heard of PTSD. I'd been living with it, not knowing its name, but I soon came to know it well.

Heidelberg Repat opened up a whole new world to me personally. I'll let Terry tell his version of events from that first meet and greet morning in October 2005.

I can honestly say that I knew very few Vietnam veterans until that day, as Terry hadn't kept contact with many old mates over the years.

At the age of seventeen, I hadn't taken a lot of interest in conscription and the Vietnam War. I was going out at the time with a boy whose family was friendly with mine, and his older brother was best mates with my older brother, Terry. Hence, I was allowed to date, under supervision. This boy became a conscript. His parents took me to have lunch with him in Seymour while he was in training. They also picked me up early one morning and we drove to Wagga Wagga for his passing out parade. No mean feat in those days from Pascoe Vale! It was all very romantic and exciting for a young girl and the young men all looked so handsome and polished in their uniforms. I still have his official photo in my album. He didn't go to Vietnam and I lost track of him after a while. I went overseas to London on a working holiday in 1971 and anti-war protests passed by me.

Back to Heidelberg and our first day. The other couples all seemed quite chatty, happy and normal, but as I'd already discovered, looks can be deceiving.

I learned that Terry was suffering from an illness, a disease – incurable as it turns out, but manageable under the right conditions. I promised myself that from that day forward I'd learn all I could about this illness and be the supportive partner. Terry needed me to rely on and see him through whatever was to come for us.

The four-week course turned out to be my personal saviour. I left Terry with the experts and I could only imagine the intense pressure he would've been under.

My one-day commitment to the partners' group consisted of meeting with the men over a yummy morning tea, a quick kiss and hug and then off to our separate sessions. The partners' group became my lifeline at a time when I felt helpless and alone in a sea of bewilderment. How can you watch the person you love suffer and have no way of breaking through that to help?

We were, as were the men, an eclectic group of ladies, all within a couple of years of each other, but all having travelled down the same road to this room. There at the Repat we were encouraged and guided to tell our own story of survival and torment, of family, love, hardship and perseverance. We loved our men and we all realised that we were each telling a similar tale. Di Cronin and her colleague Moira Healy were slowly able to tease out each of our stories. For each of us, it was the first time we'd felt safe to reveal our own personal torment. We were listened to with empathy, allowing us to speak of our worries, and with that our burdens were lightened. We forged a friendship in those weeks that is still with us today. We can ring each other at any time and have a chat, because even though our boys were put on the right track, the tendency to stray back to old habits can still surface.

The men and women of this PTSD group are still our firm friends, having made a commitment in those early days to stick together. We were the very lucky ones who forged a bond early. Able to rely on each other, we knew there was always help if things started to get out of hand.

Much has happened in twelve years, but I thank God for that phone call inviting us to participate in the PTSD Program. It gave us knowledge, support and the strength to soldier on!

The ripple effect on our children was always going to be positive and it gave me the tools to access help of my own. We've had support for the children's education needs; not to mention two Long Tan Bursaries and education allowances for tertiary studies. These have helped our burden substantially.

I can't speak highly enough of our four children, Meagan, Chris, James and Emily, who were all in secondary school while this was going on. Our children are very intuitive and we kept them abreast of everything that was happening to and with their dad. We have participated in the DVA Family Study Program and availed ourselves of every bit of information that comes our way.

Terry was initially diagnosed with PTSD and depression, but later was also deemed to be TPI, Totally and Permanently Incapacitated. He retired at the age of fifty-eight and has been good at managing his illness and seeking more counselling when needed. I'm similarly content in my progress and care.

Life was never meant to be easy and we've had our rocky times, but through it all we've stuck together and soaked up as much information and help as we can.

Our group was our saving grace and I'll always be eternally grateful for that invitation to:

- experience a turning point
- have a refreshing experience
- realise the meaning and terrifying ongoing effects of PTSD
- be with professionals who talked to me as if they could read my mind, teasing out my fears for our future together
- meet caring facilitators and counsellors
- feel great freedom at sharing the burden with someone who not only gave me that space but understood me
- meet four magnificent women who seemed to take me in and hold me close.

It brings tears to my eyes to remember those following weeks and months of catch-up and revision sessions, of which we didn't miss one. When you're on a good thing, stick to it! That was when Terry had the tools to sort himself out and was able to breathe more easily, and felt I was sharing his load.

Terry was under the care of Heidelberg Repat Hospital for some years and had regular counselling sessions. As a couple we've taken advantage of the Couples Counselling Program and the Lifestyle Program at Flowerdale. Also, since our original PTSD course, Terry's felt comfortable contacting mates from his Vietnam time and we've been to a few reunions. Terry can explain his reluctance at first to enter that particular arena, but we always make these gatherings a holiday and enjoy the catch up.

Since writing my story I've been giving a great deal of thought to my own father who served in the Second World War. I came from a family of six children, five boys and one girl. We had a very happy childhood but as I reached my teens I realised that my dad was not a particularly happy person. He seemed to be moody and uncommunicative, often relying heavily on alcohol, all of which put a great strain on his marriage. My dad was very hard on the three eldest boys, but always treated me like a princess. I cannot explain this fact, but I'm pretty certain it came about when my three older brothers became teenagers, which unfortunately coincided with my father's mental decline and his inability to deal with his own health issues. Of course this is all supposition on my part, but looking back I think I'm right.

I knew very little of my father Jack's wartime experiences. One that I can recall is of him on a troop train on his way to Canungra for jungle training, then on to New Guinea. Their train was in the vicinity of Cowra when the Japanese breakout occurred. The troops were seconded to help in the recapture of the Japanese soldiers and to secure the prison camp once more.

Having acquired knowledge of the after-affects of war through the PTSD course, I think my dad could easily have been going through similar symptoms as Terry, but didn't know it. I do, however, have a memory of visiting Dad at Heidelberg Repat on at least one occasion, and Mum and us kids catching a bus home down Bell Street at night.

I point out the similarities of my father and my husband, but the difference is that help was available to Terry and he took advantage of every offer.

Obviously family, work and relationship pressures add to everyone's life choices and health issues, but I'm convinced that wartime experiences and atrocities are outside our normal sphere of experience and add another layer to physical and psychological disorders.

Sadly Mum passed away before she was able to write a conclusion to her story.
From Meagan

POSTSCRIPT

My wife Glenda passed away on the 22nd of April 2017. She became ill in June 2013, during the last few days of a five-week holiday in Vietnam. On returning to Australia, she was diagnosed with oesophageal cancer, which caused her to have great difficulty swallowing food. She spent nine weeks in hospital, being fed intravenously and undergoing extensive chemo and radiotherapy.

Although in much pain and discomfort, Glenda's spirit and positive nature stayed with her. She had an inner strength and a great faith in a loving and caring God. As a result of treatment, Glenda's tumour reduced greatly, which allowed her to have surgery to remove the tumour completely. The operation lasted about ten and a half hours. As well as the tumour, part of her stomach and oesophagus were also removed. It took about six months for Glenda to recover from the surgery and for the following eighteen months, although never back to where she had been previously, she enjoyed reasonable health. Glenda had many friends who were of great support to her, which definitely included the partners in our PTSD group. During this time Glenda and I did a lot of travelling, by road and rail, and had some great times. Unfortunately another tumour appeared in Glenda's neck, which, being very close to vital areas, was inoperable. After another round of treatment the tumour reduced very little. A clinical trial was suggested, for which Glenda was suitable. However, it didn't start for another six weeks and during that time her health deteriorated and she was not well enough to start. In the last three months of Glenda's life, we both knew that there was not much more that could be done. I loved this woman, wife, mother and nanna even more during this time. When the inevitable is upon you, all the peripheral and unimportant aspects of life are stripped away and there's just the two of you with no distraction. During this time Glenda said to me, 'You've been my rock.' On reflection it seems to me that she was also my rock, from the very first time we got together.

Glenda loved her family and close friends dearly. I felt her love, almost to the point of sometimes feeling unworthy, but I'm so grateful to have had her in my life. We'll miss her terribly, but know that because of the way she lived she would still want us to make the most of our lives. I'm certainly going to give it a good try and I'm sure our children will. I'm also sure she'll never really leave us. For a person of small stature, she always had a large presence and I'm sure her strong spirit will be around us forever.

I'd like to thank my daughter Meagan, who tied up the loose ends in Glenda's story, as she died just before completion. There were between five and six hundred people at Glenda's funeral, which was an indication of the many people whose lives she touched. Sleep peacefully now, Glenda. I love you.

Terry Wolff

THE BOY AT THE GATE

Trevor McLean

*To the love of my life Carol for your dedicated caring of
me over recent troublesome times and the sage advice given in
the writing of my story.*

FAMILY BACKGROUND

I was born Trevor Anthony McLean on 22 June 1943, at the Royal Women's Hospital, Darlinghurst, an inner suburb of Sydney. My father, Rupert Ernest McLean, was in the Australian Military Forces at the time of my birth and was later a glassworker in Sydney with his ten brothers, and eventually an itinerant worker for the rest of his life. My mother, Ellen Agnes Rath, one of ten children, was born in Ardlethan, New South Wales. She worked as a laundry hand, and later in more dubious activities. Eventually she met an untimely end, but more on that later.

The Rath family

I have a direct Australian line back to great-great-great-grandfather Patrick Rath, who was born in County Lough in Ireland in 1797 and was a marine in the Queen's Own Regiment for some thirteen years. He was a weaver before joining the marines and transferring with his family to Australia in 1833 on the prison ship *Neva*. One of his nine children was born in-transit on the ship. Patrick was hospitalised in Australia and became very ill. The surgeon's report stated that he had debilitating bad health and was emaciated. The surgeon further said, 'From the state of this man's health he is not fit to perform the duties of a soldier.' He was discharged in 1839 and lived until 1886, to the surprise of all. He moved around regional parts of New South Wales, increasing his number of children, and eventually settled in Beechworth, Victoria. He became a prosperous farmer and owner of a hotel until his death aged eighty-nine. He survived his wife, Margaret, by thirty-six years. They're both buried in the Beechworth cemetery.

A further two generations carried on businesses as owners of hotels in New South Wales.

The McLean family

The McLeans originated from Edinburgh, Scotland, and possibly immigrated in the 1830s and settled in Surry Hills, Sydney. My great-grandfather, Walter McLean, was a sailor. My grandfather was also Walter McLean and lived until he was eighty-three, having worked variously as a bootmaker, fettler and tramway employee. My father, Rupert, was one of eleven children. He was the twin who survived when his brother and mother died during childbirth. His sister Emily, fourteen at the time, took over the role of mother. His father was fifty-two at the time of his wife's death.

Rupert married my mother, Ellen Rath, in 1942 in Sydney. I was born in 1943, their only child. Being Catholic my parents never divorced, but they did separate soon after my birth and again around the end of WWII when I was two. They eventually split in about 1950, having tried for six months to rebuild their marriage.

0-4 YEARS OLD – THE EARLY YEARS

During my first two years of life, my father was serving in the army (WWII) and my mother and I lived off army pay and welfare. We had little money and times were extremely hard. I still wonder how we got by. We lived in rented digs around Kings Cross and Paddington in Sydney. Sometime during this period, I contracted whooping cough. According to my mother's relatives, during these early years with my father away at war, my mother was unsettled and began drinking. From eighteen months old I remember my mother and me being moved around to different family homes, including to a sister in Cootamundra, and other family at Peak Hill and Ardlethan in western New South Wales. Many families did this during the Depression and post WWII to give shelter and support to disadvantaged family members. Despite very difficult circumstances, my mother did the best she could, and I was well cared for by my mother, and she loved me. I don't have any memories of my father during my infant years.

After the war ended when I was two, my mother returned to Sydney to try to be with my returned father; however, this didn't work and my parents separated again. My memory is that we had a room and shared kitchens and bathrooms. From three to four years old, I had callipers attached to my legs to help realign them. This seemed to work, and eventually helped me become a wonderful and extraordinary dancer, or so I am told.

4-11 YEARS OLD - MY PRIMARY SCHOOL YEARS

When I was four-and-a-half, my separated parents decided to place me in a boarding school in Galong in southern NSW. St Lawrence's College was run by the Sisters of Mercy (or *Show no Mercy*), and was home to some one hundred and fifty boys. This was my home until the end of primary school.

My earliest memory of school is being left at the gate of St Lawrence's with one of the nuns. My mother and her boyfriend left me there. I cried as I stood there with my suitcase. I didn't know what was happening or why my mother was doing this. Eventually I stopped crying and over time I settled in and learned to not cry or show emotion.

The students consisted of farming boys mainly from the Riverina; there were very few city boys like myself. Over the years it became obvious that many of the nuns were not suited to caring for young children – they were cruel, uncaring, mean and nasty. A small minority showed love and affection in limited amounts. Many boys had visits from their families; I did not. The farming boys returned to their families during school holidays, but because of my unsettled family circumstances, I was unable to return home so arrangements were made for me to stay at the school. In many ways I preferred this, but I was invited to go home with some of my friends to their family farms. My father came to the school on a few occasions during my seven years there to take me out for the night.

I lived at the boarding school from about 1948 to 1954. I have vivid memories of those days. The culture of the Catholic boarding school system was harsh and correction-based. My first mistake? I was left-handed. Though the nuns tried to 'belt' this out of me, I remain left-handed. I was the brightest student in the class and so they gave up on trying to change my left-handedness. Victory to the Trevster – round one to me.

The school system was demanding of little children, and I and many others suffered, no doubt with life-long effects. While I had some beltings, I probably avoided many because of my academic skills. I became dux of the school. Each year I was top of my year. I attended mass (in Latin) every morning, was head altar boy, head choirboy and top student, leaving me with skills in self-preservation. I was a deep thinker and in time understood how to exist in the Catholic system. I learned to conform to all that was required of me. I came to understand that my fees weren't paid for and so decided that to remain in what was now 'my home' I needed to be the best so that my success could allow me to remain.

A number of influences shaped me and affected my character, including the fact that I was a small boy and so attracted bullies. The bullies didn't like that I was intelligent. My family background meant that I didn't have the best social skills, though this aspect did improve over time, so a couple of large boys helped me to deal with the bullies. I felt powerful because of my brightness, but didn't understand why people were different from me. I struggled with finding sins to confess in confession so worked out that if I made up a list of acceptable 'sins' to repent, I'd be safe. The final result is that I'm a *Cath-atheist*, a Catholic atheist.

During my infrequent visits to my mother I became more aware of her problems with alcohol and of her poor mental state. I wanted my home to be St Lawrence's College, away from her. Between my seventh and eighth birthdays my parents may have reunited in Canberra for a short time. I remember visiting them for school holidays in Narrabundah in a housing commission house and being with them for a short time; however, they separated again for the final time and my mother returned to Sydney with another man. I began wanting and needing an institution-style environment to feel safe and in control.

There were some happy memories and these included staying with friends whose mothers were loving and caring; achieving great scholastic results; enjoying hot pies from the bakery in winter; the lolly hunt after a long Lent period of abstinence; and occasionally receiving some affection and caring from a few of the nuns.

In reflecting on this period of my life, I feel that it's moulded me into not easily accepting unsolicited kindness and affection. It also steeled me to be self-reliant and perhaps suspicious of unexpected affection. Love hasn't been an easy thing for me to feel or to receive and I've tended to blunt my emotions to stay safe from possible future disappointment. For the same reason I can also deflect the gift of love when it is offered to me. More recently I've softened in this attitude by learning to trust. This has come about through my family and other loved ones who have shown me unreserved love. Slowly but surely my emotional shield has started to crack. Despite this I feel that I'll always use tools such as jokes and aloofness to protect me, and that's the truth of it. As they say life is just a continual work in progress.

11-15 YEARS OLD - MY HIGH SCHOOL DAYS

After grade six I was moved to St Patrick's College in Goulburn, a Christian Brother's College, to commence form one, the first of my high school years. My time at St Lawrence's was tough, but my time at St Patrick's was like moving to B Division at Pentridge. These Brothers were brought up on raw meat and were vicious and excellent in punishment techniques.

This stage of my life was coloured by the understanding that I was from a 'poor' family, that my family wasn't like other families and I learnt what shame felt like, even though it was not a result of anything I'd done. Shame takes many guises. It's a feeling of little self-worth and not having the things that other kids have (such as visits from their families and the loving connectedness that this provides, or clothes and money). It's a feeling of embarrassment when your father, in a drunken state, turns up at the college to see you. It's the potential dread that your mother might turn up and act in the way that she usually did. Shame is the knowledge that, as told to me by nuns and brothers, your school fees weren't being paid. Shame is confusing as it makes you feel guilty without having done anything to cause it. Finally shame stays with you for many years and then subsides as the 'shamer/s' leave your life. For all the shortfalls I may have had as a father, I feel some satisfaction that I've not shamed my family.

Like all students I had my share of 'beltings' from the Brothers, but one occasion in particular stands out. I was twelve years old and was identified as having committed a misdemeanour, and so was asked to report to a Brother and stand outside his room, which was at the end of the dormitory where I slept. He took me into his room and then proceeded to dress me down for the misdemeanour and said to me that I was 'going to get a belting' from him. He must have read my facial expression as he asked me, 'You're not going to cry, are you?' I then made the mistake of my life and answered, 'No'. The end of the story was that I didn't cry and he hit me as hard as he could, for as long as he could, until he couldn't hit me anymore. Lesson learnt – don't take on self-gratifying, violent men!

Because of the school environment, my feelings about my family situation and my father not keeping up with my school fees, I began to rebel and my school results began to suffer. I was subsequently pulled out of St Patrick's School at the end of the year.

During this period my father worked as a kitchen hand at the Migrant Centre in Canberra, which was then situated up behind the War Memorial. He lived on site and was given permission for me to live with him. I was enrolled in Telopea Park High School in Canberra. This shocked me because of the lack of discipline compared to the Catholic boarding school. My father moved on to gain other work in regional NSW and so I lasted about six months before I was sent back to my mother in Sydney.

This was me: a kid about twelve years old, who'd been through the strict school boarding system, had been shifted between an alcoholic father and a raging, psychotic mother (with shifting men friends) and was being further subjected to another government schooling system. Let me describe my new environment.

12-15 YEARS OLD – MY NEW ENVIRONMENT

When I was about twelve, I returned to live with my mother in Balmain and was admitted to another public high school, Drummoyne High School. Balmain today is a millionaire's paradise; however, in the mid-50s it was predominantly occupied by waterside workers who were rusted-on Labor supporters living in little cottages close to the water between Sydney Harbour and the Parramatta River. My mother and I lived in at least three or four over two to three years. We shared a bedroom and kitchen, an outside toilet and a laundry with a chip heater with other families. Sharing often included another male adult person in the room. My understanding of sexual activities grew exponentially over this time. Studying was very difficult.

Learning about my mother

The impression that my mother loved me when she left me at the gate of St Lawrence's Boarding School at four and a half was quickly expunged by reality. Her behaviours, her screaming, her continuous line of men friends, her lack of care for me or her understanding of my needs left me with scars. I became more antisocial. I had no friends and even if I did I could never have brought them home because of the shame I felt and her antisocial behaviours. There were daily arguments between us, and between my mother and neighbours. I could never win an argument or be heard. The embarrassment I felt was overwhelming. There are no words in my language that can describe this time of my life. I was unsafe, unprotected, powerless and in great emotional pain. I survived, but it wasn't good.

The rebellious school years

At this stage, with my cloistered background, I started to rebel against my need to study, and so didn't put much effort into my schoolwork. At the same time I was growing physically and by about the age of fourteen I was one of the tallest kids in my class. With the pressure from my mother's situation I began wagging school and didn't keep up with my homework and school assignments. I started considering separating from my mother and so developed a pattern of regular absence from school. I planned to increase my level of truancy to attract the attention of the State Education Department officers, so they'd take disciplinary action against me. The plan was partly successful. I was brought before the juvenile court. The magistrate asked, 'What do you want to happen?' I stated that I wanted to be placed in a government boys' home, away from my mother. I knew it'd be a tough place but it'd provide me with an escape from her. I would have education, three meals a day and 'safe' lodgings.

Someone, however, interceded for me and stated that I needed one more chance to improve my behaviours. Once again I was returned to my mother. Things didn't improve for me, but I decided I should travel another route and 'suck it up' until I was fifteen and in the meantime do something with my life. I started to play rugby and improved my study so that I could get my 'piece of paper' and make myself employable. This was my new plan. Upon reflection, had I been placed in a boys' home, I would've received an education in toughness from the 'school of hard knocks', which wouldn't have been for my good.

During these two years in my mother's 'care', I approached my aunty who lived on the north shore of Sydney, who had a lovely home and family. I stayed with her a number of times. She treated me well and she understood exactly how my mother was. This gave me hope for my future.

When I was about fourteen, my mother gave birth to a daughter, who she gave to her sister to raise as her own. In my view this was probably the best thing my mother could've done for the baby. I subsequently met my sister about eighteen years later and we've continued to have a relationship.

15-17 YEARS OLD – I FOUND A JOB

At fifteen, I achieved my Intermediate Certificate with good results, and so worked out a plan. With my Intermediate Certificate in hand I applied for a job with the Commonwealth Employment Service (CES), and started working in administration at a Carpet Warehouse in the city. When I began looking for accommodation, my father referred me to an elderly lady who took in boarders in Marrickville. Although she was grumpy she offered me a single room, breakfast and a shared outside toilet and bathroom for three pounds, ten shillings per week. At last the jigsaw pieces were falling into place. I went straight home to my mother and said, 'I'm leaving'. She replied, 'You'll be back.' I assured her I wouldn't return. I never did, except to bury her twenty years later.

The job paid six pounds, ten shillings per week because I was replacing a twenty-four-year-old employee. At the end of the first week, I found five pounds in my pay packet. Nervously, and feeling like Oliver Twist asking for more, I approached the paymaster and asked him about the error. Luckily he remembered his offer and made the adjustment. Unfortunately my board and lodgings cost three pounds, ten shillings. I had to survive on three pounds a week. I did well in the administration position, and after about a year I switched to assistant carpet layer, got my own knife and sharpener, and enjoyed working 'with the boys'. During this time, despite lack of money, I attended night school to attain my Leaving Certificate in an attempt to improve my education. It became too hard to work full-time, travel to study and complete studies, so I didn't get it.

Although my landlady made me a hearty breakfast, my financial situation made it difficult to satisfy my ongoing hunger during the day. Those who know Sydney will be familiar with the place underneath the Central Railway Station called the Hole in the Wall. This was where the drunks and layabouts used to go for a cheap meal. I went there frequently to buy their speciality, a pie and peas with watery mashed potato, for one shilling and sixpence. There were angels in the office: one knitted me a very heavy jumper and another brought me bickies. Saved again! However, I still had trouble surviving so I started looking around for other work alternatives.

When I was almost seventeen, I saw some army advertisements promoting further education, free food, free uniforms and an adult wage. I was in. I forged my father's signature on the enrolment papers and joined the Australian Army.

17-27 YEARS OLD - THE ARMY CALLS

The basic rules of the army are: follow orders blindly while being tightly bound by rules and regulations. Generally, orders aren't to be questioned and using your initiative is somewhat frowned upon. Once trained you're to act instinctively based on what you've been taught. For a young soldier this can lead to a comfortable life in which the brain runs on automatic pilot. This worked okay for me in the early years but not so well when I discovered that I had a brain.

Recruit training began at Kapooka in Victoria. This involved twelve weeks of hard slog in the middle of summer. It also involved conversion from being left-handed to right-handed for the purpose of using a rifle and machine gun and for rifle drill. Despite the emphasis on the physical rather than the intellectual, it provided me with improved overall fitness and greater confidence. At the end of recruit training, I was transferred to the Royal Australian Army Service Corps (RAASC) and sent to Puckapunyal, Victoria for further training. From there I went to Ingleburn in NSW to my parent unit, 1 Company, RAASC, which was a supply and transport company. At Ingleburn I was trained in how to run a supply depot, air dispatch and how to drive trucks. As a field force unit, we went on many field exercises supporting other operational units. I carefully chose a small group of friends and became a skilled and competent soldier. I was in this unit for two and a half years.

In 1962, although officially too young to serve overseas, I was put on standby to be sent to Laos. As it turned out this didn't eventuate. At the end of 1963, I was transferred to a supply depot at Kensington in Melbourne. This radically changed my status from living inside the tent looking out, to living outside the tent looking in. I moved off base and shared a flat with another soldier from the same unit, which introduced me to civilian life and to the responsibility of caring for myself. Similarly it meant leaving behind my institutionalised way of life. It introduced me to social drinking because prior to this I didn't drink alcohol. I didn't, however, become a heavy drinker like my parents.

The obvious changes in moving from an army camp to going into civilian 'digs' was having to feed myself, to travel daily to my operational unit and no guard duty! Having done this from the age of fifteen, this was not a problem. Shopping with all that army money, though, made one a bit of a toff.

My army career took a new direction when I embraced the early use of computer technology in stores, supplies and purchasing. I took to this new area of work like a duck to water and soon became the leading technician on the system. I trained new staff, wrote procedures and, as more staff gained skills, became an auditor for the system. I became indispensable and couldn't be released for time off to undertake my promotion subjects. It was quite common in the army for the least efficient to be released to study for promotions, while others were held back to do the work of running departments. This was, in my view, an impediment to rewarding the brightest people.

On the social side I started socialising with the 'fairer sex' and within a short time I met a young lady who arrived to take over a flat in my apartment block. A friendship developed that turned into a relationship. Shortly after moving in, I visited her kitchen and found her with her head in the gas oven. She told me that she'd left home and that her father had been quite violent to her over the years. This young lady, Rita, eventually became my wife. She was Irish, having migrated to Australia only recently with her family. Rita was a lovely girl, however, she was a chain smoker and very nervous. I expect this was due to her father's heavy hand. I wanted to protect her. We developed a close relationship that soon resulted in our first pregnancy. We were married shortly after, aged twenty-one, and moved into married quarters in a flat in Windsor. Our first daughter, Kathleen, arrived in 1965 and within a year our second daughter, Maureen, arrived. Rita soon began to show signs that she was not coping with life, which resulted in depression.

During this time fatherhood was a bit of a blur. It was both wonderful and overwhelming. Wonderful because they were beautiful little babies who I felt responsible for and, at the same time, overwhelming because I wanted to make my mark, for which I felt a bit selfish. I'd been dealt a tough hand in having to leave school at fifteen, but at the same time still felt that I could 'make it' through my own efforts and by taking risks. Supporting my family has always been paramount to me. Support for one's family takes many guises and love displays different hues, as it did for me.

I was keen to get ahead and wanted adventure. I started looking for opportunities for overseas service. Financially it was also going to benefit us. In early 1966 I became aware that the army was looking for volunteers in the Australian Army Training Team Vietnam (AATTV). At twenty-two I applied to join. Admittedly, I didn't disclose this to Rita. This is still a point of regret on my part.

23-24 YEARS OF AGE - THE VIETNAM WAR

With the introduction of the first military contingent from Australia in the Vietnam War in 1962, it became pretty obvious that we'd be more involved as time went on. By 1965 battalions were introduced into the campaign and so the build-up began. I started considering my options, either to be involved through my specific corps, RAASC, or get more involved in a specific operational role. I chose the latter. I was advised of my acceptance into AATTV in mid-1966. Three months after being accepted I commenced a two-month course at the jungle training centre,

Canungra, Queensland. This included all physical field craft skills, taught both in the classroom and in the field, including operating as platoon commanders in simulated warfare conditions. The contingent consisted of majors, captains and warrant officers, ranging in age from twenty-three to over fifty. A lot of them were professional soldiers who had served in WWII, Korea and Malaysia. A number had been awarded bravery medals such as the Military Medal (MM), Mentioned in Dispatches (MID) and the Distinguished Conduct Medal (DCM). Some, mainly for physical reasons, didn't survive the course. It was very intense and sorted out the men from the old boys.

After Canungra we were sent to the intelligence centre at Middle Head in Sydney where we learnt all about Vietnam, including the geography, the demography, the war situation, basic Vietnamese language and capture/torture survival. For the latter old gun emplacement structures at Middle Head were converted to cells for solitary confinement. We endured torture practices, deprivation of food and amenities and humiliation. Not all survived this. I was okay. Being younger, with extensive childhood experiences, possibly helped.

At the end of all of this we went back to our units and awaited our call up to the training team.

Summary of the Australian Army Training Team - Vietnam

The team consisted of about one hundred men, including majors, captains and warrant officers who were great soldiers in war time but not so good in peace time.

- The team arrived in Vietnam in 1962 and left in 1972. The initial role was to train Vietnamese troops. After the first three years, the role changed to training company and platoon commanders of Indigenous units fighting all over Vietnam.

- Soldiers were scattered all over South Vietnam, from the Mekong Delta up to the demilitarised zone, and from the Laotian/Cambodian border to the east coast.

- Australian casualty rates in my unit from 1967–1968 were very heavy, more than fifty per cent.

- A number of groups were attached to the US Special Forces (the Green Berets).

- Our motto was Persevere.

- It was the most highly decorated unit in the Vietnam War: for example, four VCs.

My tour of Vietnam

I arrived in Vietnam on 1 April 1967. My unit was American, and part of the 5th Special Forces Group (Airborne), 1st Special Forces. Our role in the A Team in a unit called Mike Force (Mobile Strike Force) was to recruit the Vietnamese, Nungs (Chinese Vietnamese) and Montagnards (mountain people), train them, put them through Airborne and take them on operations around the Special Forces outposts, along known infiltration routes throughout all of 'I Corps' from the Demilitarised Zone down to the Cam Ranh Bay and over to the Laotian border.

A picture tells a thousand words

On the next page is a map of South Vietnam and the various corps in which we operated. You'll see the large distance between I Corp and where the major contingent of Australian Troops operated out of Phuoc Tuy Province in III Corps.

There were ten Australians attached to this unit: two officers and eight warrant officers. Our base camp was at Marble Mountain, East Da Nang on the South China Sea.

My initial job was as the S4 Logistics Officer responsible for all logistics for the companies, including rations, ammunition, transportation, setting up base camps within operational areas, and organising remedial ground and air support, including medivac. This enabled me to travel all over I Corps to provide support. The second part of my tour was as a platoon commander in a Montagnard Company, involved in a number of operations throughout I Corps, including the operational and airborne training of the soldiers.

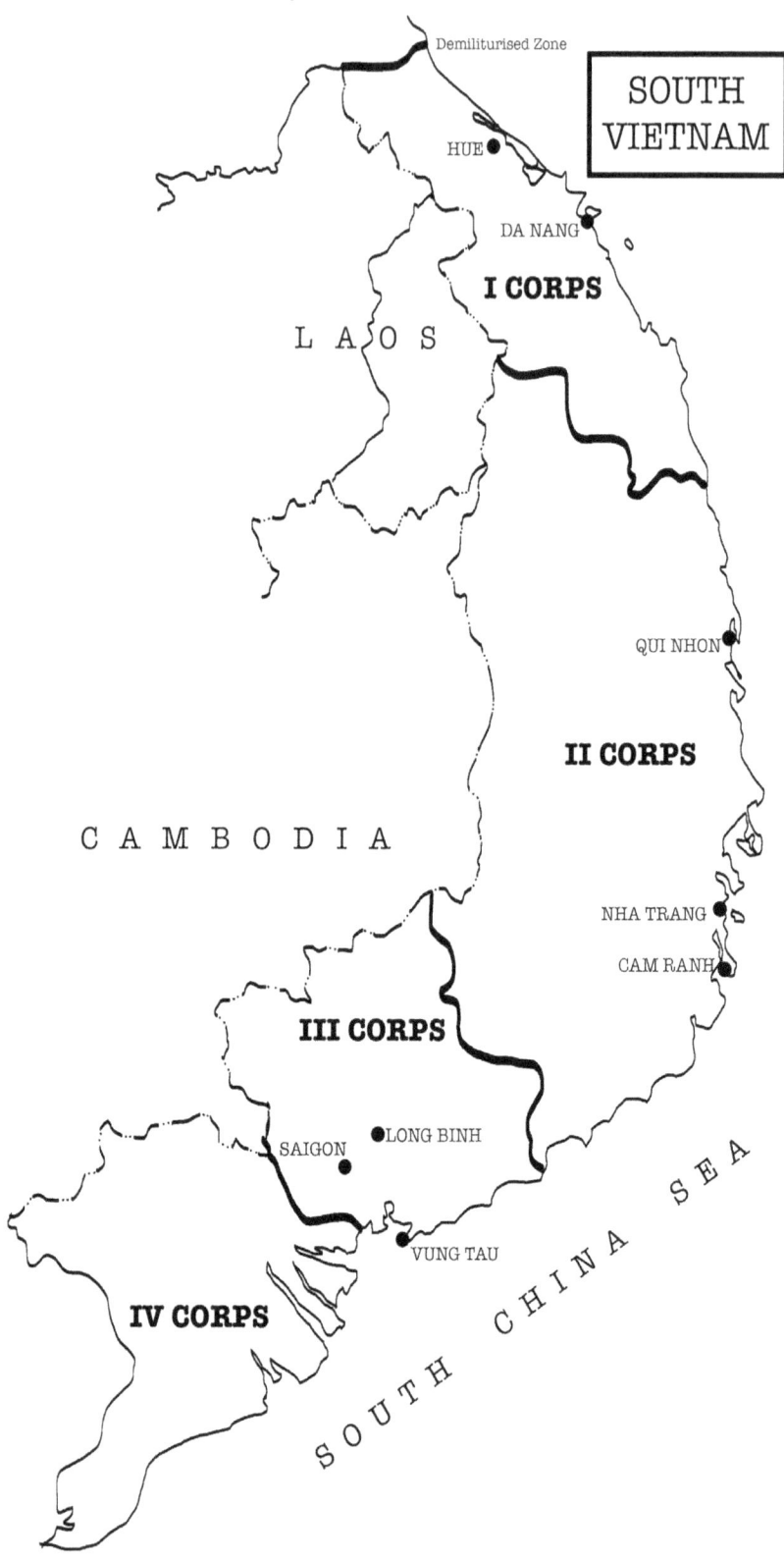

Some snapshots of my tour

The Indigenous soldiers

Our soldiers were recruited from four groups:

1. The Vietnamese who were mainly recruited from the bigger cities. This gave them street smarts but didn't make them good soldiers. They were generally lazy and didn't want to put in, in a war sense. On the other hand, they loved showing off their airborne uniforms to local girlfriends and would peg their pants to give a sharper effect. This was despite us warning them not to. As soon as they went on operations, their pants split.

2. The Nungs (Chinese Vietnamese) had migrated from the north over the years, were hardworking and became merchants and businessmen. Because of their high work ethics, they made better soldiers and were placed in separate companies to the Vietnamese.

3. The Montagnards (mountain people) were tribal people recruited from the Annamite Mountains, near the Laotian border. Because they were clansmen, they were ferocious soldiers and supported each other. As in all things, there were exceptions. In one incident during an operation close to the DMZ, a company of Montagnards, whilst under heavy fire, threw down their weapons and ran. When we finally rounded them up we had to decide what to do with them. On checking out their backgrounds, we discovered that a lot of them were only nine to ten years old. Being predominantly small people, they'd been recruited along with the rest of the tribe and were assumed to be the same age as the others. In considering what to do, we reflected on how Australian primary school children would handle being in a real operation, with real weapons, real bullets and real casualties and there was only one course of action. We sent them back to their village to be with their families, supported by their elders and given a chance to grow up.

4. Lastly, the Chieu Hoi, meaning 'open arms', a class of enemy soldier who'd been put through an indoctrination program and were deemed safe to go on operations for our side. We put together a company of these soldiers and took them on operations against their former masters. We often wondered whether they would turn on us, but they never did. They were incredibly tough soldiers used to the lifestyle.

The United States (US) soldiers
The American Special Forces soldiers were wonderfully trained. They were the elite. They tended to be specialists trained in heavy weapons and airborne, compared with the average Australian soldier who was more of a general practitioner who could turn his hand to most situations.

Many of their officers and warrant officers were African Americans and predominantly from the southern states of America. Because of this they loved country music from the south. I was able to gain an appreciation of country music from these 'good old boys'. Many of their soldiers were war-toughened veterans who had seen action in other countries including the infamous Cuban Bay of Pigs campaign. I still think of the US soldiers I was with on operations who didn't make it back home, and of the Australian Training Team companions who fell in battle.

Geographically we were located over six hundred miles north of where the Australian Task force was. Whilst this is not important and not something to boast about, it is estimated that about seventy-five per cent of total fighting and the resultant casualties took place in the most northern part of South Vietnam. Of the ten Australians in my unit, in 1967 to early 1968, five were killed in action and one died of cerebral malaria. Only four of us survived. Not a good year! All I can say is war is crap. Many decorations were awarded and many people (including civilians) were killed or badly wounded, and for what? If you think that statement above is to show you that 'mine's bigger than yours!' think again. Whilst some of the training team could've been classed as mercenaries, having helped out in private armies in Africa and taking it in their stride, I never found killing people natural and I never will. Whilst self-preservation is an incentive and reason for doing so, it doesn't totally justify this act.

1968: BACK TO AUSTRALIA

I left Vietnam in 1968 and was reassigned to the Supply Depot in Melbourne in the procurement division. This was a more senior role from the one I had prior to Vietnam. In the meantime, my wife and children, who'd lived with her parents while I was on tour, moved in with me in new married quarters in Windsor. It appeared to me that she'd been changed by my Vietnam tour more than I'd been, and that the separation hadn't been good for her. Despite this, we came back together as a family unit and I spent about eighteen months in my new army role.

In November 1969 I was reassigned to Larrakeyah Barracks in Darwin as the Senior Procurement Officer responsible for all logistical supply for Army, Air Force and Navy. As a family we settled reasonably well into the new home; however, Rita was starting to become depressed again and was finally admitted to Darwin Hospital Psychiatric Ward. I arranged for some temporary care for my children during the day. After a few weeks, she was released from hospital but this pattern recurred several times over the ensuing months. This included one time when she attempted suicide. In May 1970, I asked Rita's mother to come up to support our family. This seemed to help Rita. She did better with her mother providing support and care for her. A month later Rita's mother returned to Melbourne. For a short time there was some recovery in her condition, but then there was another admission to hospital. By this stage I'd started to apply for a compassionate transfer back to Melbourne.

After Rita returned home from hospital on this occasion, things appeared to be normal again for a short time. One night, when we were having tea, she started talking about the future in a strange way, along the lines that I was too good for her and I would be better off without her and her depression. I felt that she might have been talking like this because of the medication she was taking. I told her that this wasn't the case and that once we got her over this illness, we could enjoy life together. At the same time I suspected that she might have planned something silly, so I quietly went through the house and flushed all medication down the toilet. I suggested that she might need to sleep, that things would be better in the morning, and so we went to bed. When Rita was settled in bed and asleep, I got up to do some study. About two hours later I heard strange sounds coming from the bedroom. I went to the bedroom and attempted to wake her but I couldn't. She was unconscious. My car wasn't going, so I contacted my neighbour and asked him to take me to the hospital. His wife looked after the children. Rita was admitted immediately to Emergency and the staff attempted to revive her. I waited outside for quite some time. After what felt like a long time, the doctor came out to see me and advised that she couldn't be revived. She had died.

My feelings at that time were mixed. Obviously I was devastated at losing my wife and was a total mess. I was taken in by my Commanding Officer and medicated by the doctor. My friends on the base in Darwin took my two small daughters, four and five years of age, looked after them and escorted them back to family in Melbourne. I followed to make all necessary arrangements for the funeral.

Whilst it is terrible to say so, I was slightly relieved that the nightmare of Rita's suffering and her determination to leave this world was over. For many years I felt responsible for her demise, but over time I've lost that guilt. I remembered how unhappy she was when I met her and now understand that she'd been a tortured soul throughout our time together and, unfortunately, her life story was always likely to end tragically.

I relocated to Melbourne and was reunited with our children a few days after Rita's death. Rita was buried in Melbourne a week later.

Following some leave I was offered a new position at Victoria Barracks in Melbourne; however, I asked for a discharge on compassionate grounds and so left the army in late July 1970. This was the end of my army career after nine years and nine months. It was also the end of my marriage, and life as I knew it.

Beginning again

What to do in civilian life and what was I qualified for? I'd developed a few marketable skills that could be converted to civilian employment, but if used would put me in gaol! I'd sat the Commonwealth Public Service Third Division Entrance Examination in late 1968. Having passed my matriculation in the mid-60s whilst in the army, I phoned the Public Service Selection Committee to ask whether there were any positions available. They came back and advised that I'd done very well in the exam and they could immediately offer me a position as a Third Division Officer in Melbourne.

I commenced work with Australia Post (then PMG) in William Street, Melbourne in August 1970. The position was Examiner of Accounts in the headquarters office. So began my life in the public service. I was successful in my role and enjoyed promotions. I kept up my fitness as well.

During this time I'd agreed to live in my in-law's home and my mother-in-law would look after my children during the day. This arrangement lasted about two and a half years. In April 1973 I remarried. Suzanne and I and my children moved into a new home that I built in North Croydon. In 1975 our first son, Cameron, was born.

In 1973 I applied for and was accepted into a Bachelor of Commerce at the University of Melbourne. I was thirty years old. Life was very good and I was very happy. Having completed my degree in 1976 whilst continuing to work, I was promoted to Assistant Treasurer at Australia Post Headquarters in Rathdowne Street in 1978.

In 1980 I joined the stockbroking firm, McCaughan, Dyson and Co., Melbourne, as a money broker, where I worked for two years. I left because my liver was having 'too heavy a workout' with clients.

Other significant events occurred in the '70s. Firstly, my father died in Sydney of stomach cancer in 1972. Although we didn't have contact over the years, I visited him twice in hospital. He'd continued to be an itinerant worker, continued drinking, and didn't look after himself. He was fifty-nine years old. Being one of eleven children, my father had lived a hard life. Whilst I only had limited exposure to him over the years, when he was dying I was able to talk to him about his two granddaughters. I gave him some photos of them, and I also got to know a bit more about him and his life. I cherish those last memories of him.

Secondly, my mother was murdered in 1978 in a flat that she owned in Sydney. She wasn't found for some five weeks. I took responsibility for her funeral and end-of-life details. Her murderer was found and charged and he served time.

Though I wasn't close to my mother in any way, her ending wasn't a good ending for any person. This was the end of an era for me, as she could never haunt me again. She was fifty-six years old.

The transformational '80s

In March 1982 our twins, Michael and Stuart, were born, so in 1985 we moved to a larger property in Mt Evelyn. I was active in my children's school life as President of the Mt Evelyn School Board and active in their sporting lives. My daughters left home during these years. In 1989 our son Cameron was accepted into Melbourne High.

In 1982 I took up a position as Director, Finance/Treasury at the City of Melbourne. This covered five managers/branches involving 130 staff. This was one of the most challenging times in my career and also the most satisfying. I remained in the position for nine years. I made dramatic changes resulting in increased productivity, improved treasury gains and reduced debt. At the same time computers and electronic processes were introduced for salaries disbursements and rates systems.

In 1985 I was advised to seek an opinion on my mental state because of my work ethic and perhaps because of delayed reactions to the Vietnam conflict. I was diagnosed as having a mild personality disorder (MPD) and was accepted by the DVA. In layman's terms I was *a little bit of a nutter*. At this time the term PTSD wasn't used.

The specialist medical practitioner who diagnosed MPD sedated me and took me back through my time in Vietnam. I'd had a number of graphic experiences during this time that affected me. It was duly recorded on my DVA record.

The '90s

In 1991 the City of Melbourne had a new CEO. Changes started to occur through a full council restructure and no department was unaffected. My position was readvertised and, despite having already completed my own departmental restructure with resultant saving of money, the politics dictated that an external person be selected for my position. Not being happy with this, I began a 'campaign' to challenge their decision. I was offered me a new position with better conditions. The war was won and peace prevailed.

In 1991–1992 I became Managing Director and creator of Municipal Authorities Purchasing Scheme (MAPS) Group Limited and proceeded to set up a public company providing product brokering services for all local governments in three states: New South Wales, Victoria and South Australia, including many statutory authorities. I continued in that role until 2004, growing the company from 1992 when our sales totalled $4 million to 2003 when our brokerage sales totalled $250 million. This company continues today under the name of Procurement Australia. Not bad for a *little bit of a nutter*.

In 1994 our first grandchild was born, the first of ten grandchildren to date. In 1998 we sold Mt Evelyn and rented whilst we built. We moved to a new home in Wattle Park in 2002.

The '00s

Soon after moving into the house, Suzanne and I separated. Settlement was amicable and the twins and I lived together in our Wattle Park home for five years. The situation had been building up for a number of years. My high-pressure job contributed to it and we'd been drifting apart over time. Despite mediation, which worked for a while, our relationship reached the point where I wanted out. We still meet from time to time at family birthdays and Christmas get-togethers; family is important to us both.

I retired from MAPS in 2003–2004. I travelled, got back into fitness, socially connected with my community and generally enjoyed life. I also took my sons away with me on several trips to reconnect with them.

In 2005 I met with other Vietnam veterans through a live-in PTSD course at the Repatriation Hospital in Heidelberg. After fifteen years we still catch-up.

The group consists mainly of National Servicemen who served in Vietnam, as well as two regular servicemen, a United Kingdom officer who served in the Troubles in Northern Ireland, and a navy and an air force man. The PTSD course we attended went for about a month and, except for weekends, we lived in each other's pockets. Depending on your definition of nutter, there are a few nutters, or a whole lot of nutters, in this group.

The course covered most aspects of PTSD and how it'd generally and specifically affected each of the group members. I personally learned more from the medication sessions, as the only non-medicating nutter in the group. A challenging part of the course was at the end when we each had to draw a collage of our life and present it to the group. It was a hard but worthwhile exercise. The partners of the group members met separately one day a week at Heidelberg and this was one of the main benefits of the course. It gave them ownership and an appreciation of PTSD and so were able to join up the dots on what they'd been putting up with for years. They are the true heroes.

The rest is history. The group has maintained its connection, meeting at least five times during the year and at Christmas. It's unique in its consistent association, compared with similar PTSD groups. Being in the group I've been in a unique and privileged position. Being single has enabled me to observe and study the interplays between couples and how this has changed for the better over time. All I can say is God bless the women of the group for their sanity, intellect and understanding.

I returned to study at sixty-three years of age and achieved my Diploma of Financial Planning. I sold Wattle Park and moved to Albury/Wodonga in late 2007. I took up old-time dancing, new vogue and rock 'n roll. This kept me fit and active. I got heavily into fitness at the local gym. In 2009 I was asked to go onto the Board of Westmont Aged Care Facility in Wodonga to fill a vacancy and was then elected to the Board. In 2013 I was elected Chairperson and am still in this role. I dance, walk, ride my bike and keep fit at the gym. I live in Albury on the Hill.

During my retirement years, I've continued my love of travel and have extensively seen the world. I have a son in England, a son in New Zealand and a son and two daughters in Melbourne.

WHAT DO I GET OUT OF MY STORY?

In summary my life is a mixture of sadness, emotional turmoil, some lonely aspects, traumatic experiences, and many joys. Though I didn't always get the results in my personal life that I wanted, I did try to invest myself in what was best for my family. I strived to produce unexpected and outstanding results in my work. During my childhood I learned not to give up and this continued throughout my personal and professional life.

With the help of wonderful people, I've been able to turn the negative aspects of my childhood into positive traits of self-reliance, strategic planning skills, pursuit of knowledge, how to care, and how to fight back when all seems insurmountable. I've developed good values regarding achieving education and obtaining the seemingly unattainable. I've passed these values onto my children, who've adopted and passed them onto my grandchildren. I recognise that being a father and grandfather is a work in progress, and I continue to believe that I can always improve in this area. I've felt great pride in my children's achievements and who they are as people. They've partnered with good people and my grandchildren are being raised in loving, caring homes. They all contribute to the world in positive ways. The mothers of my children and I have fostered good citizenship in our children and hopefully taught them that they are lovable and loved. I hope they feel this.

I broke the cycle of my parents' legacy. What more could that little boy at the gate have asked for from his life? My race is nearly run but I have much to do.

Epitaph from collage created during PTSD course with the Vietnam vets

I'm revisiting my original collage created during the 2005 PTSD course. In particular, the two possible epitaphs I wrote about myself at the time. These were:

Future 1: Lonely and reclusive	Future 2: Love, happiness and contentment
Epitaph 1 Trevor was a determined individual who was insufficiently nurtured in the early years, which led to a rejection of the social norms of life (love, affection, etc.). He developed corporate but not life skills. **SUMMARY** He tried, but the black dog turned up too early in life.	**Epitaph 2** Trevor fought the good fight while behind at the end of the third quarter. He gained momentum while expunging the demons to win in a tight finish. **SUMMARY** He finally shot the black dog.

In 2005 I was possibly closer to Future 1 because of my circumstances – my marriage break-up and lack of a job. Since then I've relocated to a regional city, created many social opportunities, moved heavily into dancing and now chair a growing aged care facility. I've become closer to my family both locally and overseas. I've developed some personal relationships and, although not all have succeeded, this is still a work in progress and no doubt is likely to bear fruit over time. All in all I consider that my future is leaning further towards Future 2. The black dog is in ICU and his parents have been called in to turn off his life support. Amen to that!

JUST A FEW MORE WORDS

Having read and re-read our stories we decided that if, as we sincerely hope, this book is to be helpful to others, there are a few loose ends to tidy up. In view of this and our personal experiences dealing with trauma we felt we should offer some of our own insights. We have also compiled a list of some of the many organizations that offer help and support in recognising women as well as men.

Firstly, an overview. It is important to make it clear that PTSD does not discriminate. It is not a condition that only happens to others, and has nothing to do with 'weakness' – the old sayings "just get on with it" or "she'll be right mate" simply don't work. PTSD is not necessarily related to factors such as age, gender, education, socio-economic status, or in our case, whether military service was voluntary or conscripted. Some of us clearly had our childhood challenges which increased our susceptibility to PTSD, while others in our group related positive memories of their growing up, yet have also been deeply affected.

The experience of PTSD is specific to the individual. Although, as a group, some of our general symptoms such as flashbacks, extreme anxiety, sleeplessness, easily angered, nightmares and reliance on alcohol have similarities, nevertheless they are unique in their manifestations to each.

Although first formally recognised following the Vietnam War as a mental disorder with specific diagnostic criteria, PTSD is not exclusive to military service. The statistics on the DVA website indicate that between five and 20 percent of Australian Defence Force (ADF) veterans are likely to develop PTSD in their lifetime. However, as a community, we now know that other groups (men and women) are also at risk of work-related PTSD, in particular first responders, such as police officers, fire and rescue, and paramedics.

In researching resource and support services, we learnt that police officers in Victoria, for example, experience symptoms that are characteristic of PTSD at a very similar rate to military veterans, compared to the general public. We can only imagine the numbers of firies, many of whom were volunteers, families and even members of the media who have experienced fallout due to our all too common, devastating bushfires.

There are many stories about WW1 and WW2 servicemen and women (as nurses or in other active service duties) whose lives were forever changed by war-induced trauma. As with all wars where PTSD is unrecognised and untreated the lives of veterans, wives, families and friends can be severely impacted. To this we can certainly contend.

The second loose end is a sort of recipe for action! Starting with the absolute imperative to seek help as soon as possible – it is never ever too late. The onset of PTSD is not always immediately apparent. It starts slowly and often may be noticeable to others long before you realise it's there taking over your life. And like some other long-term conditions, the symptoms of PTSD can be managed. There is no shame in seeking help but there is potential for great sadness and loss if you don't.

We cannot overstate the benefits of involving partners and other family members as much as possible in learning about PTSD and as participants in treatment. Apart from completing the course at the Heidelberg Repatriation Hospital, having the support of each other and our partners to this day helps us all to maintain our purpose and direction. Not everyone with PTSD will need or be able to access a program such as the one at Heidelberg, but our wish is that everyone who has been significantly affected by trauma will not only seek help from a suitably qualified health professional but also have the opportunity, with a bit of assistance from organisations such as those below, to form their own networks and friendships for additional support.

Our third loose end is to provide some general information on support services and resources for people living with PTSD. The list below is tailored primarily to the subject of combat trauma, given the nature of our personal stories, and has a national focus; so, it is by no means exhaustive. However, many of the websites include information about a wide range of services and resources across Australia, which will also be relevant to other groups, such as police and people working in emergency services. Of course, don't forget your GP – he or she is usually a good starting point.

Resource and Support Services - alphabetical

*Note, an asterix indicates our understanding that 24-hour crisis support is available

ADF All-hours Support Line: 1800 628 036*
Helps ADF personnel and their families access ADF or civilian mental health services

Alcohol and Drug Foundation: 1300 85 85 84 or visit **www.adf.org.au**
Delivers evidence-based approaches to minimise alcohol and drug harm (initially established to support post-war veterans)

Beyond Blue: 1300 224 636* (support service line) or visit **www.beyondblue.org.au**
Supports people affected by anxiety, depression and suicide

Black Dog Institute: visit: **www.mycompass.org.au**
An interactive online self-help service that promotes resilience and wellbeing

Carers Australia: (02) 6122 9900 or visit **www.carersaustralia.com.au**
Advocates on behalf of Australia's unpaid carers

Department of Veterans' Affairs (DVA): 1800 VETERAN (1800 838 372) or visit **www.dva.gov.au**
Supports those who serve or have served in the defence of our nation

headspace: Visit **www.headspace.org.au**
Tailored and holistic mental health support to 12 - 25 years old

Head to Health: Visit **www.headtohealth.gov.au**
Lists digital mental health services and resources from some of Australia's most trusted mental health organisations

Kids Helpline: 1800 55 1800* or visit **www.kidshelpline.com.au**
Provides an online and phone counselling service for young people aged 5 to 25

Lifeline: 13 11 14* or visit **www.lifeline.org.au**
24-hour crisis support and suicide prevention services

MensLine Australia: 1300 78 99 78* or visit **www.mensline.org.au**
A telephone and online counselling service offering support for men

National Sexual Assault, Domestic and Family Violence Counselling Service: 1800RESPECT (1800 737 732) * or visit **www.1800respect.org.au**
Supports people experiencing, or at the risk of experiencing, violence and abuse, their friends and family, and professionals

Open Arms – Veterans & Family Counselling (formerly VVCS): 1800 011 046* or visit **www.openarms.gov.au**
Mental health assessment and counselling for Australian veterans and their families

Phoenix Australia: Visit **www.phoenixaustralia.org**
Experts in posttraumatic mental health and wellbeing

ReachOut: **www.reachout.com**
Online mental health service for young people and their parents in Australia

SANE Australia: 1800 187 263 (helpline) or visit **www.sane.org**
Supports people affected by complex mental health issues

This Way Up Post-Traumatic Stress Course: Visit **www.thiswayup.org.au**
8-lesson online course based on Cognitive Behavioural Therapy (CBT) which may be completed for free with an appropriate clinician referral

If you need to speak to someone urgently, please call Lifeline on 13 11 14*. If life is in danger, or police attendance is required, call 000.

For a list of hospital-based trauma recovery programs funded by the DVA, please refer to the Open Arms or Phoenix Australia websites.

(Details of organisations listed above in 2020 are correct to the best of our knowledge but maybe subject change without notice.)

ACKNOWLEDGMENTS

Herewith are the people and organisations that have enabled our group of veterans, wives and partners to write of our unique life stories, torn by abuse, war and fractured relationships. This project, with the assistance of others, has taken some five years to complete. We offer our thanks for all those who gave so much of their time to this enterprise, which has culminated in a collection of thirteen unique stories.

Firstly, our sincere thanks to John Ramsdale for reading the first drafts of the stories, thereby providing us with positive comment and guidance, plus grammatical suggestions.

We are indebted to Dr Tarni Jennings for reading every story for context and asking us questions to consider including more details to give a clear voice to our feelings and to encourage us to write well of our troubled lives. As she was involved with our group and the PTSD Program (October 2005 at the Heidelberg Repatriation Hospital Melbourne) we were delighted when she agreed to write an introduction to this anthology.

We owe Sandra Cahir our sincere appreciation and thanks for editing our stories. With such a diversity of life experiences detailed in the thirteen stories her task of editing was a challenge, which also tested us with many rewrites and questions. However, with her belief in our project and long hours, our stories were shaped with clarity and structure.

Our sincere appreciation to Anna Bilbrough, Writer and Editor for Busybird Publishing, for the proofreading, extra detailed editing and styling of our stories for this anthology.

A special thank you to Robyn Pritchard (FACN CF) for agreeing to read our final manuscript and for the subsequent detailed comments and suggestions.

To free us from the plague of our trauma and relationship turmoil, we have the staff of Ward 18, Austin Health at the Heidelberg Repatriation Hospital, to thank. The professionalism of the staff and their commitment to our wellbeing was beyond reproach and it's to them we owe our heartfelt gratitude. They gave us the opportunity and the ability to survive against the odds. Our group met on 17 October 2005 and now, nineteen years later, our togetherness is testament to the care and dedication given to us during the Residential PTSD Program.

We'd also like to acknowledge the critical role played by staff of Ward 17, who care for traumatised patients at the Repatriation Hospital. As some of us spent time in Ward 17, we'd like to extend our thanks and gratitude for their help when our lives seemed so pointless. We found the courage, within ourselves, to write of our experiences and to say with reasonable confidence that 'we have made it'.

From the men in our group, a special thank you to our wives and partners who were always nearby to offer support and smooth the way in troubled times. Their participation within the group and in particular their stories have given extra meaning and insight into our relationships. The partnering of the men and women's stories in our anthology will perhaps give the reader an appreciation of how important and necessary it is to foster and maintain ongoing good relations with each other.

Finally, a special acknowledgment from the authors of this book to John Marks who has tirelessly driven this project from the beginning when, some 5 years ago, the idea was to publish our stories to give hope and help to others. With John's focus, energy and infinite patience in keeping us going, our stories became a meaningful reality.

Vale: It is with great sadness we acknowledge the passing of Christine Marks and Glenda Wolff.

Footnotes

I'm the Guy Who Buries His Head in the Sand
[1] My number two, the bloke who assisted me with getting into the bomb suit and preparing weapons, took the photograph. Little did I know that it'd become an iconic image representing EOD operations in Northern Ireland during the Troubles. The picture appeared all over the place, most notably in *Time* magazine (according to a friend) and on the cover of a book. Snozzer 2006, 'Bomb disposal', <https://en.wikipedia.ord/wiki/Bomb_disposal>.

Beyond the Brokenness
[1] Tull, M 2019, 'Why people with PTSD use emotional avoidance to cope', *Verywell Mind*, <https://www.verywellmind.com/ptsd-and-emotional-avoidance-2797640>.

[2] 'Relationships' n.d., PTSD: National Center for PTSD, <https://www.ptsd.va.gov/family/effect_relationships.asp>.

[3] Fothergill, N 2001, DVD, *You're not in the forces now: An informational video for Vietnam veterans and their families*, DVD, Vietnam Veterans Counselling Service (VVCS), Victoria.

[4] Snozzer, 2006, 'Bomb disposal', <https://en.wikipedia.org/wiki/Bomb_disposal>.

[5] Nic Fothergill, op. cit.

[6] ibid.

[7] Bemelmans, L 1939, *Madeline*, Abridged edition, Viking, Penguin Young Readers Group, Camberwell, Victoria, Australia.

[8] Beks, T 2016, 'Walking on eggshells: The lived experience of partners of veterans with PTSD', *The Qualitative Report*, vol. 21, no. 4, pp. 645–660.

[9] ibid.

[10] American Psychiatric Association 2013, 'Diagnostic Criteria for Posttraumatic Stress Disorder', *Diagnostic and Statistical Manual of Mental Disorders, Fifth Edition (DSM–5)*, American Psychiatric Association Publishing, Psychiatry Online, DSM Library, <https://dsm.psychiatryonline.org/doi/book/10.1176/appi.books.9780890425596>.

[11] Ratcliffe, M, Ruddell, M, Smith, B 2014, 'What is a "sense of foreshortened future?" A phenomenological study of trauma, trust, and time', *Frontiers in Psychology*, vol. 5, <www.frontiersin.org/articles/10.3389/fpsyg.2014.01026/full>.

[12] Pai, A, Suris AM, North, CS 2013, 'Posttraumatic Stress Disorder in the DSM-5: Controversy, change, and conceptual considerations' *Behavioral Sciences*, vol. 7, iss.1, article 7, <www.ncbi.nlm.nih.gov/pubmed/28208816>.

[13] Tull, op.cit.

[14] Ratcliffe, et al., op. cit.

Candle in the Window

[1] Nott, R, Payne, N 2008, *Vung Tau Ferry: HMAS Sydney and Escort Ships, Vietnam 1965–1972*, Rosenberg.

[2] Foster, J 2003, *Hands to Boarding Stations: The Story of Minesweeper HMAS Hawk: Confrontation with Indonesia 1965–1966*, Australian Military History Publications, New South Wales, pp. 74–75.

[3] Department of Veteran's Affairs 2002, 'Examination of the potential exposure of Royal Australian Navy (RAN) personnel to polychlorinated dibenzodioxins and polychlorinated dibenzofurans via drinking water: A report to the Department of Veterans' Affairs Australia', reported by Müller, J, Gaus, C, Alberts, V, Moore, M, National Research Centre for Environmental Toxicology

For What It's Worth

[1] Lieutenant John Burrows has granted permission to use a condensed version of 'A Platoon Commander's Perspective – Operation MASSEY HARRIS'.

A Platoon Commander's Perspective – Operation MASSEY HARRIS 2006, The Red Rat: HQ 1ATF Association Newsletter, <www.diggerz.org/-hq1atf/>.

NOTE: Some amendments to spelling and capitalisation in the original story have been made. In particular, 'BINH TY PROVINCE' has been amended to 'Binh Tuy Province' and 'MAO TAY' has been amended to 'May Tao'. Other examples include amending 'op' to 'Op' and 'D & E' to 'D&E'. The excerpt has also been condensed.

Glossary of Acronyms and Terms

AATTV (Australian Army Training Team Vietnam)
ADG (Airfield Defence Guard a mustering in the RAAF)
AK47 Automatic Assault Rifle (developed by Russian Mikhail Kalashnikov made in 1947)
APC (Armoured Personnel Carrier)
AO (Area of Operation 1st
ATF (Australian Task Force)

3rd CAV (Cavalry Regiment – APCs)
CHQ (Company Head Quarters)
CO (Commanding Officer)

DCM (Distinguished Conduct Medal)
D & E (Defence & Employment Platoon)
DMZ (Demilitarized Zone – 17th parallel Vietnam)

EOD (Explosive Ordinance Disposal)
ERA (Engine Room Artificer)

FESR (Far East Strategic Reserve- established in 1955. A joint military force of British, Australian and New Zealand armed forces based in South East Asia and tasked with protecting Commonwealth interests in the region from communist forces. Sarawak, North Borneo, Malaya and Singapore. FESR was suspended in 1971.)
FSB (Fire Support Base)

GH (General Hand, a mustering in the RAAF)

HMAS (Her Majesty's Australian Ship)
HQ1 (Head Quarters – damage control, fire, flooding, engineering issues- Navy)

IRA (Irish Republican Army)

LAC (Leading Aircraftsman)
LME (Leading Mechanic Engineer)
LZ (Landing Zone)

MBE (Member of the British Empire)
ME1 Mechanical Engineer 1st class)
ME2 (Mechanical Engineer 2nd class.
MEQ (Mechanical Engineer Qualifying)
MID (Mention- in-Despatches)
MM (Military Medal)
MP (Military Police)

NBCD (Nuclear, Biological & Chemical Defence)
NCO (Non-Commissioned-Officer)
NVA (North Vietnamese Army)

OC (Officer Commanding)
OOW (Officer of the Watch)

POME (Petty Officer Marine Engineer)

QGM (Queen's Gallantry Medal)

RAAF (Royal Australian Air Force)
RAASC (Royal Australian Army Service Corps)
RAN (Royal Australian Navy)
RAR (Royal Australian Regiment)
RTA (Return to Australia)
R&R (Rest and Recreation)

SAS (Special Air Service)
SEATO (South East Asian Treaty Organization. Established in 1954 by Dwight Eisenhower and John Dulles. An international organization for collective defence of South East Asia. Ceased in 1977.)
SLR (Self Loading Rifle – Aust. Army)
SQN (Squadron)

UC (Underwater Controller-seaman)
USN (United States Navy)

VC (Viet Cong – communists)

Non- Military

DVA (Dept. of Veterans Affairs)
PTSD (Post Traumatic Stress Disorder)
REPAT (Repatriation Hospital Heidelberg, Melbourne, Victoria.)
TPI (Totally & Permanently Incapacitated Ex-Servicemen & Women)
VVCS (Veterans & Veterans' Families Counselling Service – now called Open Arms)

www.ingramcontent.com/pod-product-compliance
Lightning Source LLC
Chambersburg PA
CBHW071304110526
44591CB00010B/768